Colleen McCullough is the well known author of *The Thorn Birds*, *Tim* and *An Indecent Obsession*. She was brought up in Sydney and worked as a neurophysiologist in Australia, London, Birmingham and at Yale University before turning her hand to writing novels. She now lives on an island in the South Pacific.

Jean Easthope was Colleen's first teacher in the techniques of neurophysiology research. She lives in the Wollombi Valley in N.S.W.

Cooking with
Colleen McCullough
and Jean Easthope

Futura

A Futura Book

First published in Great Britain in 1982 by
Macdonald & Co. (Publishers) Ltd
London & Sydney

First Futura edition 1985

Copyright © 1982 Colleen McCullough and Jean
Easthope

Line drawings by Janet Kenney

ISBN 0 7088 2877 9

Set in IBM 9/10 Century by 🅰 Tek-art, Croydon,
Surrey

Printed in Great Britain by William Collins, Glasgow

Futura Publications
A Division of
Macdonald & Co (Publishers) Ltd
Maxwell House
74 Worship Street
London EC2A 2EN

A BPCC plc Company

CONTENTS

To our mothers,
Laurie McCullough
and May Easthope.
We thank you for teaching us to cook.

INTRODUCTION

When our publisher in Sydney first threw this project at Col, he requested a colonial cookbook. Col countered that she should prefer to make it a joint effort with her former teacher and long-standing friend, Jean Easthope. And a colonial cookbook we set out to write. However, books have a way of shaping themselves and we found ourselves with a manuscript filled with old and proven recipes using simple ingredients, a straightforward cooking manual angled towards sensible advice and an attempt at answering some of the 'why' of cooking.

Let's be honest! So-called colonial cooking was English cooking transported across the oceans and in most cases only poorly adapted to radically different climatic conditions. Can you think of many truly Australian recipes? There are peach Melba and meat pies; pavlova and kangaroo tail soup. The New Zealanders also claim Pavlova and these days kangaroo tail soup is definitely out.

However, over the years Australians have learnt the art of adaptation and throughout you will recognise where we have used the basic recipes of long-established cuisines, changing some of the ingredients to others more easily available in Australia. We have endeavoured to use nothing that was not available on the supermarket shelves.

Professionally we are not cooks. The only professional cooks are those who earn their livings at cooking, and except for a few short-term pinch-hits, that we've never done. But it puts us with the majority of those who use cookbooks, because the kind of cooking which is performed in homes is by definition amateur cooking. No diplomas, degrees or even basic educational requirements.

Both of us belong to the era where girls, and boys, learnt to cook in their mother's kitchen, Col on the tail of that era admittedly. When we were children we vigorously dodged domestic science and cooking classes at school, for both of us were more interested in physics and chemistry. Not because physics and chemistry were where the boys were, but because those subjects fascinated us.

When Jean sought paternal support for her plea to substitute science for cooking and sewing, her father said, most irate: 'Do you mean to tell me that I'm supposed to pay school fees for having you taught something your mother does better than anyone else in the village? Go right ahead and enrol in physics and chemistry, Jean! I'll talk to the school principal. There's one condition — you tell me you will be the only girl in the classes; you've got to beat all the boys!' So Jean took chemistry and physics, and did come in the top grading. Col did not have to seek parental sanction; she went to an extremely academic school which did not offer domestic sciences.

So we trained as teachers and later as laboratory technicians; and now we are writers. We never missed those domestic science courses, for our mothers taught us the basic principles of cooking (and all the other facets of housekeeping), and our scientific educations filled in the gaps which our mothers could not. Indeed, those expensive and hardfought scientific educations of ours proved a great asset. We discovered that we were better equipped to understand the chemical basis of cooking (for it is a kind of chemistry, if not an exact science) and to understand what happens to food when it is cut, diced, minced, marinated, beaten, combined, folded, squeezed, crushed, pared, chopped, sliced, whipped, mixed, strained, pulverised, blanched, peeled, boiled, roasted, fried, steamed, disjointed, eviscerated, and lots more. Aren't they interesting terms? Most of them seem to belong to a torture chamber! However, they are all apt in a cooking context, which should tell us a great deal about what we eat and how we prepare it for eating.

When it came to writing this cookbook, we found too that our early home backgrounds enabled us to split much of the work logically between us; Col grew up in a meat-and-potatoes environment, Jean in a vegetarian environment. So while Col concentrated on meats and starches, Jean did vegetables, salads, soups, bread. However, since our childhoods both of us have learnt that there are many other ways to live, and both of us have had the good sense to regard the way other people live (and what they eat) with respect. It is a form of bigotry to condemn the living habits of those with whom we do not agree.

You will find many of the chapter introductions as long, if not longer, than the recipes which follow; the teacher in us came out, so that we found ourselves anxious to explain as simply as possible some of the fascinating phenomena which underlie cooking methods. For to understand is to do well, to understand is to have enthusiasm. Cooking becomes a bore when it is routine, automatic, and conducted in ignorance. Once the principles underlying it are fully grasped, boredom can be easily avoided by the possession of sufficient confidence to try new things, and the ability to produce familiar things with ease gives confidence.

HEALTH AND FOOD

Over the decades since the Second World War, figure-consciousness has increased in direct proportion to income. This is a direct result of mass media propaganda combined with the lack of exercise which comes with cars, dishwashers and all the other appurtenances of living in the second half of the twentieth century. A new adage has emerged: *you can't be too thin or too rich* (at which Col indulges in a quiet chuckle). Cuisine minceur (which is the fancy French name for low-calorie cooking) has become all the rage, even in restaurants. And certain interesting things have happened as a result of figure-consciousness. First, the kind of family cooking which has lots of variety and a distinctly exotic flavour, light dill sauces, the thinnest of crêpes, wild rice, satay meats. This is marvellous fare for a change, but our observation reveals that families grow tired of exotic fare rapidly, and crave something closer to the kind of food they were served in earlier days. Then again, there is the dieting cook who strictly curtails the menu she serves to her family, but when guests come to dinner indulges her frustrated desire to eat by laying on a feast which would tempt a flagellant saint to commit the awful sin of gluttony. But day-by-day the family members sneak out to fill up their empty corners with fast-foods, if the cook is determined the whole family is going to diet also, or with full consent, even encouragement, if the cook is interested in her own figure but disinterested in the fate of her family.

We can't see why an interesting and well-cooked meal every day, complete with a gorgeous dessert once or twice a week, is any worse for the family than monotony and saccharine. Perhaps the cook would be better advised to concoct a programme of healthy exercise for all? Bodies were meant to consume and to burn their fuel-food in decent proportion. It is not good for human beings to feel perpetually hungry, whether they live under a regime of famine or with a dieting cook.

Dieting to reduce weight from aesthetic motives seems to progress fairly logically in this introduction to dieting from other motives, with or without loss of weight — we mean dieting for the preservation of good health, as in the management of diabetes, hypertension (high blood pressure), formation of sclerotic plaques on blood vessel walls (tendency to throw clots, or in milder form, hardening of the arteries), and other disorders.

Disruption of healthy bodily function on the part of a family member inevitably leads to headaches for the cook. We would encourage her by saying that if she searches she will find many current cookbooks designed for specific dietary needs. We offer only one word of warning on a subject which seems oddly neglected, and that is in the region of the salt-free diet. A salt-free diet is usually prescribed for persons suffering from high blood pressure or other circulatory disorders, and almost invariably it is a diet which simultaneously demands either weight reduction or rigid weight control. Unfortunately the family cook, who bears ultimate responsibility for policing this regime, is all too often not made aware of what exactly a salt-free diet means. Free of salt, you say. But what it really means is free of *sodium*. Common salt is a compound of sodium and chlorine, its chemical name being sodium chloride. NaCl. In disorders like high blood pressure, the body has a tendency to retain its sodium due to metabolic malfunctioning; normally we need to replace our body's sodium quite lavishly, for we lose it, chiefly in sweating. In any life-situation where sweating is profuse, sodium intake needs to be high, and the most convenient form we have of obtaining sodium is via common salt. In the old days of steam engines, stokers for instance had to supplement their dietary intake with salt tablets. Even today, if you are planning to walk across the desert, you had better not forget to take along an ample supply of salt tablets.

A problem can arise for the cook faced with concocting a salt-free diet which is also a weight-reducing or weight-controlling diet, for most sugar substitutes contain sodium, as do baking power and bicarbonate. Used in small quantity such products are harmless, the amount of sodium they contain being minute. But if artificial sweetener is added lavishly to a dozen cups of coffee or tea a day, the total amount of sodium can pile up. Artificial sweeteners which are small in volume are by far the best to use, such as the tiny tablets of simple saccharine. Beware of sugar substitutes measured by the spoonful, unless the label says the sodium content is low.

OUR KITCHEN

All our recipes were either personally tried out during our three-month cooking/writing stint, or are recipes from sources well known to us and well tried (although these are in a minority).

Neither of us possessed a kitchen which could cope with the volume of cooking we needed to do, so we rented a flat in a harbourside suburb of Sydney for three months. Ours was still far from the ideal kitchen. In fact, it was a kitchen designer's nightmare, having only two things to recommend it — lots of space and a gas stove. (All concentrated cooking projects are done on gas stoves, as you will soon discover if you prowl into restaurant kitchens).

Our rented kitchen was a converted front verandah; it faced due west, was one storey up on the high side of the street, and was entirely glassed along its very long front. The floor was uneven, there were no blinds or curtains, it had one battered bench with two cupboards underneath, a tiny single-basin stainless-steel sink wedged into a corner so tight it was impossible even for tiny Jean to stand straight-on to it. And oh, that gas stove! It was a 1952 four-burner single-oven Metters Early Cooka, minus one knob (we never did get to use all four burners on its top, because the Gas Company said there were no more knobs around to fit it — we had an antique!), with an oven so cantankerous we could never put more than one tray-rack in it.

We are telling you all this because we don't want you to despair if your kitchen doesn't look like something out of a glossy housekeeping magazine.

For a minimum of monetary outlay when compared to the cost of a complete new kitchen, we made our horrible kitchen not only bearable but actually workable. It did have advantages we hadn't seen when we rented the flat — a hot water system which produced unlimited scalding water, for instance.

We went to a local whitewood shop and bought two unpainted benches with drawers and cupboards underneath, and two unpainted whitewood bookshelves. Our last, most important purchase, was a plain rectangular table (also unpainted whitewood); it had two comfortable rungs underneath, one which accommodated tiny Jean's legs beautifully, and one which suited huge Col's legs beautifully. We can do without a lot in a kitchen, we discovered, but a good worktable — never! Including a role of Contact paper with which we surfaced all tops and shelves, our furniture outlay was about $300.

Seriously, you do need good tools to produce good food. To help you here is a list.

MAJOR EQUIPMENT

1. The single most important piece of gadgetry in a modern kitchen is undoubtedly a first-quality, heavy-duty electric beater-mixer-blender-mincer-food processor on a permanent base. We didn't choose to have a hand-held mixer because they are too fragile, and many of our cooking tasks we felt were better executed on a mixer we could walk away from and leave steadily beating. In fact, our mixer proved to be a godsend. The motor was so powerful it could beat for an hour at medium speed without heating even to warmth. The disc on which the bowl sat turned no matter how thick the mixture was. We could make butter-cream on it, or meringue egg whites, or fold the flour into a cake like thistledown. The food-processor attachment worked like a dream. With the blender top on it instead of the mixer, our gadget behaved better than single-function blenders. With the mincing attachment, we ground meat for sausages, brawn, shepherd's pies, etc., and again the motor never so much as ran warm, even while grinding raw meat; at times we ran it for hours without resting it. This super-duper mixer of ours cost about $150.

2. An equally expensive outlay was a set of the very best pots and pans — a Dutch oven, three saucepans ranging from large to small, and two frying-pans of different sizes, each with a lid. All these were of heavy-duty cast aluminium with machine-ground steel bottoms, and were lined with the newest and best of the non-stick compounds, ironstone. In three months of intensive use, albeit tender loving care, there was not a scratch on the non-stick surface. The lids fitted ring-on-ring instead of inside the rim of the pots, a system which doesn't look tight, but on heating of the contents, the two finely ground surfaces resting against each other produced a near-vacuum which was quite hard to break. We had opted for

these more routine pots rather than any of the so-called gourmet cookware because we felt we should cook with utensils more in keeping with the pockets of most of our readers, and because, quite frankly, we feel most gourmet cookware is grossly over-priced for what it offers. Enamel-lined pots are difficult to clean, the contents tend to stick, and they scratch; cast iron of any description may be wonderful, but you need to have the brawn and reach of a weight-lifter to move them around or lift them off the stove. Our set cost us about $200, and performed splendidly. Heat was uniform right through and across the bottoms, the ironstone coating prevented any kind of sticking, and the handles never got hot, nor did the knobs on the lids. Considering that a similar array of gourmet cookware can cost $800, we felt we did very well.

3. When buying ovenware, you will naturally be guided by the size of your family and your cooking aspirations, but remember that if you are a working person, casseroles are wonderful to have. Good-looking casseroles save on serving china, for they can be brought to the table. We feel one deep large casserole with lid, one shallow casserole with lid, one large oval casserole with lid, and two rectangular lasagna dishes, one smaller than the other, are all you will need. Make sure all but the lasagna pans have lids. Our cost was about $80.

4. Don't be tempted to buy expensive and gorgeous ceramic or glass canisters, especially if they have Tea and Coffee and Flour and so forth stamped for all eternity on their gleaming sides. Don't be seduced by fancy cork lids and complicated vacuum lids, either; mostly they don't fit if they're cork, or if they are vacuumised can't be undone without a wrestling match. We bought clear plastic canisters with screw-on or snug fit-in lids in various shapes and sizes from one for spaghetti to one for cream of tartar. It is so useful to be able to see at a glance what's inside something, not to mention that simultaneously you will see how much you have left. If some substances look confusingly alike, buy a role of adhesive blank white labels and keep track of contents that way. Our canister outlay was surprisingly modest — about $30 for a truly formidable assortment.

5. We didn't buy a set of mixing bowls, but simply bought what we decided we would need. In the matter of two blue-and-white striped Cornish pottery bowls we confess we succumbed to a love of this Cornish ware which goes back to

childhood, but the smaller had a projecting rim which made it ideal for doubling as a steamed-pudding container, and the larger came with a lip which made it ideal for pouring cake and batter mixtures. We bought one gargantuan bowl for wedding cakes and the like. Also, four melamine (a very hard, durable plastic) bowls with lips, each on a rubber base which steadied its intrinsic lightness. These proved excellent investments too. All in all, we wound up with one huge bowl, two large bowls, four or five medium-sized bowls, and about eight small bowls, each of which held about a cup of liquid; some of these small bowls were melamine, some pottery. You can't have too many little bowls because they are extremely useful for holding all the left-overs, as well as for having minor ingredients on hand. Our total outlay for bowls was about $80.

6. Jugs, spoons and knives. Ordinary ceramic or glass jugs with good lips on them are invaluable in a kitchen, and we think you should have many on hand. Several good glass measuring jugs, both small and large, are essential. Of one thing we urge you to take note — the formation of the lip on a jug. Col noticed during her years in the United States that in spite of American know-how and technical brilliance, one thing they fell down on badly was a jug's lip. Of all the jugs she acquired there, only the Corning Pyrex measuring jugs poured without liquid running down the side. The lips on Australian jugs tend to be much better, but beware of a lip which is too flat and too short!

Our taste in kitchen spoons has veered away from wood and towards melamine, this plastic being both very hard and quite heat-resistant. The modern wooden spoon is poorly finished, with handle so rough your skin will blister and chafe until the newness wears off unless you sand it down yourself. Melamine spoons look beautiful, and are as good to work with as a wooden spoon. They come in all shapes and sizes, and as well as spoons there are forks, spatulae, egg flippers and slotted spoons. We got some of all varieties. varieties.

And now to kitchen knives. You cannot operate a kitchen well without an assortment of the very best knives, manufactured from the very best tooled steel. As a minimum you need two or three little ones (usually called vegetable knives), a serrated one, a long thin filleting knife, and a large heavy-bladed carving knife.

You should also have a steel for sharpening them, as this

isn't hard once you know how. And to learn how, don't ask an amateur. Many a family man has pretended to know the technique when he really doesn't. Go to your butcher and ask him to show you. A steel, incidentally, is a long tapering rod with a heavy rounded handle, the rod itself being minutely scored like a file. It is made of super-hard steel, and will sharpen and keep sharp any kind of knife. Never, incidentally, leave time and much use between sharpenings of your knives; we make it a rule to sharpen a knife before every use. That way it never dulls. Once the edge goes off a knife, a steel can't replace it.

If you are buying meat in bulk, or are ambitious to bone or section your own cuts of meat, you will also need a boning knife, a chopper and a meat saw. In this respect we yielded to the professionals, and had our butcher perform these tasks for us. Most butchers are only too glad to oblige, grateful for the fact that you aren't buying your meat wrapped in a plastic sheet from a supermarket cold-bin.

The cost of our jugs, spoons and knives came to about $250, the knives costing more than two-thirds of this.

7. Do acquire a pair of kitchen scissors. Until you own a pair, you will not realise how many things you can do with them. Cutting up a whole chicken into segments, for instance; a good pair of kitchen scissors will go through chicken, rabbit and tiny chop-bones easily. They never dull like dressmaker's scissors, and have a hundred and one uses. Ours are Swedish stainless steel, hand-tooled, rust-resistant, and perpetually sharp. The amount we paid: US$30.

MINOR EQUIPMENT

Aside from these major expenses, there are lots and lots of minor tools which are load-lighteners (and some indeed essential) in a kitchen. Among them:

French whisks
Conical strainer
Food tongs
Graters
Pastry sheet
Chopping boards
Powder shakers
Measuring cups
Can opener, non-electric

Bottle opener
Strainers of all sizes
Colanders
Egg flippers (what is their proper name?)
Pastry blender
Iced-water rolling-pin
Pepper mill (an easily turned one!)

Measuring spoons
Kitchen scales
Punch for canned liquids
Corkscrew
Metal spatula
Bottle brushes
Jelly moulds
Baking dishes
Rubber gloves
Egg or crumpet rings
Assorted steel skewers
Mortar and pestle
Icing bags and nozzles
Oven thermometer
Wire cake-racks
Baking trays
Various cake tins
Pie dishes
Steamed pudding bowl
Potato masher
Dish towels
Fly swatter
Washing-up drainer
  basket

Pastry brushes
Oven cloths and mitts
Plastic storage containers
Kitchen papers (foil, etc.)
  dispenser
Small hand mouli for
  slicing, grating
Griddle
Garlic crusher
Pastry bags and nozzles
Flour sifter
Meat thermometer
Scoops
Loaf pans
Patty-cake tins
Bread tins
Deep-frying saucepan
  and basket
Good wall clock with
  second-hand
Good kettle
Wooden block for
  holding knives
Lemon Squeezer

There you are! None of the above may be as pretty or decorative as a spice-rack, but all are more useful. Among this list ought to be something in the price-range of most bridal shower donors. For those of you not in a bride-to-be situation, drop hints to families if you have them, and not necessarily very subtle or gentle hints. No electrician or surgeon would dream of working without the right tools; why should the cook?

Now to discuss some of the items on our list of minor utensils.

We found the best kitchen scales we have ever seen, and we do urge you to shop around for the same kind. And remember that the term is 'a pair of scales'! Our kitchen scales have two dials, one in metric grams and kilograms, the other in imperial ounces and pounds. The mixing bowl sits on the top and the scale can be adjusted to zero so that you can weigh directly into the bowl.

Bottle brushes. Have you ever had a bottle or a vase with the kind of neck you can't get past? Buy yourself several different sizes of bottle brush, with flexible wire handles that can be bent around corners. They clean small tubes and bottles and vases beautifully.

Buy a timer with an alarm if you feel you must, but nothing ever takes the place of a large wall clock placed within sight of the stove. If for any reason you forget to set a timer before you start to cook, it becomes useless, but it is very easy to train yourself into glancing up at the clock the moment you've started something cooking.

Kettles, we learnt, are not cheap, at least not good ones. Ours was of anodised aluminium with a machine-ground steel base; its quiet matte gold finish blended beautifully with the grease spots it collected from the frying-pan, and we experienced no frantic urges to polish it every two seconds. It had a high wooden handle which never heated up, its lid was large and had a steam vent which didn't scald us as we poured; admittedly it didn't whistle, but it had a proper swan-like spout which poured perfectly.

A fly swatter: what an odd thing to have in a kitchen! But it is a useful, practical thing, we assure you. Since most mass-spraying of insecticides is now banned, the flies are back with us in swarms. And no matter what the instructions are on the can, you cannot spray insecticide around a kitchen, with food scattered everywhere and the canary chirping blithely in its cage, whereas you can down your tools at a convenient moment to chase a stray fly with your swatter. It is a fly fly which can avoid a well-aimed swatter, believe us.

There is one further kitchen outlay which we made and which we do not regard as a luxury. For three months we lived, save for sleeping-time, in our rented kitchen. From about two every afternoon in the height of Sydney's summer (we cooked during January, February and March), our kitchen absorbed the full strength of the sun. For the first week we endured it, then we bought a large, efficient air-conditioner. From that first blissful moment after installation when we turned on our new air-conditioner, life was extremely comfortable.

Air-conditioning a kitchen is not so very extravagant. In fact, when a household budget can run to an air-conditioner, we advocate that the first choice of site should be the kitchen, not the bedroom or the living-room. It is from the kitchen that most of summer's unwanted heat comes, and it is also the room in which most of the household's physical work is done.

Though we don't want to spend our entire book merely discussing the room in which cooking occurs, we do want to mention disposal of kitchen fumes and smells. Many a cook and group of prospective diners have been so saturated by smells during the cooking process that by the time the meal is on the table, appetite has quite vanished. The first choice is proper venting of stale and smoky odours from the interior to the air outside, which means not only a hood above the stove, but an exhaust fan at the top of the hood's funnel. Hoods which merely 'deodorise' and recirculate the same air are not satisfactory. Failing installation of a vented hood, which can be costly, a large exhaust-fan placed as near to the stove as possible works very well. To some extent an air-conditioner will perform the work of an exhaust-fan if placed on 'suck' instead of 'blow', but this means losing its cooling properties.

WORKING METHODICALLY

Do you have a method when you cook? Devising a method was something we didn't have to do when we began our three-month session, for each of us had done that long years before, largely due to our scientific training. It is so much easier to carry a cooking task through from start to finish if you assemble everything in a convenient location before you begin. We weigh all our ingredients and set them out in order on the counter, we grease our cake or bread tins ahead of time, we make sure we have all the utensils we are likely to need, and have them to hand also. Truly it is worth the effort in the time it saves, the dishes which can be completed because we have checked on all our little ingredients such as specific herbs or spices beforehand, and the sensation of proficiency and mastery of the subject which it unconsciously promotes. And this last, a sensation of proficiency and mastery, is so important to any cook's morale, not to mention her enjoyment of the task.

WEIGHTS AND MEASURES

In this book we give both metric and imperial quantities, though mostly we have adhered to an even older form of gauging amounts — cups and spoons.

First, let's consider cups. All our old books list the imperial cup as containing 10 fl oz, or about 310 ml. The metric measuring cup contains 250ml, and the American measuring cup also 250ml.

But how many cooks actually possess or use a proper graduated measuring cup? In our experience, most cooks use a good old teacup (a teacup is the one included in dinner services; coffee cups tend to be smaller, even if not actually classified as demitasse). To satisfy our curiosity, we compared the capacities of twelve differently shaped teacups, and discovered with surprise that whether the cup was bell-shaped, tubby, bowl-shaped or straight-shaped, it still contained much the same amount of fluid, between 7½ and 8floz, or about 250ml. Thus the household's routine teacup turns out to be the same size as a metric or an American measuring cup. This is the cup we have used in all our recipes, and where possible, everything is given in cups. Any teacup will do.

If measuring fluids by teacup, you may differ by about a tablespoon from the originator of the recipe, and this is not enough to worry about. If measuring solids like flour or sugar, you will err from the recipe's originator anyway, for exactly how much the cup holds depends upon how firmly its contents are packed, and whether it is sternly levelled with a knife, or heaped, or rounded.

Spoons were a more difficult problem, but not insuperable. Because Col travels so much, we acquired sets of measuring spoons (most of which included large spoons labelled ½ cup, 1 cup, and even 2 cups) from the United Kingdom, France, the United States and Australia. Then we compared them.

One interesting fact emerged: every single set — and we had two American, two British, one French, and three Australian sets — measured slightly differing amounts. There is no guarantee when one buys a measuring set that it conforms to the National Standards Bureau.

However, the most serious discrepancy occurred in the tablespoon. The metric tablespoon should hold 20 ml, which is exactly the amount held by an old kitchen-drawer made-in-Sheffield tablespoon. American, old imperial and old Australian tablespoon measures seemed to hold between 15ml and 17ml of fluid. This is from half to one teaspoon less than the metric.

If you consider the substances usually measured by tablespoon — sugar, butter, flour, cornflour, rice flour, arrowroot, etc. — this is not a significant difference. Where essences are measured it might be, as they impart high flavour, but we cannot think of any occasion upon which we have used a whole tablespoon of any essence. If the need should ever arise, we feel you should choose the smaller quantity tablespoon. When water or milk is measured by tablespoon, you are usually adding it to batters to smooth them out or thin them down, so again the difference is not important. Our advice is always to use your common sense, and not to worry too much.

At this point it might be advisable to emphasise a fact emerging out of the discussion on measures above.

Cooking is more an imprecise art than a precise science. There are virtuosi of the pots and pans, just as there are the virtuosi of violin or piano. Anyone who possesses a television set must have begun to understand the very real artistry of cooking, while watching some brilliant and breezy cook go through the various movements of a dish's preparation. The complete symphony is practised, polished and performed with a uniquely individual style. Were cooking a true science, there could be no virtuosi — to us, after so many years in laboratories, there is a delicious joy about visualising Professor Poddle performing on the gas chromatograph, or Professor Boop giving a masterly rendition of column-packing. In any science, individual style is sternly subjugated to an absolutely formal, stereotyped ritual. Burettes and pipettes having capacities calibrated to 0.005 per cent of error by 1000 ml volume would take the place of a particular cook's favourite set of measuring spoons, and instead of scales there would have to be balances so delicately calibrated that a hair on the weighing platform could lead to a crucial error.

That is because scientific experiments (we are using chemistry because we feel this lies closest of all the sciences to cooking) are performed upon a minute scale. Substances are weighed in milligrams, poured in millilitres, measured sometimes in micros and nanos. The substances used in most chemical experiments are extremely expensive, so the very tiniest amount of them necessary to conduct an experiement will always apply.

Cooking is quite different. The cook works in pounds or kilograms, measures in pints or litres, and the very smallest amount of any substance you are likely to use is a pinch, or about one-eighth of a teaspoon. And one-eighth of a teaspoon of ingredient is gigantic when put alongside the quantities a chemist employs.

Scientists talk about something called a margin of error. The margin of error is the amount by which you can safely deviate from the amount stipulated. It's easy to see that the larger the amounts used, the larger the margin of error will be. In cooking, with its relatively vast quantities, the margin of error is relatively vast.

The best cooks don't measure much at all. They grab a handful of this, a pinch of that, a glug from a bottle, the first cup they see full of an ingredient. Yet they turn out magnificent food, and it always works. They rarely exactly duplicate the taste or texture of the same dish when they repeat it, for each time they make it they add something else, or forget something, or use a slightly different cooking method. Which is the right way to go about eating, if you think about it, for it avoids monotony.

We have included the imperial equivalents as well as the metric, but we have done the sensible thing and made 1 oz equal 25 g rather than 28 g, 1 lb equal 450 g rather than 453 g. The margin of error in cooking is capacious enough not to notice.

Flour
4 cups equal 450 g (1 lb)
2 tablespoons equal 25 g (1 oz)
Flour is measured gently rounded on top

Sugar or butter
2 cups equal 450 g (1 lb)
1 tablespoon equals 25 g (1 oz)
Sugar and butter are heaped on top

Eggs
1 medium-sized hen egg equals 40 g (1½ oz)
1 large hen egg equals 50 g (2 oz)
10 medium-sized hen eggs equal 450 g (1 lb)

The final appearance and texture of most recipes will tell you how right your measurements have been:
● Batters pour easily.
● Cake batters pour sluggishly, and need a little push.
● Steamed pudding mixtures have to be pushed.
● Scone or damper dough is slightly sticky, but can be shaped into a sort of ball.
● Pastry or bread dough is never sticky, and can be moulded into shapes which stay shaped.

STOVES AND TEMPERATURES

We have included both temperature scales in our baking or cooking times. The first thing to remember is a most reassuring fact. Like weights and liquid measures, cooking temperatures are rough estimates, and a few degrees either way will make little difference to whatever you are cooking. If our stove is anything to go by, thermostats themselves can be highly inaccurate instruments. Our oven was a full 27°C (50°F) colder than the thermostat indicated.

We do emphasise that you ought to invest in a little oven thermometer (ours was graduated in both metric and imperial scales), and keep it sitting in the oven at the same position as the food to be baked. After lighting or turning on your oven, it takes a certain time to reach the desired temperature, and this varies from oven to oven, too. Electric ovens, be warned, generally take longer to heat than gas ones.

Ovens have hot spots and cold spots, and it is a mistake to go by the 'hot air rises, cold air stays at the bottom' principle. The hottest portion of our oven was its bottom the coldest the top. Even at the level of the particular rack you choose to bake on, most ovens are hotter on one side, or at the back or at the front.

So use an oven thermometer, and learn the quirks of your oven. In ordinary cooking this may not worry you overmuch, but for an item which needs delicate, uniform browning, for instance, knowing your oven can make all the difference.

Fahrenheit thermostat		Celsius thermostat		Actual celsius
200		90		94
212	water	100	boils	100
225		110		107
250		120		122
275		130		133
300		150		148
315	sugar	155	boils	157
325		160		162
350		180		177
375		190		191
400		210		208
425		220		218
450		230		233
475		240		243
500		260		260

A point worth remembering is that altitude affects cooking times. The higher the place where you live, the lower the temperature at which water boils. Under 1 atmosphere of pressure at sea level, water boils at 100°C (212°F) exactly, but at 5000 ft (over 2000 m) water boils at a lower temperature. So if you live high up, cook things for a slightly longer time rather than increase your oven temperature. If you have any doubts, consult your local town council for help. In Australia altitudes are rarely a problem with cooking, but in the United States it is common to see on the side of widely marketed cake mixes, for example, sets of baking times for various heights above sea level, up to plus 10000 ft.

We think it's germane to close our introduction with a grumble directed at stove manufacturers in particular, and builders and house designers in general. Why, we want to know, is it beyond the resources of stove manufacturers to make an oven level? It seems they have no difficulty in charging enough for their products! After an oven shelf, tray, rack, call it what you will, is slid in and out of a new oven some ten or twelve times, it becomes permanently warped. And nothing is more irritating to a good cook than to see her cakes come out thick on one side, thin on the other, not to mention the mess on the bottom of the oven because a full dish tilted downhill and dripped.

House builders or kitchen specialists mostly don't even bother to make sure they have installed the stove evenly, though one presumes these people do own spirit levels. Jean and Col can both use a spirit level, so why can't they?

We feel all of this slipshod manufacturing and slipshod installation dates back to the times when cooks were female and secondhand citizens at best, chattels at worst. We are not blindly fem-lib, but we are female, and well aware of how women used to be regarded, still are, in some circles. Women should demand level stoves, level refrigerators, level counter-tops in their kitchens, among many other practical things. The trouble is, how many women are ever consulted during the construction of a kitchen, except perhaps in the choosing of its colour scheme? Some of this inertia is due, we freely admit, to women who do not think beyond a kitchen's colour scheme and decorative trinkets. So let everyone become more aware — the men who in the main design, build or manufacture or install kitchens, and the women who in the main use them.

COOKING MEAT WITH WINE

Because of its acidity, wine aids in the tenderising of meat, therefore it does serve a legitimate purpose above and beyond palatably altering the taste of dishes.

We feel it is a mistake to use cheap wines in cooking, as cheap wines tend to be very vinegary and may impart a bitter flavour.

Alcohol is an extremely volatile substance at cooking temperatures, and we can assure our most sceptical readers that wine included in a cooked dish will entirely have lost its alcoholic content by the time the dish is served. However, if there is an alcoholism problem in the house, we do advise *not* using any liquor, for there are aromatic esters and other substances which may not disappear during cooking and which may trigger a wish for alcohol even in its absence. Not to mention that a bottle of cooking wine tucked on a shelf is just as attractive or tempting as other liquor. Religious scruples should not extend to wine in cooked food, but if they do, substitute grape juice. Since grape juice is very much sweeter than wine, add 1 teaspoon of vinegar or lemon juice per cup of grape juice.

A wonderful amateur chef of Italian extraction told us about cooking with vermouth rather than wine, and after experimenting, we tend to recommend vermouth over wine in many of our recipes. Vermouth is a wine-based aperitif with a most distinctive flavour, and is available in several varieties, red and white, sweet and dry. It also has the advantage over wine of keeping once the bottle has been opened, so that if bought for kitchen use, none of it is wasted.

We have never liked sherry in food; it 'disappears' rapidly, and has a less appealing flavour than other wines. Vermouth 'stays' better than either sherry or table wines, and possesses a herbiness which complements stews and casseroles splendidly.

Cognac, a brandy, is a grape-based member of the spirits family, and can also be employed in cooking. If you want to impart a special richness to a cream sauce, add a couple of tablespoons of cognac. When added to a cream-based stuffing mixture for fowl or joint, cognac imparts a grand richness and a special delicacy. Three-star hospital brandy is no substitute, however!

1. SOUP AND STEWS

SOUP

More years ago than we care to remember, we worked at different hospitals but occupied adjoining bed-sitters in an old, old weatherboard house in Mosman. It was the kind of accommodation so familar to the working girls of Sydney: one large room, share a bath-room, sometimes a small kitchen, sometimes just a gas ring. Jean had a proper kitchen, having inherited the kitchen of the original home, but Col's cooking inconveniences were at the end of an enclosed balcony and consisted of a sink without draining-board and a two-burner gas stove. So for company and economy we often shared meals cooked in the larger kitchen. At the time we were both heavily involved in training EEG technicians and on occasions would bring them home after work for extra tuition. The meals we provided were simple: grills and salads in the summer, and in the winter bowls of thick soup and homemade bread. One lass in particular always ate heartily; we knew that she 'batched', but we had doubts about her cooking abilities. One night we had a large Dutch oven brimming with thick soup and our little protégée, passed up her bowl for a third helping with the question, 'What brand of soup do you buy? I have never tasted anything so good!'

Jean's astonished reply of 'We made it ourselves!' was almost drowned by Col's cheerful cry of 'Well, kid, if we all fail at EEGs, we can open a soup kitchen and go into business!'

Our pupil's response was an amazed gape: 'But I'm serious. I didn't know people made soup. Don't you have to start with a tin?'

So we proceeded to give a lesson on soupmaking. Said Col, 'You saw the big beef bone and chunks of cooked meat Jean gave the dog? Well, that's how we start it.'

'But you must buy the meat just before the butcher closes for the weekend, and always go to the same butcher,' Jean chipped in. 'Just ask for a large meaty bone for the dog and you'll usually get a few hunks of good skirt or brisket thrown in. You see, it's not worth their while to put such scraps back into the cool room over the weekend.'

Col continued, 'If you ask your butcher nicely, he'll saw the bone into two or three pieces — you just say it's for a small dog and you want the bones to last him for several days. When you bring it home, put the whole lot, scraps and all, into a large boiler, cover with cold water and bring it to simmering point. Turn the gas down low and let it simmer for hours and hours. You don't add any onions or seasoning, because the dog doesn't like such flavourings. When the meat has fallen off the bones, lift the pot off the stove and save the bones and any large bits of meat for the dog. Leave the liquid to get cold.'

Jean continued: 'This part is very important. You must let it cool, overnight preferably, until the fat has risen to the top and solidified. Then lift off the fat. You can save this fat for cooking if you like, but we usually discard it; although I often save a bit to cut into the dog's share. After you've removed all the fat and taken out any bits of gristle, put the pot back on to the stove and heat it again. If you want clear stock, pour it through a hair sieve to take out all the little bits and pieces of meat. But if you want a thick stock force the whole lot, liquid and meat, through a colander and then through a fine sieve.'

'And this job is usually mine,' said Col. 'I've got more muscle. And while I'm doing this, Jean is getting the vegetables ready.'

Our poor little stunned student managed to ask, 'What sort of vegetables do you use?'

'Anything that is left in the vegetable box,' said Jean. 'Swedes, carrots, turnips, parsnips, celery, beans, peas — anything at all — but unless it is to be cabbage soup, which is done differently, we don't use cabbage or cauliflower because they drown the other flavours. If you want it to cook quickly grate all the vegetables; but if there's no hurry, just cut them into small cubes. By the time I have these ready, Col has puréed the stock. Then we put the stock and vegetables back into the pot, add salt, pepper and any herbs if we feel they're needed; and simmer gently until the vegetables are cooked. If you want a fine purée type of soup, put it through the sieve again.'

'And that's your soup,' said Col. 'Want another bowl?'

The lass became a good technician, but we never were invited to sample her cooking.

We still make our soups the same way — no additions to the basic stock while it is simmering, so that you have a neutral base from which to develop any particular flavour you want in the final product. And now we have been able to invest in a food blender, we have eliminated the hard labour of forcing the soup through a hair sieve.

If you have never made your own soup stock, you may be wondering about quantities of meat and bone to water. The water should be about 3½ cm (1½ in) above the meat. Using a large, high-sided boiler, 1 kg (2 lb) of meat and bone will take approximately 8 cups of water, but there is no hard and fast rule. You will lose a lot of water with evaporation in spite of a lid, because the stock is going to be simmered for several hours.

Another important point: always start off with cold water. The reason for this is fully explained in Chapter 3 (Meat); but briefly, meat is protein, and high temperatures toughen protein. So start with cold water, bring to the simmer and never, never let the stock (or the soup for that matter) boil. Remember Grandma's stockpot standing on the back of the fuel stove where it never boiled.

And thinking about Grandma's soup, you know it never tasted the same, not even on consecutive days. It just sat over a very low heat accumulating various flavours from whatever leftovers Grandma threw into it. You should never worry whether your soup is going to taste exactly the same as the last time you made it. Unfortunately, we have become so brainwashed with advertising — 'Our soups always taste the same' — we have lost our sense of adventure when it comes to taste. The following recipes are very basic, and we hope you will let your imagination run riot and give your families some interesting surprises whenever you serve soup.

BEEF STOCK

1 shin of veal, cut into 3 or 4 pieces (our butcher never minds doing this for us)

Cover the meat with cold water and simmer for several hours until the meat is falling off the bone. Remove from the heat and allow to cool. When the fat has solidified on the top — it will do this more quickly in the refrigerator if you have room to put the boiler in — lift off the fat.

If you want clear stock, strain through a sieve to remove all the pieces of meat.

If you want a heavier stock that is not clear, put the meat and liquid into your blender.

Now re-simmer the stock until it has reduced to about one half of its original volume. It is now ready for use as your basic stock for any soup calling for beef stock.

MUTTON STOCK

1 neck of lamb (or mutton), cut into 3 or 4 pieces
1 lamb knuckle cut into 3 pieces

Method as for beef stock.

CHICKEN STOCK

the carcass of 1 or more chickens, together with any bones and
scraps from the roast chicken or you can buy 1 kg (2 lb) of
chicken thighs

Follow the method for beef and mutton stock, but you will
find that chicken fat is much softer than the fat from beef or
mutton and is more difficult to skim from the surface at room
temperature. Therefore put the stock in the refrigerator for 1
hour or 2 and you will find the skimming much easier.

FISH STOCK

fish heads, bones and scraps after you have filleted your fish,
or you can buy about 1 kg (2 lb) of small fish

If using whole fish, chop them roughly before simmering.
Otherwise the method is the same as for the other stocks.

Note about fish stock. Because of the fish bones and the
odd scale or two, never force this stock through the sieve or
put it in the blender — just drain it, keeping the clear juices
and discarding the solids.

Vegetables or yeast extract can be added to soup stock, but
be very careful with quantities, starting with half a teaspoon
and tasting as you go. These products are usually rather strong-
flavoured and often very salty and can easily drown all other
flavours. A more subtle flavour is obtained by dissolving a
tablespoon of Torulla yeast in the soup 10 minutes before
serving. (Torulla yeast is an *inactive* dry yeast, obtainable from
health food stores.)

Always remember that vegetable soups depend for their
flavours on the vegetables used, together with the addition of
appropriate herbs, rather than on strongly flavoured stocks.

STORING SOUP STOCK

Sometimes we get carried away when making stock and

finish up with enough to make soup for a regiment. Of course there is never room in the refrigerator, and anyway your family will complain if you serve soup every day for a week. So we make iceblocks.

Reduce the filtered stock further by returning it to the stove and simmering gently without the lid so more of the water is driven off. When it has cooled, pour the liquid into iceblock trays and freeze. Once frozen, the stock iceblocks can be removed from the trays and stored in plastic bags in the freezer. If you want small quantities of stock in a hurry for soup or for making gravies, use a cube or two. They surpass bought stock cubes any day, and what is more, you know what they are made of, that they do not contain too much salt, and that they are not over-seasoned.

We hope that all this talk of stocks will not deter you from putting together your own soups, because soup can be made without previously prepared stock. Stock is used to provide flavour and body, rather than to give additional nutriment to your soup. After all that simmering, straining and filtering there can't be much nourishment left, particularly in the liquor of clear soups. With a little judicious use of herbs, spices, grains for thickening, your soups will taste grand made on water. (But don't tell your mother.) And don't forget to save the water if you are boiling a fowl; keep any leftover gravy for both thickening and flavour.

In these days of energy crises, making soup is probably an expensive waste of fuel. This is obvious when you compare the modern gas or electric stove with the wood or coke stoves used by our grandmothers. On the old stoves there was plenty of room on the cooking plate; there were cool and hot areas and all degrees in between; so it was no problem to move the soup pot around while the main cooking was in progress. You can't do this on a modern stove. You will use one burner for your soup and that immediately restricts your cooking area. Also, who is going to go off to work with one gas jet burning, even if it is covered by an asbestos mat? Insurance companies don't like it. If you have a crockpot, it is a different story — crockpots are marvellous for making stock and soup. But apart from all that, we don't believe any cook should spend 6 or 8 hours in the kitchen just to make soup, unless she is being paid award wages.

We are not giving many soup recipes because we feel that soup is very much a thing of the moment — depending on what is in the vegetable basket, what scraps of meat are lying around asking to be used up, and your own imagination in the use of herbs and spices. Never be afraid to make substitutions. If you are unsure of the resulting flavour, remove a couple of tablespoons of the unfinished soup from the pot and add a little, a very little, of the substitute and taste. If you like the result, go ahead and finish the soup. If you don't like what you have done, try something else. And as you have used only a little of the soup, you are not going to waste much if you throw out 2 tablespoons of soup; or as it is only a very little of the soup, you won't really spoil the end result if you return the sample to the pot.

In the recipes that follow, we have given a few traditional ones requiring the long slow method of cooking, but for most of them, you will find shortcuts have been made, and the results are more than comparable. As we said before, don't tell Grandma you made the soup in under an hour because she won't believe you, or if she does, she will accuse you of using packet soup from the supermarket shelves even if she can't find the tins in the garbage can.

TO THICKEN SOUP

There are lots of things you can use to add body to your soup. Throw in a handful of barley, or for that matter any of the grains; just be sure you allow sufficient time for the grains to cook.

Flour made from any of the grains can be used to thicken soup: plain white flour, wholemeal flour, rice flour, rye flour, etc. Mix 1 or 2 tablespoons of the flour with cold water to make a thin paste. Then add half a cup of the hot liquid from your soup, stirring all the while. Now return the pasty mixture to the soup, stirring it vigorously to prevent lumping. If you pour the thickening in slowly, whisking all the while, you will find lumps do not form. Allow a good 10 minutes for the flour to cook and thicken your soup before serving. It does not matter if you let it simmer longer; as long as you have thoroughly mixed the flour paste through the hot soup, it will not become lumpy.

Thick cream folded through the soup after you have served it not only thickens but adds a delicious creamy texture. But do not use cream in this manner with soup made from acidic vegetables or fruit such as tomato, as the cream curdles.

Dumplings are as good in soup as in stews. Here are three simple recipes.

SUET DUMPLINGS

1 cup plain flour
½ teaspoon baking powder
½ teaspoon salt
1 tablespoon chopped suet (or butter or margarine)
water (or milk)

Sift together the flour, baking powder and salt.

Using either your fingers or the pastry blender, work the suet into the flour.

Add sufficient water (or milk) to make a firm dough, the same consistency as you use for scones.

Pinch off small pieces of dough and roll them into balls about the size of large marbles.

Drop the dumplings into the simmering soup about 20 minutes before you are ready to serve.

CHEESE DUMPLINGS

½ cup breadcrumbs (we prefer wholemeal breadcrumbs)
½ cup grated cheese
pepper and salt
pinch mixed herbs (optional)
1 beaten egg

Combine the breadcrumbs, cheese, pepper and salt, and the herbs if you are using them. Bind the dry mixture with a well-beaten egg.

Pinch off small pieces and form into balls the size of large marbles and drop into the simmering soup about 15 minutes before serving.

GLUTEN FLOUR DUMPLINGS

2 tablespoons gluten flour
1 tablespoon Torulla yeast
pepper and salt
pinch of dried rosemary
water

Mix together the flour, yeast, pepper and salt, and rosemary.
Add sufficient water to make a very dry dough.

Pinch off marble-sized pieces and form into balls.

Drop into the simmering soup about 30 minutes before
serving.

CREAMED SOUP

When making any creamed soup — for example, cream of
asparagus, cream of onion — we find the following an easy and
effective method. While your basic ingredients are cooking,
prepare the liaison, which is really a thin white sauce made
from the following:

1 tablespoon butter
1 tablespoon plain flour
1 cup milk

Then slowly pour the liaison, while it is still hot, into the
simmering soup, stirring briskly until the two are well blended.
And that is your creamed soup. If you want to make it richer,
use cream instead of milk; instant powdered milk can be substituted for fresh milk; or you can add 1 or 2 tablespoons of
the dried milk to the fresh milk to enrich it. Exception: When
making cream of tomato soup, pour the soup into the liaison
(see recipe page 34).

Eggs can also be used to give body to your soup. There are
two ways of doing this: crumbled, hard-boiled eggs are added
just before serving, or 1 or 2 eggs are lightly beaten and then
whisked into the soup. Never let the soup boil after you have
added the beaten eggs.

THE ACCOMPANIMENTS FOR SOUP

For clear soup or consommé

Either grate or dice finely root vegetables such as carrots,
turnips, parsnips, etc.; you will need about 1 to 1½ cups to
serve six people. In a separate pot, quickly bring the pieces to
the boil; strain and refresh by immersing in ice-cold water and
draining. Add to the soup a few minutes before serving, just
long enough for the shredded vegetables to heat through.

Fresh green peas, tiny florets of cauliflower or broccoli, or
sliced leeks can be used in the same way.

Italian pasta cooked until tender in boiling salted water can be added to the soup just before serving. By using pasta in fancy shapes such as letters or shells, you can add interest to a plain clear soup. If you have run out of pasta, make a savoury pancake and cut it into tiny shapes and add these to the soup just before serving.

Put 1 spoonful of plain boiled rice into each soup bowl before pouring the consommé over it. This is known as *consommé au Riz*.

Garnishes for thick soup and broth

If you have any leftover sausages from breakfast, cut them into 1cm (½in) rounds and drop them into plain vegetable soup. Or use raw sausage-meat (i.e., very finely minced or ground meat): roll small pieces about the size of a marble in flour and drop them into the soup 15 minutes before serving.

Dumplings have been mentioned. These are good in either thick or thin soup.

A sprinkle of fresh herbs floating on the top of any soup improves both its appearance and flavour. Try fresh mint with pea soup; with cream soup, float a few fresh watercress leaves on the top; and there is always parsley.

Macaroni, spaghetti, noodles can all be added to the soup, allowing about half an hour for cooking time.

Croûtons are made from slices of bread, either fresh or old. Remove the crusts and cut the bread into dice about 1cm (½in) cubed. Fry them in very hot fat and then drain. You can either float these on top of each soup bowl or serve separately for the diners to add if they so desire.

Pulled bread goes well with soup. You will find the recipe in the chapter on breads. But if you do not want to make your own bread you can get something almost as good by tearing apart a fresh loaf of bread and drying the rough pieces in the oven until they are crisp and light golden in colour.

If you are too busy for any of these, plain dry toast is always acceptable.

BEEF TEA

450g (1lb) lean beef, very finely minced (ground)
2 cups cold water

The only secret for making good beef tea is the temperature — never let it get above 55°C (130°F). For this reason always use a double boiler, or if you do not have a double boiler, use a heat-resistant bowl of such a size that it will sit neatly on top of your pot with its bottom about 5 cm (2 in) above the bottom of the pot. Place cold water in the bottom of the double boiler (or the pot, if using a basin and pot), and put the meat and 2 cups of cold water in the top half of the boiler. Heat very slowly, and stir occasionally. When you make beef tea, it is wise to use a thermometer for the first few times until you get used to using the low temperature for cooking. If the meat changes colour and goes dark, you have over-heated it. Keep it at this low temperature for about 20 minutes and then strain using a coarse strainer. Season with pepper and salt, and add a teaspoon of chopped parsley to float on the top.

If you are going to re-heat the beef tea, use your double boiler. Over-heating destroys the delicate flavour.

OXTAIL SOUP

1 oxtail
6 cups cold water
1 large carrot
1 small turnip
1 medium-sized onion
1 stalk of celery
1 bay leaf
bouquet garni
pepper and salt

Oxtail soup is better if you take two days to make it.

Ask the butcher to cut the oxtail into 3½ cm (1½ in) pieces. Remove as much fat as possible from the pieces. Place the oxtail pieces in a large saucepan and add the water. Simmer slowly for 3 or 4 hours; by this time the meat should be tender and be coming away from the bone.

Remove the meat from the heat and let stand overnight to allow the fat to rise to the surface.

Next day, skim off all the fat. Add the prepared vegetables and the herbs. As this is a hearty soup, cut the vegetables into large bite-sized pieces. Simmer until the vegetables are tender. Remove the bouquet garni and the bay leaf. Taste and season with pepper and salt.

If the butcher has supplied you with a very large oxtail you will need more water and on the first day cooking time will be 4 to 6 hours — the bigger the tail, the older the beast from which it came and therefore the longer time.

Grandma went to more trouble with this soup. After the fat had been skimmed off, she strained the soup. The meat was reserved and the liquor cleared (egg shells and egg white method). The meat was then returned to the cleared stock and the vegetables added.

There is no reason why you cannot use good beef stock instead of water in making oxtail soup. Also, if you want to thicken the end product, barley can be added or you can thicken with flour as explained in the earlier part of this chapter.

Kangaroo tail soup is made in exactly the same way. As kangaroo is rather lean meat, you do not have the problem of skimming the fat, and the soup can be made in the one day.

PEA SOUP

Traditional pea soup is made from dried peas and a ham bone.

1 ham bone, with meat
1 cup dried peas

You should start the soup the day before you want it. Simmer the ham bone in 6 to 8 cups of water for several hours. Remove the bone and the meat and let the stock stand overnight so the fat can rise to the surface.

Overnight, soak the dried peas in 2 cups of water.

Next day, skim the fat from the stock and to this stock add your soaked peas together with any water they have not absorbed. (Dried peas vary considerably, and you may find you do not need this much water, or you may even need more.)

Simmer gently for 1 hour, or until the peas are tender, without a lid so as to reduce the liquid content.

When the peas are cooked, put the whole lot into the blender or force it through a sieve. Australian split or dried peas always require puréeing, but American ones almost literally melt and do not need puréeing.

Just before serving, add some of the shredded meat from the original ham bone.

Add salt and pepper to taste. We cannot give exact quantities for salt because the saltiness of the ham varies so much.

Either in place of the ham bone, or in addition to it, you can use bacon bones or a pig's trotter.

Diced onions and carrots are sometimes added to this soup when you put in the soaked dried peas. We have given the basic materials and method, and after that it is up to you to try some variants.

LENTIL SOUP

1 cup of lentils (soaked overnight in 2 cups water)
4 cups beef stock (or stock made from bacon bones or salt pork or plain water)
1 carrot, diced
1 medium-sized onion, diced
1 stalk celery
1 small piece turnip (or a piece about the size of an egg)
1 cup milk
2 tablespoons margarine
salt and pepper
herbs — sage, thyme and parsley

Sauté the vegetables in the margarine for 5 minutes.

In a large pot, place the lentils, sautéed vegetables, sage and thyme; add the stock (or water). Cover and simmer for at least 1 hour, or until the lentils are soft.

Purée the soup by forcing it through a sieve or putting it in the blender.

Return the purée to the pot, season, and add the cup of milk. When it is reheated, serve with chopped parsley sprinkled on the top.

BARLEY BROTH OR SCOTCH BROTH

1 neck of mutton (or knuckle of veal)
2 tablespoons pearl barley
6 cups cold water
1 carrot, diced
1 onion, diced (or 2 leeks, sliced)
1 small turnip, diced
2 stalks celery, chopped
2 tablespoons fresh parsley, chopped
pepper and salt

In a large saucepan place the neck of mutton (or veal knuckle), the pearl barley and the 6 cups of cold water. Simmer for 1½ hours.

Add the prepared vegetables and simmer another half an hour, or until the vegetables are tender and the barley is cooked.

Using kitchen paper, remove any fat from the surface of the broth — a few sheets of paper gently passed across the soup will absorb most of the fat that has risen to the surface.

Just before serving, taste the soup and season with pepper and salt. Add the freshly chopped parsley last so that it will not lose its green colour.

If you are using hulled barley, that is, barley with only the outer husk removed, the cooking time must be lengthened to 3 hours.

COCK-A-LEEKIE SOUP

Wherever Scotsmen have settled, they have demanded that their good wives produce cock-a-leekie soup at least once a month, and more often if the ingredients are available. And rightly so, because it is a meal in itself.

1 old boiling fowl
1 neck mutton (or knuckle of veal)
2 cloves
12 cups cold water
6 to 8 leeks, depending on size
1 tablespoon rice
pepper and salt

In a large boiler place the fowl, the mutton, the cloves and all the cold water. Allow to simmer for 1 hour (longer will not matter).

Add the leeks cut into 5 cm (2 in) lengths, and sprinkle the rice into the simmering broth. Continue to simmer for another hour.

Season with pepper and salt.

The meats can be served separately with parsley sauce made from some of the broth, and the liquor served as a broth. Or you can serve meat and broth together.

MULLIGATAWNY SOUP

This is a mild and fairly sweet curry soup which tastes good hot or cold. Although many people think of this as a very British soup, its origins are Indian. The name is a corruption of the Tamil milagu-tannir, meaning 'pepper water'. We can thank the British Raj for introducing it to English (and Australian) kitchens.

6 cups chicken stock
1 large apple, grated
1 medium-sized turnip, grated
1 large onion, grated
1 cup pre-cooked rice, with saffron if possible
1 cup raisins
1 teaspoon salt

Bring the chicken stock to a simmer in a large saucepan, then throw in the apple, turnip, onion, rice, raisins and salt. Keep it simmering, and stir in the following mixture:

2 tablespoons lime juice (or lime cordial)
2 tablespoons sugar
1 tablespoon cornflour
3 teaspoons curry powder
½ teaspoon garlic powder (or 2 cloves crushed garlic)

Mix the dry ingredients in the lime juice (or cordial) until they form a smooth paste, thin it if necessary with a little extra (and cold) chicken stock, then pour it into the simmering soup, stirring constantly until it returns to a simmer. Simmer it for 2 hours.

This gives good-sized servings for six people.

Like all Indian soup, mulligatawny is a thin soup but full-bodied in flavour. If you chill any hot Indian soup for a day or two and then reheat it, the flavour is greatly enhanced.

TOMATO SOUP

4 cups tomato juice
½ teaspoon salt
4 tablespoons sugar
2 teaspoons sodium bicarbonate
2 teaspoons Worcestershire sauce
½ teaspoon sweet basil
2 teaspoons lemon juice
4 teaspoons cornflour (corn starch) — optional

Dieticians are strongly opposed to the use of sodium bicarbonate in cooking, but with tomato soup it is really necessary unless you like the strong acidic flavour of cooked tomatoes.

Being an alkali, it neutralises some of the acid and the small amount used does not leave any objectional taste. However, if you don't like using sodium bicarbonate, ignore this ingredient; you can still make tasty tomato soup.

In a saucepan combine the tomato juice, salt, sugar; bring this to simmering point and remove from the heat. Now add the sodium bicarbonate. It will froth up (this is why you remove the pot from the stove) as the bicarbonate and acid react.

When the frothing stops, add the Worcestershire sauce, sweet basil and lemon juice, and return the soup to the stove.

The soup can be served at this stage, or you can thicken it a little using the cornflour (corn starch). Mix the cornflour with a little cold water to make a smooth paste. To this paste add 2 tablespoons of the hot soup, mixing it well to prevent lumps forming. Now add the thin flour paste to the hot soup, stirring constantly. Allow another 4 to 5 minutes for the flour to cook thoroughly, and at the same time it will thicken the soup. Vary the amount of thickening to suit your own taste.

Taste the soup, add more seasoning if necessary, and serve with croûtons. This quantity will serve four to six people.

Perhaps you are wondering what kind of tomato juice to use. When tomatoes are plentiful we make our own and bottle it for future use. But there is no reason why you cannot use any tinned variety of tomato juice — some brands are thicker than others, and you will use your own judgement as to whether water should be added, or the thickening omitted.

HOMEMADE TOMATO JUICE

Ten kg (25 lb) of ripe tomatoes will yield approximately 4 litres (7 pints) of tomato juice. The tomatoes must be ripe and juicy. It saves a lot of bother if you skin them before starting the cooking. To do this, immerse 5 or 6 tomatoes at a time in boiling water. Insert the prongs of a fork into the stalk end and with a sharp knife make a cut in the opposite end — the skin will peel away very easily. If you have a good supply of very hot water to the kitchen, just hold the tomato on the prongs of the fork and put it under the tap.

Having peeled your tomatoes, chop them roughly and put into a large boiler. *You do not need any water because the ripe tomatoes are full of juice.* Using a low heat to begin with, bring to the boil and boil gently until all the fruit has gone to pulp.

Now force the pulp through a sieve to extract the seeds. Do not be tempted to use a blender for this, because although it will give you a smooth paste, the seeds do not enhance either the flavour or the colour.

Return the sieved pulp to the boiler and bring back to the boil. Bottle the pulp in sterilised bottles and seal them. To sterilise bottles, fill them with cold water; place in a large boiler and cover with cold water; and bring to a rolling boil; boil for 20 minutes. Don't forget to sterlise the bottle-tops as well.

When filling the bottles with the boiling juice, stand the bottles in a sink of hot water. This keeps everything at much the same temperature and thus lessens the likelihood of the glass breaking.

Stand the filled and sealed bottles on the kitchen bench for a few days and watch for the development of any gas bubbles. If the juice does start to bubble, it is fermenting, either because the bottles are not air-tight, or the juice was not boiling hot and sterile when you bottled it. If you catch them quickly, you can open the bottles and return the juice to the pot and re-boil. Re-sterilise the bottles before using them again.

When you are happy that everything is air-tight, that is, after three or four days, store the bottles in a cool place. The juice seems to keep almost indefinitely. In fact, we have occasionally found a bottle that has been pushed to the back of the cupboard and been there for 2 or 3 years. On opening, the juice was as fresh as when first bottled. It is a good idea to put the date of bottling on each bottle, so that you can use the oldest first.

We never add either salt or sugar, or any seasoning to our homemade tomato juice. In this way, we have plain tomato juice without additional flavouring that can be used in any recipe calling for it.

To make a pre-dinner appetiser, open a bottle of your homemade tomato juice, add pepper, salt and sugar and a dash of Worcestershire sauce, and then chill. Garnish the appetiser with a slice of fresh lemon and a sprig of watercress. A quick method of disolving the sugar is to use a spoonful of hot water to make a sugar syrup and then add this to the juice.

CREAM OF TOMATO SOUP

Many people seem to have trouble making cream of tomato soup because their soup always curdles. Tomatoes are very acidic and will curdle milk or cream. But there is an easy way to make excellent cream of tomato soup: you need two pots, one for the tomato and one for the cream mixture. When both are cooked and of equal temperatures, carefully blend the two, adding the tomato to the cream a little at a time and stirring all the while.

3 cups tomato juice
¾ teaspoon salt
3 tablespoons sugar
1½ teaspoons sodium bicarbonate
½ teaspoon sweet basil

This is the tomato part of the soup. Combine the juice, salt and sugar in a pot and bring to the simmer. Remove from the stove and add the sodium bicarbonate. When frothing has ceased, add the basil and return to the stove.

2 tablespoons of butter
2 tablespoons plain flour
2 cups of milk

In a larger pot make a thin roux sauce. Melt the butter and remove the pot from the heat; add the flour, stirring until you have a smooth paste. Return to the heat and cook for 2 to 3 minutes over low heat, stirring all the time. Again remove the pot from the stove and add the milk a little at a time, stirring all the time. Return to the stove and bring to the boil, but still stirring. Boil for 3 minutes until the flour is cooked and the sauce is smooth and has thickened.

Now slowly add the hot tomato juice, whisking briskly. Simmer; do not boil.

Serve immediately with croûtons, or any other soup accompaniment you like. A sprinkle of chopped fresh parsley or a few leaves of watercress floated on the top gives your soup a professional appearance.

You will have noticed that we use a goodly amount of sugar in both our tomato soups. The exact amount will vary with the variety of tomatoes you have used for the juice because some are sweet, for example, Tom Thumb and egg tomatoes, and others are acidic.

Another little note of warning: if you are using canned tomato juice, taste before adding either sugar or salt because both of these may have been added before canning.

POTATO SOUP

Or for that matter, any root vegetable or pumpkin soup.

3 medium-sized old potatoes (or 2 large ones)
1½ cups water (or stock)
sprig of mint
1 small onion, chopped
1 tablespoon butter
1 tablespoon flour
1 cup milk (or ½ cup cream and ½ cup milk)
pepper and salt
1 tablespoon chives, chopped

Peel and slice the potatoes into 1 cm (½in) pieces, place in a pot and use sufficient stock or water to just cover the potatoes. Add the mint and bring to the boil, cooking until the potatoes are soft.

Meanwhile sauté the onion in the butter and add to the cooking potatoes, reserving the butter.

Make a thin roux sauce by stirring the flour into the butter, returning to the stove to cook for 2 or 3 minutes; remove from the heat and add the milk or milk and cream, stirring continually. Return to the heat and continue to stir for 4 or 5 minutes, until the flour is cooked and the sauce is smooth.

Mash the potatoes in their cooking water (or stock) and force them through a coarse sieve or use your blender.

Add the puréed potatoes to the thin roux. Season with pepper and salt, add the chopped chives and reheat.

If you have a plentiful supply of chives, use all chives and no onion; this produces a potato soup with a very delicate flavour.

ROOT VEGETABLE SOUP

A creamed vegetable soup can be made from any of the root vegetables, either using just one kind or mixing. A combination of carrot and parsnip will surprise you, particularly if you add a pinch of Chinese Five Spices. Be adventuresome and play around with the herbs and spices with any of these soups.

PALESTINE SOUP

Palestine soup is made from Jerusalem artichokes. These are a root vegetable and are not to be confused with the globe artichokes (see further notes on page 117 in Chapter 5 — Vegetables and Salads). Peeling these ugly tubers is a tedious job, so scrub them clean using a stiff bristled brush. Cook the required amount in sufficient water to cover. Then, while the tubers are still hot, you can squeeze the soft pulp out — this is the part you use — and discard the skins. Use rubber gloves while doing this squeezing because it is much easier to do while they are still hot. Discard this first cooking water because it is usually discoloured and a bit gritty — it is difficult to remove all the surface dirt. Mash the pulp and combine with the thin roux. Chives, parsley, chervil are all good herbs to use with Palestine soup.

PUMPKIN SOUP

Pumpkin soup is made the same way as potato soup, but instead of the sprig of mint, grate a little nutmeg into the creamed mixture.

CREAM OF ASPARAGUS SOUP

1 bunch asparagus
2 spring onions
2 cups chicken stock
2 tablespoons butter
2 tablespoons plain flour
salt and pepper
½ cup cream
chopped parsley and grated lemon rind for garnish

Wash the asparagus stalks and cut into 1 cm (½ in) pieces, reserving the tender tips. Finely chop the spring onions, including the green leaves. Simmer the asparagus pieces and the onion in the chicken stock until tender, adding the tender tips towards the end of simmering time. Cover the pot so as not to lose too much liquid. Remove the pieces when cooked, and set aside the tender tips.

Make a thin roux as follows. Melt the butter in the pot, remove from the heat and add the flour. Return to heat and cook for 3 or 4 minutes. Remove the pot from heat and stir in the liquid you have saved from the asparagus. Return to heat and continue stirring until it is thickened.

Add the asparagus pieces you lifted out of the stock, and then put the whole lot through the blender or force it through a fine sieve.

Season with pepper and salt and reheat. Carefully fold in the tender tips of asparagus and just before serving, fold in the cream and garnish the soup with the chopped parsley and lemon rind.

This soup is delicious if chilled and served cold. But if you do this, do not add the cream until you serve the chilled soup, having it the same temperature as the creamed soup. Add the parsley and grated lemon rind after you have folded in the cream.

Using the same method, creamed soup can be made from lots of vegetables and fruit. Briefly, cook your chosen vegetable in stock or water; make a thin roux using this cooking water; combine the cooked vegetables with the roux; purée; season and reheat.

MINESTRONE

It seems that every recipe book must include this most cele-brated Italian soup. And every Italian momma has her own secret ingredient that makes her soup special. However, it is a soup you can vary as long as you use these basic ingredients: dried beans, fresh beans, zucchinis (courgettes), tomatoes, macaroni and Parmesan cheese. Here is a recipe that works for us and uses canned beans (saves soaking overnight and 2 hours' cooking before you start on the soup proper).

*one 300g can of beans (haricot, red, butter or any kind of
    bean, but not in tomato sauce)*
2 onions
2 stalks celery
225g (8oz) fresh green beans
2 zucchinis (courgettes)
2 medium-sized potatoes
2 large ripe tomatoes
1 clove garlic
6 cups beef stock
6 tablespoons olive oil
¾ cup macaroni
½ teaspoon each of chopped fresh oregano, basil and parsley

pepper and salt
freshly grated Parmesan cheese

Prepare all the vegetables by washing, peeling (or stringing where necessary), and chopping into bite-sized pieces.

Heat the olive oil in a large saucepan. Add the crushed garlic, onions and celery and sauté until the onions are translucent, but not browned.

Add the remaining vegetables, the can of beans and the stock. Cover and simmer for about 30 to 40 minutes.

Take off the lid and bring the soup to the boil. When boiling add the macaroni, the chopped herbs, the salt and pepper. Cook the soup for a further 20 minutes uncovered, or until the macaroni is tender.

Taste and adjust seasoning if necessary.

Serve. We always serve the grated Parmesan cheese separately, as there are people who do not like cheese with soup — for ourselves, we love it.

You can vary this soup; in all truth, ours never turns out the same. We use whatever vegetables are in season, and although we prefer fresh herbs, dried herbs work just as well, but their flavour is slightly different so be sure to taste as you go. We have even substituted egg noodles for the macaroni, but we have not found a name for this variant. Have you any suggestions?

VEGETABLE SOUP

Although all dishes are better when prepared from fresh ingredients, it is surprising what you can do with the odds and ends that accumulate in the vegetable basket. If you are in a hurry, grate the vegetables first so they will cook more quickly.

2 onions
2 large potatoes
2 carrots
1 parsnip
1 small turnip
1 large piece pumpkin
handful green beans
handful green peas
2 large ripe tomatoes
any other bits and pieces, but not cabbage or cauliflower as
    these tend to drown the other flavours

stock or water
vermicelli (or macaroni, or noodles), optional
pepper and salt

Prepare the vegetables; either cut them into bite-sized pieces or grate them. Place in a large pot and add sufficient stock or water to cover. Simmer the vegetables until tender; then increase the heat to a rolling boil and add the vermicelli. Cook the soup for about 20 minutes at the higher temperature.

Taste and season; have fun and games with herbs here.

If you haven't got any stock, use plain water and be generous with herbs and spices. The addition of a tin of beans with their liquor will help to give body to a thin soup. The main thing is to *taste*; don't serve up a watery tasteless concoction that looks like dishwater. If you add dumplings to this soup, you will have a meal-in-one-course. Sliced cooked sausage will improve a dull soup, but of course it is no longer a vegetable soup.

AVOCADO SOUP

1 ripe, but still firm, avocado
6 cups rich chicken stock
1 cup bite-sized cooked chicken pieces, preferably breast
2 tablespoons chopped chives
pepper and salt
a few watercress sprays
1 cup cream

Chop the avocado flesh into bite-sized pieces, or smaller if your guests say they do not eat avocado (a little deception in cooking never hurts). Bring the chicken stock to a simmer, add the avocado and chicken pieces and continue to simmer for 5 minutes. Add the chives, pepper and salt. Before serving, fold in the cup of thick cream. Decorate each soup bowl with a few leaves of watercress.

STEWS

This is probably as good a place as any to write about stews. Do you know the difference between a stew and a soup? We find this a bit hard to explain because if our soup is too thick we call it stew, and if the stew gets too thin we rechristen it soup. The principles of making both are really the same: long, slow cooking processes at low temperatures, always less than boiling, except perhaps for the few minutes after flour thickening is added.

In a stew the bits of meat and vegetable are usually bite-sized and identifiable, whereas in soup these are often blended into an homogeneous mass. But the same ingredients are used. If you take the time to brown the meat pieces and the onions in hot fat (we prefer using butter) before you throw them into the stewing pot, your final product will have that lovely rich colour rather than the dirty grey of meats cooked in water. However, if your stew ends up rather grey-looking, you can always cheat and add a little gravy browning.

Probably the most famous of all stews is Irish stew, and although some books give fancy recipes for this, true Irish stew is made from mutton, potatoes and onions seasoned with pepper and salt and the only herb used is parsley.

IRISH STEW

450g (1lb) middle neck of mutton
900g (2lb) potatoes
2 large onions
salt, pepper
chopped parsley

When you buy the neck of mutton, ask your butcher to chop it into joints. Remove as much fat as possible, but do not worry if you can't get it all off. A true Irishman likes his stew with fat floating on the top — just ask Col.

Peel the potatoes and onions and cut them into 1cm (½in) slices.

Use a pan with a tight-fitting lid or a casserole dish with a lid. Starting with the meat, place all the ingredients in alternate layers, that is, a layer of meat, a layer of onions, a layer of potatoes, and finish with a layer of potatoes.

Sprinkle the pepper and salt over the top and carefully pour in sufficient cold water to only half cover the contents of your casserole, without dislodging any of the pieces. Put on the lid and simmer very slowly for about 2½ hours.

It is easier to control this low temperature if you put the pan or casserole in the oven. Crockpots are ideal for this kind of cooking, as you can maintain low heat without constant watching.

The parsley is sprinkled over the stew when you serve it.

Although you can use lamb in place of the mutton, the latter makes the best stew because it has much more flavour. We hope you can find an Australian butcher who still sells mutton; if you do, let us know. It is a great pity that mutton has become unfashionable and only lamb is offered to the housewives of Australian cities. We became very excited when we found both hogget and mutton in New Zealand butcher shops.

2. FISH

Though Australians are mainly coastal inhabitants of an island continent, we do not eat fish as often as you would expect; and yet we can boast more fishing widows (and sometimes widowers) than most countries. Sure, they are seldom widows for long periods of time as are the fishing widows of Lisbon or Taiwan, but these are the widows of professional fishermen. When fishing fleets put out from Bermagui or Eden in New South Wales, they are seldom at sea for more than a week, and unless the prawn trawlers are heading north for the Gulf of Carpentaria, they usually cross the bar from Ballina in New South Wales, and Yeppoon in Queensland, on the afternoon high tide and return on the morning tide. It is to the weekend widows of amateur anglers that we refer. Any beach, any rocky headland, any sleepy lagoon, any inland creek has its devotees of this most ancient of sports. They come from any and every suburb. So what happens to all the fish — not the ones that got away, those that are caught?

There is nothing wrong with these fish, which range from pilchards to jewfish, from Australian whiting to man-eating sharks. After asking questions and listening to fishy stories, we have decided there are two main reasons why most of these fish are either thrown back or fed to the cat.

'Fish stink!' (And so does boiling cabbage.) If fish are fresh, the only smells are of seaweed and sea, and the faintest of fishy odours. Rub your hands well with salt both before and after handling fish and there will be no clinging fishy smell.

'But they bring home such weird-looking fish, I don't know what to do with them.' And that is the real reason. Look in any fish-shop window and you will see whiting fillets, snapper, tailor, flounder; the cook knows what to do with these. But what does the fish widow do when presented with a catfish, an eel, a snook, a long Tom, a mulloway?

When we began this book, we didn't know either. We didn't even like fish very much. So we talked to fishermen who are their own cooks, and most fishermen are, and to government fishery experts. We do not pretend to be experts in this field because we have not had sufficient practice, and neither of us are fishermen these days. But for what it is worth, we will tell you what we have learnt.

There are many more edible Australian fish than most people realise — both salt and fresh water. The Aboriginal peoples knew them all, and the early journal-keepers such as Tench and White all have references to hauls of fish caught off beaches and in estuaries. But our pig-headed British ancestors don't seem to have learnt much from the original Australian cooks. This is probably because Australian fish are warm-water fish and differ greatly in appearance, texture of flesh and flavour from the fishes of the colder northern hemisphere waters. If a fish did look a bit familiar it was given a familiar name; but the Australian sea salmon is a member of the perch family and no relation to its northern namesake; Australian whiting don't even look like North Sea whiting and are related to the breams and bass. This leads to unfair comparisons and in some cases unjust criticisms of the quality of Australian fish. Sea salmon are frequently caught by surf fishermen and thrown back because of the coarse texture and dark colour of the flesh. This is a terrible waste because properly prepared baked Australian salmon is a delicious dish. We tell you what to do in our fisherman's recipe of that name.

Further confusion is added by the use of varying local names for the same fish. Luderick is called sweep in Tasmania, nigger in New South Wales, rock perch in Victoria and black bream in Queensland, while the New Zealanders call it *parore*, which is the Maori name.

There are local prejudices. In Queensland shark is used only for bait, and in Victoria it is sold under the name flake and often at high prices. Catfish caught in the tidal Norman River of north-west Queensland are thrown back to feed the crocodiles, but some estuary anglers on the east coast are delighted when they land a catfish. It is the same with our fresh-water fish; of the fish caught in the vast inland river systems of the Murray — Murrumbidgee — Darling, the locals will only eat Murray cod and yellow belly and sometimes redfin; carp (introduced from Europe) and tench are sent to the Melbourne markets.

Your bewilderment when presented with a strange sea creature is fully appreciated, but there are only two decisions to be made. Is it edible? How is it to be prepared? First, make certain your fish is not one of the poisonous kind. The commonest of these that your children will bring in is the toad fish. It is an ugly little grey fish that blows itself up when caught. There are a few others to beware of: catfish have poisonous glands on their fins at the base of needle-sharp spines. An experienced fisherman, however, will cut these out before bringing home the catch. As for the rest, if the fish is unfamiliar, ask another fisherman. He may not like that particular variety of fish, but he will tell you whether it is edible or not. Having assured yourself that your fish is fit for food, how should it be cooked: baked, grilled, steamed, fried or poached?

The method of cooking fish depends on a number of factors, including what cooking facilities are available, but the most important is what kind of flesh the fish possesses. Fish (as opposed to shellfish) can be classified into three basic groups as regards their flesh:
● the degree of oiliness
● texture (fine or coarse)
● whether the flesh is soft or firm.

A few examples from fish with which you may be familiar: anchovy, mullet and Murray cod are oily; Australian whiting, flathead and shark are dry; and in between you have bream, flounder and jewfish. Carp, now very plentiful in some of the western rivers although not an indigenous fish, has extremely coarse flesh. In fact, most fish which grow to a great size have increasing coarseness of flesh with age. The rule of thumb: the bigger the fish, the coarser the flesh. Firm-fleshed fish is easier to handle during preparation and cooking; salt-water cod and luderick have very soft flesh and need careful handling, but both are delicious eating.

Oily fish are best either baked or grilled. If it is a dry fish, use plenty of butter and baste throughout the cooking time. If it has delicate flesh, pick a method that requires little handling, such as poaching. All fish can be fried, either with or without batter, but if the flesh is fine and tends to break up, coat the fillets with batter or egg-and-crumb them. Don't try to boil, grill or fry coarse-fleshed fish such as carp or shark; either braise or stew them, slowly and gently. Before we detail the cooking methods, here are a few hints.

● Don't overcook fish. Cooking times are short — about 5 minutes for frying fillets and a little longer for whole fish; 30 to 40 minutes when baking fish, again depending on size and whether you are baking whole fish or fillets. The fish is cooked when the flesh has changed from the semi-translucent pink-white-grey of the raw fish to an opaque white. If you cook it any longer, the flesh becomes hard and the flavour is destroyed. You will get an idea of the short time required to cook fish if you think about the methods used in serving raw fish. Raw fish fillets are soaked in a marinade of vinegar and oil with added spices and herbs for anything from 30 minutes to 12 hours, depending on the size of the fillets and the temperature of the marinade — the shorter time for room temperatures, and the longer time for the refrigerator. Again, the fish is ready for eating when the flesh has become white.

● By rubbing lemon juice over the fish before cooking, the colour is preserved.

● All anglers proclaim loudly that fish must be cooked and eaten as soon as they are taken from the water. But this is not always the best way. Small fish, for example, will tend to curl up if cooked immediately after being caught, but if you refrigerate these tiddlers overnight, you will find this does not happen as you cook them.

● Dry the fish or fish fillets thoroughly before dropping them into hot oil to fry. (This applies to any food that is to be fried.) The ugly burns that result from splashes of hot fat can be avoided if you take this simple precaution. Because oil or fat is at a much higher temperature than boiling water, when you drop in the chips or fillets any moisture on the surface of the pieces is immediately turned into rapidly expanding superheated steam; this is what causes the spattering. *So dry food that is to be dropped into hot oil or fat.*

● If you are going to crumb your fillets, add 1 tablespoon of oil to the beaten egg; this helps the crumbs to stick to the surface.

● Dry the fish before dipping them into batter — because the batter will stick better.

TO GRILL A FISH

Whether you are grilling at the kitchen stove, on the barbecue in the garden, or over an open fire on the beach, remember you are subjecting the fish to intense, direct heat, which will rapidly dry out the fish no matter how fresh it is. To prevent this, score the surface with a sharp knife and brush liberally with melted butter or oil, dip the fish lightly in flour, and then apply more butter or oil. Grill them for 1 or 2 minutes to seal the outside. Now reduce the heat (if you are cooking over an open fire, raise the griller a little farther away from the embers) and finish the cooking. If you are grilling whole fish, split them open.

TO BAKE A FISH

The preparation will depend on the size of the fish. They can be left whole, filleted, or cut across the backbone into 3—5 cm (1½—2 in) cutlets. The casserole should be well oiled and large enough not to cramp the pieces. If it is a dry fish, make some shallow cuts in the surface and brush it liberally with lemon juice and melted butter, and baste it with this mixture throughout the cooking time. Oily fish are better left alone. The oven temperature should be high, that is, 210—230°C (400—450°F). The cooking time will depend on the thickness of your fish or cuts, but when you can easily flake the thickest part with a fork, the fish is cooked. Small fillets take about 10 minutes.

TO POACH A FISH

This is a useful method for handling fish with fine delicate flesh, particularly if you have an old fish kettle. These are oval in shape with a perforated tray, fitted with handles, that sits inside, just above the bottom of the pot. The fish is laid on the tray and gently lowered into the simmering liquid, which is never allowed to boil. There must be sufficient liquid to cover the fish. Cooking time is about 6 to 10 minutes per ½ kg (1 lb) of fish. Again, don't overcook: the flesh must not become soft and mushy and begin falling to pieces. The poaching liquid can be plain salted water if it is a very flavoursome fish, or a *court-bouillon*. A basic fish-poaching stock is made as follows:—

FISH-POACHING STOCK

6 cups water
¼ cup white vinegar (or wine or cider)
3 teaspoons salt
2 medium-sized onions, sliced
1 medium-sized carrot, sliced
1 bay leaf
1 small sprig of rosemary
4 to 5 whole peppercorns

Simmer all the ingredients, except the peppercorns, for half an hour; add the peppercorns and simmer for another 10 minutes (by adding the peppercorns last, you will stop the mixture from becoming bitter). Strain, and use the liquid for your fish-poaching stock. The stock can be stored in the refrigerator.

If there has been a good catch of fish, make a fish-poaching stock using the heads and any bits and pieces after filleting. These can be added to the above liquid, simmered and strained; or you can simmer the bits and pieces in water, add pepper and salt, strain and use this plain fish stock. (Try making this poaching stock with clean sea water but do not add additional salt — that is, if you know of a clean patch of sea.) Also vary the herbs to suit your own palate: thyme and parsley and marjoram go well with fish and so does a faint flavour of cloves. And, of course, lemons, either juice or rind, or both.

TO FRY A FISH

To sauté fish

Using a heavy-based frying-pan, melt sufficient clarified butter to cover the base, but do not let the butter brown. Small fish or fish fillets are fried quickly, being turned once. If the fillets are very thin, there is no need to turn them. Remove the fish and add a little more butter; now increase the heat so the butter browns but does not burn; add chopped parsley and pour over the fish before serving.

The fillets can also be coated lightly with a mixture of lemon juice, salt and pepper before frying. Or you can dip them in beaten egg and roll in seasoned flour or breadcrumbs to form a thin coat before frying.

(To clarify butter: Gently heat a slab of butter — it is easier to use large quantities, at least ½ kg (1 lb) — until all bubbling stops, being careful not to brown or burn the butter. Remove the butter from the heat and pour into a Pyrex container; allow to stand until all sediment has settled; pour off the clear butter oil and discard the water and white fatty sediment that has settled on the bottom. The clarified butter will be a clear yellow and keeps exceptionally well.)

To dry-fry fish

Use a non-stick pan. This method is good for oily fish fillets. To check the heat of your pan, carefully splash in 1 or 2 drops of water, which should sizzle and disappear as steam. Lightly brush the fillets with lemon juice and place in the pan, with their cut surface down. Thin fillets should take only 4 or 5 minutes, and as the flesh breaks easily do not turn, just fry on the one side only. If you are careful in turning them you can give the skin side 1 minute to brown it slightly. Serve with a sauce made from equal parts of melted butter and lemon juice, to which you have added pepper and salt and a pinch of freshly chopped parsley.

Both sautéeing and dry-frying are quick methods of cooking fish, and they are ones which you can vary by using herb butters. Col makes a delicious sauce béarnaise (see Chapter 3 — Meat) and if Jean is around she has to make extra because Jean loves flounder fillets sautéed in sauce béarnaise. Another subtle variation in flavour can be achieved by throwing into the pan a handful of blanched almonds or macadamia nuts. We find it is best to do this after you have lifted out the fillets and before increasing the heat to brown the butter. A few of the sautéed nuts are put on each fillet before the butter sauce is poured over them.

To deep-fry fish, or fish à la fish shop

The cooking utensils for deep-fried fish are important. You must have a deep heavy-based pot with matching frying basket. We like a pot 20cm (8in) deep but if you have a deeper one, so much the better. By starting with 7½cm (3in) of oil in this pot, when the fish is added the level of the hot oil will only rise to about half way up the pot. This saves a lot of splattering and reduces the danger of oil burns. Oil is the only medium in which the fish should be fried. Although more expensive, olive oil is undoubtedly the best; however, many people do prefer the blander flavours of other vegetable oils such as sunflower or safflower. Eastern cooks prefer soya bean oil. Certainly the vegetable oils are usually cheaper, but you do not have to discard the oil after you have finished frying — strain it when cool and return to the bottle, but keep this oil for fish only or you will have fish-flavoured meat or meat-flavoured fish!

Oil can be raised to much higher temperatures than water, but how hot should it be for frying fish? Every writer and every cook to whom we referred gave different temperatures and different methods of testing the temperature. Some say 'when the oil begins to give off blue smoke'; others recommend dropping in a 2½cm (1in) cube of dried bread and if it browns in 30 seconds the temperature is correct; still others say 'a drop of water should spit' (we don't like that method because it is too dangerous: oil, being so hot, can cause nasty burns). So Col waits for the blue smoke and Jean checks with the piece of bread. What everybody seems to forget is that different oils do different things at different temperatures. We suggest you find the oil of your choice, and experiment as to the temperature, the easiest way being to try one small fillet and see if it cooks the way you like it; but *never, never* use the 'drop of water' method. The temperature should be about 190°C (375°F) for good results.

Keep the oil at a constant temperature throughout the cooking process, so don't over-fill the frying basket with the pieces of fish. Don't crowd the pieces because you want the hot oil to contact every surface of each fillet as soon as you immerse it. And we repeat, make sure each fillet is dry before dropping it into the hot oil. In this way you will avoid the dangers of splattering oil. If you are using frozen fillets, always allow time for them to thaw to room temperature and then dry thoroughly with kitchen paper.

BATTERS

Although all fish may be fried naked, many people do prefer a coating of batter, but make certain you have removed all bones and scales before battering the fillets. Please yourself about removing the skin — some people claim it improves the flavour. The batter should be only a thin coat because it is fish you are supposed to be serving, not fried flour. So many good fried fish are ruined by soggy overcoats of batter that would have been better used to paste pictures in a child's picture book. If you use self-raising flour or plain flour with a pinch of baking powder in your batter it will be much lighter.

BASIC RECIPE FOR FISH BATTER

½ cup self-raising flour (or plain flour with a pinch of baking powder)
1 beaten egg
½ cup milk
pepper and salt

Beat all ingredients together with a whisk until you have a thin batter without any lumps. Allow to stand for 1 hour before using.

BEER BATTER

½ cup plain flour
½ cup beer

Beat the flour and beer with a whisk until there are no lumps. Allow the mixture to stand for at least half an hour. You can add an egg if you like. The beer will work the flour in the same manner as the yeast does for bread dough, and you have a very light batter which fries crisply.

Make the batter in a deep bowl because this makes dipping much easier. Dry each fillet with kitchen paper and double-check for scales and small bones. Dip the dry fillet into the batter, allow it to drain for a moment, and then place it on the bottom of the fish basket. Repeat the procedure with more fillets until the bottom of the basket is covered, but be sure none of the fillets is crowded. Check the temperature of the oil and lower the basket into the pot. When the batter has become golden brown all over, the fish will be cooked. Remove the basket and drain the fillets on absorbent paper. Continue with the remainder of the fish. There must be sufficient oil in your pot to cover the contents of the basket.

TO STEAM A FISH

Steamed fish cooks in its own juices. Because the fish is not subjected to any agitation, such as in simmering stock or frying oil, it is an excellent way of handling fine-textured fish which tend to break up. If you do not have a double boiler, it is easy to make one up. Look through your pot cupboard and find a large pot and a shallow pie dish that will sit comfortably on top of the pot. You also want a lid to fit over the pie dish. Bring about 5 cm (2 in) of water to a rolling boil in the pot. Having prepared your fish or fish fillets, place them in the pie dish with a generous dab of butter. Cover the pie dish with a lid and then sit the dish on top of the pot of boiling water. Cooking time is a little longer than when sautéeing fish, but as soon as the flesh flakes easily, the fish is cooked. If you are cooking a bland fish with little flavour, use a herb butter. When you serve the fish, pour over it the liquor that has collected in the dish.

Rather than give a swag of recipes for all the numerous fish that are available in Australian and New Zealand waters — that sort of thing would belong to a book devoted to fish alone —

we offer a few of the butters and sauces we like and some suggestions for stuffings if you are baking a fish. These are followed by some recipes for specific fish that we have found successful.

SAVOURY BUTTERS

Nothing can equal butter when cooking fish. (We prefer unsalted butter.) The only thing to remember is that butter burns at lower temperatures than other cooking fats, and it is for this reason we always clarify it before grilling or frying with butter. If you cannot get unsalted butter, the clarifying removes the salt along with any moisture.

BEURRE MANIE (KNEADED BUTTER)

One tablespoon of butter is kneaded to a smooth paste with 1 tablespoon of plain flour. Tiny knobs of the butter are pinched off and stirred one at a time into liquid you wish to thicken; have the liquid *just below boiling point*, and never allow it to boil. Stop adding the kneaded butter knobs when the sauce has reached the desired thickness and continue cooking for 5 minutes, *but never let it boil.* Beurre manie can be used with fish stock, plain water, milk or any other liquid you wish to thicken. Any of the herbs can be added to achieve a particular flavour.

BEURRE MAITRE D'HOTEL

This is probably the most useful of the butters, not only for fish, but with grilled meats and many of the vegetables. It keeps in the refrigerator so we usually make up 225 g (½lb) at a time. If you have an electric mixer, use it. Warm the mixing bowl and the beaters in hot water; then add 225 g (½lb) of unsalted butter and 4 heaped tablespoons of chopped parsley. Using the lowest speed, cream the butter and parsley together, and add lemon juice a teaspoon at a time, until you like the taste. Remove from the bowl and form into a roll; wrap in greaseproof paper or polythene wrapping and store. You can then cut off a quantity as needed.

HERB BUTTERS

Try some of the herbs, preferably fresh, and as a change from lemon juice use the juice of an orange or of a lime. Tarragon butter is made using fresh tarragon leaves and a few drops of tarragon vinegar in the unsalted butter.

OTHER BUTTERS

Anchovies, prawns, lobster, crab meat, smoked salmon, can all be used to flavour the butter. Pound the meat to a paste and work into the butter. These add flavour to otherwise rather ordinary fish. The exact quantities are up to you: if you want a subtle hint, use a little of the chosen meat; if you want a more definite flavour, use larger quantities.

SAUCES

Sauces may be either hot or cold; they can be simple such as melted herb butter, or the more complicated sauces of the French cuisine.

BASIC BUTTER SAUCE

We find this basic sauce useful because you can add whatever flavouring you like — a spoonful of oyster sauce, hard-boiled eggs, pounded crab or lobster meat, a few drops of anchovy essence, and so on, and don't forget the old standbys of chopped chives and capers.

2 tablespoons butter
1 tablepoon plain flour
½ teaspoon salt
1 cup milk (or water)

Cut the butter into tiny pieces.

Mix the flour and salt with the cold milk (or water) until you have a smooth paste. Drop the pieces of butter into the flour/milk paste and slowly heat, shaking the pot continuously. *Do not let the mixture boil;* as the butter melts and blends with the flour the sauce will slowly thicken. Simmer for 2 to 3 minutes. Serve at once. The additional flavourings are added to the flour/milk paste before you heat it with the butter.

SAUCE BÉCHAMEL

This is another basic from which you can develop many sauces, for example, caper, parsley, crayfish, mornay, mussel, and so on. If you follow the rules, it is not difficult.

slice of onion
piece of carrot
bay leaf
2 sprigs parsley
2 cups milk
2 tablespoons butter
3 tablespoons plain flour
salt
freshly ground pepper

Put the flavourings — onion, carrot, bay leaf and parsley — into a pot with the 2 cups of milk and slowly bring to simmering point. Remove the pot from the heat and let it stand for a few minutes. Strain the mixture, reserving the seasoned milk.

In another pan melt the butter, stir in the flour and cook for 2 to 3 minutes. Remove from the stove and add a few spoonfuls of the seasoned milk and beat it until you have a smooth paste. Return to the stove and add the remainder of the milk, stirring all the time. Simmer gently for at least 20 minutes. Add salt and pepper to taste. To be quite sure the sauce will not boil, use a double boiler with boiling water in the bottom half and the sauce in the top half. The above quantities will make approximately 1 cup of creamy sauce bechamel.

If you want it to be richer and creamier, use thin cream instead of milk, or half cream and half milk. You can vary the basic milk flavourings, too.

SAUCE MORNAY

This is a cheese sauce often served with lobster. Grate ¼ cup of Gruyère cheese and ¼ cup of Parmesan cheese; and add to the bechamel sauce about 5 minutes before the completion of the 20 minutes' simmering time.

CAPER SAUCE

One tablespoon of chopped parsley and 2 tablespoons of capers together with a little of the liquor in which the capers are bottled, are added to the bechamel sauce just before serving.

SAUCE BEARNAISE

See page 80 in Chapter 3 (Meat) for bearnaise butter, which is even tastier than sauce bearnaise.

SAUCE HOLLANDAISE

This is really a hot mayonnaise and here is a quicker method for making sauce hollandaise, although it may not be approved of by professional sauce chefs.

3 tablespoons white wine vinegar
2 tablespoons water
10 peppercorns
6 tablespoons unsalted butter
3 large egg yolks
salt and lemon juice to taste

Put the vinegar, water and peppercorns in a small pot; boil down until you have about 1 tablespoon of liquid. Strain into a basin and allow to cool.

Melt the butter and leave it to cool.

While the butter is cooling, beat the egg yolks into the reduced vinegar.

Set the basin with its beaten egg yolks over a pot of very hot, *but not boiling*, water. (Use an asbestos mat if cooking on gas.) Keep beating the egg yolks and vinegar and pour the melted butter, which should now be tepid, in a very slow stream into the egg yolks, as if you were making mayonnaise.

The sauce is cooked when it looks thick and it coats the back of the spoon. Remove from the heat and beat in the salt and lemon juice to taste.

It is best used immediately; but you can hold it if you put the basin over the pot of hot water, and give an occasional stir. Don't let the water boil.

CAVIARE SAUCE

For the choicest of fish. Try it with John Dory. Into the sauce hollandaise fold ½ cup of very thick cream and 4 tablespoons of caviare.

STUFFING FOR BAKED FISH

When making stuffing for fish, always maintain a low key with herbs. Remember that fish has a delicate flavour of its own and the stuffing should enhance not mask, this flavour. It is difficult, in fact impossible, to give exact amounts for herbs, because their pungency varies so much. If your herbs come from a hot, dry climate they will be much stronger in flavour than those grown in cool moist climates. If using dried herbs, remember they do not keep forever, but gradually lose the aromatic oils on which their flavours depend. You must *taste*.

ROE STUFFING

½ cup soft roes, chopped
½ cup soft white breadcrumbs soaked in milk
1 small onion
2 tablespoons butter
herbs: parsley and chives (or sweet basil)
salt and pepper
lemon juice

Sauté the onion in the butter.

Combine all the ingredients, adding sufficient lemon juice to give a sharp taste.

This stuffing can be used in any fish that you are going to bake.

RICE STUFFING

Very good in large mullet.

1 cup cooked rice
1 small onion, chopped
10 or 12 button mushrooms
125g (4oz) butter
1 lemon, juice and 2 teaspoons grated yellow rind

freshly chopped marjoram (or oregano)
salt and pepper

Sauté the chopped onion and the button mushrooms in the butter. Combine with the rice, lemon juice and lemon rind, and the freshly chopped marjoram (or oregano). Salt and pepper to taste.

If your cooked rice is very dry, mix a cup of hot water with the stuffing mixture and let stand for a few minutes for the rice to absorb more water. Use any water that is left over in the baking dish with the stuffed fish.

BAKED AUSTRALIAN SALMON

It is a great pity that these beautiful fish were ever called salmon; they belong to the perch family and because their flesh is dark and rather coarse in texture, unhappy comparisons are made with the true salmon of the norther hemisphere waters. Next time your surf fisherman catches a sea salmon, ask him to prepare it properly and bring it home. The Australian salmon must be bled as soon as it is landed. To do this, sever the backbone behind the gill covers by inserting a sharp pointed knife at the back of the head. Clean the fish and rub the inside with fresh salt, or sea water or lemon juice, and then bury it in wet sand with just the tail showing so you can find it again. It will continue to bleed, and be protected from flies and drying winds. Young Australian salmon are often called salmon trout.

½—1 kg (1½—2 lb) Australian salmon
clarified butter to oil the baking dish
1 medium-sized onion, sliced
½ teaspoon salt
pinch ground ginger
4 or 5 peppercorns
1 small chilli, chopped
garnishes: lemon slices, tomato wedges, pickled cucumbers, fresh herbs

Oil the baking dish well with the butter.

Wash the fish thoroughly to remove any sand that is still clinging to it as a result of its recent interment, and place it in the baking dish, skin side down. (If your fisherman has not cut the fish wide open, do this yourself, so that it will lie flat on the dish.)

Lay the slices of onion over the fish, and then all the herbs and spices: that is sprinkle the salt, ground ginger and peppercorns, and top with the chopped chilli. Pour the cup of wine vinegar over the whole lot.

Cover the baking dish with greased greaseproof paper and bake in a moderate oven at 190°C (375°F) for 15 to 20 minutes.

Although baked Australian salmon can be served hot, we prefer it cold. Remove the baking dish with its fish from the oven after the 15 or 20 minutes (depending on the size of the fish) and let it stand in its own juices until cold. Very carefully lift the whole fish from the baking dish and place it on the serving platter. Strain the liquor and pour over the fish. Garnish with the wedges of tomato, sliced cucumber, and sprinkle with finely chopped herbs such as parsley or chervil, or even sweet basil.

Any other large, coarse-fleshed fish can be used in this recipe. If you like the flavour of cloves, add 3 or 4 to the spices before you put the fish in the oven.

FRIED BARRACOUTA FILLETS

450g (1 lb) barracouta fillets
1 can beer
seasoned plain flour (or breadcrumbs, or rolled oats)
oil (or clarified butter) for shallow frying

Dry the fillets and dip them in the beer. Now coat each fillet with the seasoned flour (or breadcrumbs or rolled oats).

Fry in the pan using oil (or clarified butter).

BARRAMUNDI

*If you have ever been served barramundi cooked by an Aborigi-
al fisherman, you will never want to eat it prepared in any
other fashion. The whole fish is wrapped in fleshy leaves and
buried in the hot ashes of the campfire, where it slowly cooks
in its own juices. For most of us, however, the only barramundi we will ever handle are the steaks or cutlets from the
fish shop. To savour their full qualities these should be grilled.
The flesh is firm, but tender and white, and can be used in
any recipe calling for quality fish.*

TUNA AND MUSHROOM PIE

200g can tuna
125g can mushrooms (or fresh mushrooms sautéed in butter)
2 cups hot mashed potato
pepper and salt
marjoram (or oregano)

We find this is an excellent emergency dish. You can halve, double or treble the quantities depending on the number of unexpected guests. It goes well served with plain vegetables or salads. But the important thing is that it can be made so quickly: 20 minutes to cook the potatoes and 10 minutes in the oven.

Boil the potatoes in the minimum amount of water. Mash them well and season with pepper and salt, beating in a generous quantity of cream or butter so that you have a fluffy potato mixture, but not too wet.

While the potatoes are cooking, sauté the mushrooms in butter if you are using fresh mushrooms, otherwise use the can opener. Combine the mushrooms and the tuna in a casserole dish, flaking the tuna flesh; add the marjoram (or oregano) and 1 tablespoon of fresh parsley if you have any.

Heap the hot mashed potatoes on top of the tuna/mushroom mixture and place in the oven at 190°C (375°F). In about 10 minutes the potatoes are browning and ready to serve.

OVEN-FRIED FISH

The average frying-pan will hold sufficient fillets for four people at the outside, so you have the problem of holding the first batch cooked until you have fried the second, or you serve your guests in relays. Here is a way whereby you can fry them all at once. And there are two side-benefits: the fish can be prepared in advance, and the kitchen never smells of cooking oil.

8 fillets Australian whiting
1 egg
¼ cup melted butter
1 tablespoon oil
herbs for seasoning (optional)
dry breadcrumbs
½ teaspoon salt

*1 baking tray large enough to hold all the fillets without their
touching each other.*

Beat together the egg, melted butter and oil.

Mix the herbs, if you are using them, through the dry breadcrumbs together with the salt.

Dry each fillet and, using a pastry brush, coat each with the
egg and fat mixture. Then dip in the breadcrumbs.

As each fillet is coated, lay it in the baking tray, but do not
crowd them together — it is better to use two trays. There is
no need to grease the trays. Having prepared the fish, you can
cook them immediately, or the tray can be left in a cool place
until required.

Heat the oven to 200°C (400°F); slide the tray of prepared
fillets into the oven and cook for 15 to 20 minutes, depending
on the thickness of the fillets. Do not turn the fillets.

Serve the fish immediately with wedges of lemon and
sliced cucumber.

Any kind of fish fillets that you would normally fry in the
pan can be cooked in this manner.

MARINATED MULLET

1 kg (2 lb) mullet fillets

For the marinade you will need:
2 spring onions, chopped using all the green tops
¼ cup white wine
1 tablespoon soy sauce
1 bay leaf

For the sauce you will need:
*8 to 10 Tom Thumb tomatoes (or 225g) — use canned plum
   tomatoes if fresh are out of season*
2 tablespoons butter
2 tablespoons brown sugar
¼ teaspoon oregano
pepper and salt

For the garnish you will need chopped parsley

The marinade Place the dried fillets in the bottom of a large
casserole and sprinkle the chopped spring onion over them.
Combine the wine and soy sauce and the bay leaf and pour
over the fish. Let them marinate for at least 2 hours, turning
the fillets several times.

To prepare the sauce Skin the tomatoes by immersing them in boiling water for 1 minute, and then peeling off their skins using a sharp-tipped knife. Melt the butter in a pot and add the whole tomatoes, brown sugar and oregano, stirring gently so you don't break the little tomatoes. Drain the marinade from the fish and add to the sauce. Add the pepper and salt and simmer for about 5 minutes or until the sauce has slightly thickened.

Re-arrange the fish fillets in the casserole and pour the sauce over them. Cook in the oven at 200°C (400°F) for 20 minutes — no longer.

Remove the fish from the oven and liberally sprinkle the fillets with chopped parsley before serving.

This recipe can be used for other varieties of fish including, in the northern hemisphere, cod, haddock and hake.

TAHITIAN FISH

450g (1 lb) fresh thin fish fillets (trumpeter, or similar)
1 large cup unsweetened grapefruit juice
2 tablespoons mayonnaise
2 tablespoons onion, finely chopped
1 tablespoon coconut milk
2 tablespoons capsicum (red for preference), finely chopped
2 tablespoons celery, finely chopped
½ teaspoon salt

Slice the fish extremely finely.

Place the fish in a jar or crock and pour the grapefruit juice into it. Cover it with a tight lid. Store in the refrigerator for 48 hours, swirling occasionally. By the time the marinating period is over, all the little pieces of fish should have turned an opaque white.

Drain off the juice and discard. Place the fish in a bowl.

Add the onion, mayonnaise, salt and coconut milk, cover the bowl and store in the refrigerator for a further 24 hours, longer if you like, up to 48 hours.

Before serving, add the capsicum and celery, and stir well. Dish up in individual portions on beds of lettuce.

This is sufficient for four small appetiser portions.

YABBIES

Do you remember spending the school holidays fishing for yabbies? The only equipment was a piece of string and bits of very dead meat, and a billycan in which to cook the catch. Fortunately for hungry kids, our mothers did not have the same confidence in our fishing abilities as we did, and by mid afternoon we would rather self-consciously pretend to find a packet of sandwiches 'Mum must have put in my haversack.'

Yabbies are freshwater crustacea found in dams and billabongs in Australia. The New Zealand koura, a small freshwater crayfish, is caught and cooked in the same manner. Both are very much the same as the French ecrivisses. Although yabbies are seldom if ever, seen in city fish shops, we were interested to hear recently that the State Fisheries of New South Wales is investigating the feasibility of harvesting these fresh-water delicacies. Once you have tried them, you, with us, will wish them success.

Having caught your yabbies, put them in a bucket of clean fresh water into which you have emptied a 100g packet of Epsom salts, and leave them there for 24 hours. This will get rid of the muddy taste. (This is a good trick with any 'muddy' fish such as carp.)

Now they have to be killed. There are two methods and we prefer the more humane one of piercing the head with a nail; death is instantaneous. The other way is to dump the live yabbies into the cooking pot and let them slowly die as the heat is increased.

TO COOK YABBIES

For 24 yabbies you will need:
8 cups cold water
½ tablespoon vinegar
1 teaspoon salt
½ tablespoon sugar

Put the whole lot, dead yabbies and all, in a large pot and bring to the boil. The yabbies are cooked as soon as they turn red. Wash under cold running water until they are cool and then remove the outer shell and the heads. The flesh is now ready to be used in any way you wish. For starters, try some of your favourite crab recipes. Our favourite is cold yabby meat and avocados.

YABBY ENTRÉE

the meat from 24 boiled yabbies
1 large ripe avocado (or 2 small ones)
1 tablespoon brown sugar
1 cup wine vinegar
salt and pepper
lemon juice and slices of lemon
brown bread and butter

Place the pieces of yabby meat in a large deep bowl. Dissolve the brown sugar in the wine vinegar and pour this over the yabbies. Refrigerate for 12 hours, but not in the freezer.

Mash the avocado meat with pepper and salt and a little lemon juice to form a smooth, creamy paste.

Take the yabbies from the refrigerator and drain. Arrange the pieces of meat on a bed of crisp lettuce leaves (or fresh watercress). Serve the avocado paste in a separate bowl. With a plate of fresh home-made brown bread and home-made butter, you have a feast fit for a king, or a queen. To make it a friendly meal, supply each guest with a small fork. The idea is to take a piece of yabby, dip it into the avocado cream and pop it into your mouth, then take a bite of bread.

SOME THOUGHTS ON SERVING FISH

We believe many cooks spoil the eating of fish by overdoing the decorations. A whole bream sitting in the middle of an elegant fish plate and surrounded by a pile of chips, a serving of mashed potato, assorted lettuce leaves, a radish or two, onion rings or a couple of spring onions and quarters of tommato may be appealing to the eye. But how do you eat it? If you start by eating the rabbit food and then attacking the various forms of potato, you will probably keep out of trouble; but by this time you are full and the fish is cold. If you start with the fish, before you know where you are the head has slipped dangerously over the edge of the plate and is about to take a dive on to your lap, and the potatoes are full of bones.

The fish should be served on a plate by itself, the only decorations being the sauce and perhaps a sprig of parsley or watercress. All accompaniments should be on a separate plate, either as a side salad, or as another course of vegetables alone.

And a thought on the tools used in eating fish. The Duke of Bedford claims that he eats with two forks because there are no Georgian fish-knives to match the Georgian forks, but he really has the right idea. Try it yourself: fish is much easier to handle with two forks than with a knife and fork. Also, why don't we use finger-bowls when eating fish? If it is all right to use your fingers with chicken bones, why can't you remove an unexpected fish-bone with your fingers? Much easier and safer than poking around with the fork and ending with a hasty visit to the emergency department of the nearest hospital to have the bone removed from your throat.

In choosing the foods to serve with fish, always remember that fish has a delicate flavour which should be enhanced but not drowned by the accompaniments. For this reason, it makes a good entrée dish. The elusive tastes can be savoured before the palate has become jaded by the stronger-flavoured main meat course. If it is to be used as the main dish, select the salad or vegetables according to the method you have used for cooking. Chipped potatoes always seem to be served with fried fish, but you know there is no law that says you *must*. They go equally well with poached fish, and mashed potatoes or fried rice are a welcome change with fried fish. But do serve either a plain side salad or one or two steamed vegetables if you are using both fried fish and fried potatoes.

3. MEAT

Meat has always been a staple of the vast majority of Australian people from the very earliest days of the Sydney colony. The soil was sandy, the rainfall in those years sparse, and a great many of the seeds brought out proved to be unsuitable for local growing conditions. At one stage there was a riot because the governor forbade settlers, convicts, troopers and officers to eat a shipment of seed potatoes. The incident culminated in large numbers of people being thrown into gaol, while the governor tried to explain that everyone would have to learn to be patient, that the seed potatoes must be planted and only their crop consumed, for there was no guarantee when the next shipment of potatoes might arrive.

During their days in Britain most of the new colonists, voluntary or otherwise, were lucky to eat meat once or twice a year.

But for those who had settled in Australia, there was little to eat save meat; kangaroos abounded, the Aborigines taught the new people how to bake in clay ovens, and livestock brought out from Britain thrived where vegetables and fruit didn't. And the early settlers liked eating meat, still deeming meat a luxury. By 1880, one new settler (a minister) was complaining in his letters to the editor that the predilection Australians had for eating meat had resulted in the ruination of their characters, intellectually and morally! At that time the same dissatisfied settler quoted figures of 100lbs (45kg) of meat consumed by an Englishman in one year, compared to 264lb (119kg) of meat consumed by an Australian.

Until relatively recently, lamb (or mutton) and beef were the cheapest and most-consumed kinds of meat in the average Australian home; since Jean came from a strictly vegetarian home, we can only quote Col. During her childhood, pork was so expensive and hard to come by that it was the meat for Christmas/Easter or other special occasions, and chicken or turkey followed close behind. Veal too was not popular, though possibly due to distaste rather than to unavailability. It took our post-war immigrants from the European mainland to show us how delicious veal was. However, beef, lamb and mutton were so plentiful and cheap that by Col's girlhood Australians in general had a hearty contempt for the meats they called offal — heart, liver, kidney, sweetbreads, tripe, brains. Only the striated muscle-fibre meats were really popular.

Red meats, including veal, chicken (and fish!) are movement muscles of the animal body. This tissue is highly vascular and fibrous, and depends for its flavour on the juices contained within it. Generally speaking, the main basis of meat flavour is salt, for these tissue juices are a combination of various salts, proteins and fats, and the predominant natural flavour is a salty one.

Meat, including fish, has a high protein content. Except for any fat it may contain, when digested meat breaks down to protein which is utilised by the body, and wastes which are eliminated by the body. Protein is a complicated substance, built up of smaller units called amino acids; the human organism requires eleven different amino acids in order to build up its tissue proteins and only three of these amino acids are synthesised by the body, the remainder must be supplied by way of the food we eat. (Tissue is made from protein and growing children must therefore have adequate protein in their diets.) Meat does contain these essential amino acids, as do many other foods — eggs, cheese, nuts, peas and beans. However, only meat, eggs and soya beans contain all eleven amino acids. Therefore with a vegetarian diet it is essential that all available sources of protein be used, because what one food does not supply another will. Over a week it is very easy to provide a balanced diet; don't become a faddist and attempt to exist on only one type of food. If you are the cook for a meat-eating household and one member suddenly renounces meats, construct a substitute diet which is adequate in its amino-acid content and variety. The type of vegetarian diet followed by the Seventh Day Adventist church is infinitely preferable to those recommended by health faddists who lack proper nutritional and biochemical training.

Once the human body has finished growing, its need for protein declines but never ceases. Theoretically, an adult human being can subsist entirely on carbohydrate, since this is the chief source of glucose, the body's energy fuel. Practically, the result is the kind of body seen in impoverished European and American areas, where bread, potatoes or pasta form almost the entire food intake — overweight rather than underweight, listless and prone to disease. A good adult diet must contain adequate calories to provide energy, proteins to replace dying cells in the tissues, vitamins, and some fat (for fat-soluble vitamins, good skin and hair and healthy maintenance of metabolism).

As well as having a basic knowledge of protein, it is essential to know how to store meat correctly. Never store meat tightly wrapped up, in the refrigerator, unless you plan to use the meat within a day. Meat intended to be stored unfrozen longer than that should be either uncovered, or covered in a way which permits some access of air to the surface. Because it is muscle tissue or internal organ, meat is highly susceptible to the growth of anaerobic bacteria — that is, bacteria which cannot survive in an atmosphere rich in oxygen. Anaerobes like an airless environment. So when you wrap up meat tightly, you give the anaerobes a perfect climate in which to work, and they will, much faster than ordinary aerobic bacteria can. Anaerobes are the chief agents of putrefaction, so that even if you leave well-aired meat so long in the refrigerator that it goes off, it will never smell or look as offensive as meat which has putrefied while tightly wrapped. Botulinus, for instance, is an anaerobic organism, which is why it can only thrive in tins which were once vacuum-sealed.

The same rule applies to cooked meats stored in containers. If you leave the lid off, or cover them loosely, they will last much longer. Cooked meat stored in a container with a tight lid will decay rapidly.

We would like to put in a word for people who happen to like their meat well cooked. Modern society with its dogmatic and sometimes rigid attitudes tends to despise the 'well done' brigade as gastonomic imbeciles; waiters sneer, gourmets look down their noses, and the poor soul who demands meat well done may either be refused this service in a so-called better class restaurant, or else be nauseatedly obliged from politeness to eat rare meat when entertained in a private home. Since people come in different shapes, sizes, colours and personalities, surely it is wrong to inflict under-done meat on those who find under-done meat distasteful. We have also noticed than when a child takes a dislike to meat, it is often possible to make meat more palatable to that child by cooking it more thoroughly. Because we ourselves bleed, the sight of blood in food may be off-putting, especially to children.

Always salt and pepper your meat *before* you cook it. Since the meat's natural flavour is a salty one, you will find you need to use less salt if you salt before you cook. Meat which is not salted before cooking will taste flat and bland, and those who are eating it will tend to smother it in salt from a shaker. Remember that the amount of salt sprinkled on the outside of a piece of meat will depend upon its thickness: it is a matter of the surface area, since the surface is the only part of the meat you can salt. A thick piece of meat will take more salt than a thin one. We have served to guests the plainest of meals, such as a thick rump steak pan-fried in the tiniest amount of clarified butter, with its outside well salted and peppered (adding pepper is purely a matter of individual taste) before frying, plus boiled potatoes and young peas. And people will always ask what sort of seasoning we have put on the steak, and be enormously surprised when we say, 'Oh nothing much, just salt and pepper, actually.' Add a pat of bearnaise butter, and you have a meal fit for a king.

Don't be afraid of meat fats. These days the use of ex-cellent kitchen papers and non-stick pans makes fat far less a danger than many people realise. You need only a trace of fat to pan-fry meat in a non-stick pan, and if you drain the meat afterwards, it will actually have less fat content than a piece of grilled meat. Not all the fat goes into the pan under grilled meat; fat pools on its top, and since it is generally less heated through than pan-fried meat, there will be more fat left in the meat itself. Remember that certain vitamins (A, D, E and K) are soluble only in fats, so you must incorporate a small amount of fat in your diet for good health. Use your common sense about fat as about most things, and you will be all right. So will your heart.

Like fish, a good cut of meat doesn't need doctoring. Fancy ways of cooking meat were devised for poor cuts.

The older the beast is, the cheaper its meat is to buy, and the tougher that meat will be. As muscle tissue grows older, it becomes thicker-walled and its concentration of cellulose, collagen and other indigestible proteins increases. So tough meat, that is, old meat, or poor cuts of meat, have to undergo intensive preparation in cooking. Ground (minced) meats, for instance, are rarely the best bits of the beast, nor even the best beasts, which is why the meat is ground in the first place. Grinding breaks down the fibrous elements in the tissue, thus rendering it more tender.

There are several ways to deal with poor meat. You can pickle (corn) it, marinate it in substances such as wine or weak vinegar (these are acidic liquids, and acid attacks the fibrous husks of meat cells), smoke or dry it, or simply subject it to a long, slow cooking process.

Meat tenderiser, which is simply an enzyme obtained from

the pawpaw (papáya), is very good, provided you use the un-seasoned variety, and don't use it wrongly. We haven't seen any health reports on it, but since apparently it doesn't contain artificial or chemical (in the manufactured laboratory sense) substances, it is probably fine from a medical point of view. It is certainly effective. The enzyme it contains starts breaking the meat down, that is, digesting it, before it is cooked, let alone eaten. So the meat is softer, less fibrous. We have found meat tenderiser excellent for people who have had an amount of intestine or stomach removed, as it lessens the digestive process.

If you use meat tenderiser, you must get it into the interior of the meat as well as all over its surface. Wet the meat by holding it under a running tap, and just shake off the excess water, don't blot the meat dry again. Lay it on a board and sprinkle the tenderiser over its surface much as you would a good quantity of salt, then drive a fork through it all over its surface, not gentle little pricks but big deep stabs. Then turn the meat over, sprinkle tenderiser on that side, and repeat the stabbing. This drives the tenderiser into the depths of the meat. If you refrigerate the meat or it was cold when you actually put the tenderiser on it, you can wait for an hour before cooking, but if you work with warmish meat and then don't refrigerate it, you must cook it within 15 minutes. For what you've done is to start the digestive process, and it will spoil very quickly.

The unseasoned variety of tenderiser does nothing to alter the flavour of meat, so you cook tenderised meat using salt and/or other condiment as you would normally.

Accent, Chinese taste-powder, MSG, or, to use its chemical name, monosodium glutamate, is *not* a tenderiser of meat. A curious substance, it has the property of enhancing flavours already present, though it has no taste of its own. We use it where a Chinese recipe calls for it, but not otherwise. It is well to remember that some people seem to have a physiological idiosyncrasy for it, experiencing signs of allergic reaction. *Never use MSG as a salt substitute in preparing food for those on salt-free diets!* As a salt substitute it is worse than useless, for it too contains sodium just as salt does, and the body will treat MSG sodium exactly as it does ordinary salt sodium. (It is a point to remember about artificial sweeteners, by the way, that they too contain a lot of sodium and should be used with caution by those on salt-free diets.)

There are many fallacies about the way meat should be cooked: the author of one of the more popular cookbooks insists that all roasted meats should be basted at least every 20 minutes. We find too that recipe books still seem to recommend relatively short cooking under high heat, and that grilling is still considered healthier than frying. You don't have to agree with us, but we do have some thoughts on these matters.

Basting was a technique used to keep the outer surface of the meat soft when it was being roasted in the open air on a spit. Since there was no enclosure of any kind around the meat save the kitchen walls or the sky, all the moisture in the outer layers of the meat tended to evaporate, and it did dry out drastically unless continually basted. Very little meat is cooked that way now; even when spit-roasted, it tends to be done inside an oven or a high-temperature glass case. For those who do own an outdoor spit (made from an old model-T Ford crankshaft, or the crankshaft of a windmill), then baste the meat; for those cooking inside an oven, *do not baste!* All you are doing by basting is forcing fat back into the meat, and preventing the formation of a nice crisp brown outer crust. We don't even baste our poultry, and a better duck than the one we ate the other night we have seldom encountered.

Generally speaking, the slower meat is cooked the more tender it will be, and this is true whether you like your meat rare, medium, or well done. Most older cookbooks suggest that meat should be roasted in a fairly hot oven, but of late nutritionists recommend increasingly lower temperatures for the roasting of meat, with a correspondingly longer cooking time. It makes sense to us. Slow and gentle heat penetrates the fibres more gently, and doesn't cause them to give up their moisture content as readily.

Grilling still holds sway over frying, but dry-frying is actually more fat-free than grilling, and kinder to meat.

Roasting, frying and grilling are techniques reserved for the best cuts of meat only, and it is a mistake to attempt to do any of these to a piece of meat which isn't good enough. If you have a doubtful cut, then pot-roast it rather than oven-roast it, or braise it rather than grill or fry it.

We have our own preferences when roasting meat. We dislike sitting it on a rack. If meat is placed on a rack, it is the rack which collects all the lovely oozings and droppings which made such marvellous gravy. We like to place the joint flat on the bottom of the pan, and use only sufficient lubricant to prevent its sticking. Choice of lubricants is purely personal; Jean likes vegetable shortening, Col clarified butter. Other alternatives include vegetable oil (the only trouble with oil is that if it spits, the marks it makes on oven walls or pan are well-nigh impossible to remove) and meat fat saved from a previous roasting. The old-fashioned name for such a collection of fat is 'dripping', but we notice that the term is rapidly disappearing from cookbooks.

A meat thermometer is a handy gadget, and the only sure way of telling when a piece of meat is done exactly the way you want it. Thrust into the very middle of the roast, it registers the temperature at the deepest point in the meat, indicating its 'doneness'. In our experience, roasts always tend to take a little bit longer to get to the point we want than the tables in books recommend. After all, tables in books can be at best an approximation: what are your personal definitions of medium-rare, medium-well done? They are likely to be several shades pinker, redder or browner than the next person's. Ovens vary tremendously, too. Even in a new stove, there is no guarantee that the thermostat is accurate, or that the oven's temperature is uniform. Our stove wasn't new, but we placed an oven thermometer in it and discovered its quirks. The thermostat turned out to be 27°C (50°F) cooler than it said, and the bottom of the oven was 54°C (100°F) *hotter* than the top, against all the laws of nature.

Grilling is not a technique for those who like their meat well done, as the meat is usually unpleasantly burnt on the outside by the time the inside is properly cooked. However, cuts no more than 13mm (½in) in thickness will grill to a well-done state before turning to cinder. The surface of the meat should be close under the source of heat, otherwise it loses too much juice, and most grillers don't work well unless turned up high.

An inferior cut of a size suitable for roasting can be pot-roasted instead of open-pan roasted. The meat is first browned all over, then it is placed on a low rack in the bottom of a high saucepan. The bottom of the pot is covered with water, but only the very lowest portion of the meat ever sits in the water. The lid must be absolutely tight.

Braising is an excellent way of cooking less expensive cuts of steak, or chops. The meat is greyed in a frying-pan first, and then placed on top of a layer of vegetables in a casserole with a good lid. Sufficient liquid to keep the vegetables moist is then added, but the meat remains about the level of the liquid, and cooks gently in the steam released from the fluid when it heats to simmering point. To prevent steam escaping, make sure the lid fits well (if you don't have a crock or casserole with a tight lid, take 2 cups of plain flour, enough water to make the flour into a stiff dough, form the dough into a rope, place all the way around the top rim of the pot, and press the lid down on to it — guaranteed escape-proof, and the dough tastes delicious too).

Casseroling is another slower cooking process for less expensive cuts of meat, but it differs from braising in that the meat sits covered by liquid. As with braising, the container must have a tight lid.

Stewing implies the use of cut-up meat, usually with vegetables, simmered in a pot on top of the stove for several hours, and is suitable for the poorest meats.

In Australia, most boiled meats have first been treated in some way, either corning, smoking, or marinating.

A word about pre-frying meat which is to be braised, pot-roasted, casseroled or stewed. Unless you're working with very good meat, don't brown it too deeply while frying, as this tends to toughen it. Grey it rather than brown it. This was told to us by a butcher, and we agree with him.

Also, when adding liquid to a stew or a casserole, use tepid liquid: three parts cold to one part very hot. If liquid too hot or too cold is used, it shocks the meat and toughens its tissue fibres instead of tenderising them.

CURRYING

Curries are a special category, the recipes for which are probably best obtained from an Indian or Oriental cookbook. The curries included here are anglicised and do not pretend to be authentic. However, for many Australians they are the preferred kind, and hearken back to days when the difference between a curry and a stew was a tablespoon of curry powder added to the gravy thickener.

Father McCullough had only two dislikes among food: vinegar and curried sausages. Vinegar is self-explanatory, but curried sausages is not, for apparently it wasn't the flavour of curry Father disliked. It was simply the combination of curry and sausages. As far as we know Mother McCullough is the only sausage-currier in the world. We admit there must be others lurking somewhere, but she *is* the only one in our experience. Mother's curried sausages didn't look good at all; pale bloated cylinders floating in a thick sea of bilious yellow. Nevertheless they tasted wonderful, and with the noted exception of Father, the McCullough family adored curried sausages.

Now Father had a hearty appetite, but when curried sausages appeared he would quit the dining table in a huff to eat elsewhere, and wouldn't come home until the rest of the family was in bed. It was always easy to tell when Mother had quarrelled with Father, for that night curried sausages would appear on the dinner menu, and would continue to appear with disastrous regularity until the rift was healed. We don't intend to include a recipe for curried sausages, because Mother says she has forgotten how to do it, but if you would like to try them, just substitute sausage for the beef or lamb in one of our plain, bush-style curries.

Turnips boiled and mashed with lots of fresh-ground pepper make a wonderful accompaniment to any kind of curry.

STEAK DIANE

1½ kg (3 lb) round or topside steak, very thinly sliced, no fat or gristle
1 teaspoon salt
1 cup cream

Marinade
2 teaspoons garlic powder (or 4 cloves garlic, chopped)
salt
2 tablespoons pink (or green peppercorns)
6 heaped tablespoons tomato paste
4 tablespoons Branston (or other fruity steak sauce)
4 tablespoons Worcestershire sauce
1 cup dry white vermouth
1 cup sweet red vermouth
6 bay leaves
water if necessary to make up to volume

To make perfect Diane, the steak must be very thin, no more than 13 mm (½ in) thick, and quite free from fat, gristle and tendon. Because the marinade is in effect a tenderiser, it is not necessary to use the fattier, better grades of frying or grilling steak, such as rump or fillet. Round or topside is better.

Mix the garlic, salt and peppercorns into the tomato paste, then begin to thin this down by first adding the Branston, then the Worcestershire sauce. Finally add the 2 vermouths and the bay leaves.

Place the steaks in a flat dish and pour the marinade over them, if necessary diluting with sufficient water (and mixing it in) to ensure that the top surface of the steak is adequately submerged. Lift for a second to let the marinade run underneath.

Refrigerate for at least 24 hours (48 hours is not too long) in the marinade, the dish well covered (the marinade acts as a preservative, so there is no need to worry about possible deterioration).

When ready to cook the dish, remove the steaks from the marinade, pick any bits off them, and strain the marinade into a jug.

Quickly fry the steaks in a very hot pan, no more than 5 minutes a side for medium rare, 10 minutes a side for well done. Remove the steaks from the pan and place in a warm receptacle.

Into the pan, pour sufficient of the marinade to just cover its bottom, and thoroughly stir the pan drippings into it. Bring to the boil, stirring, then turn off the heat. Add the cream, mixing well.

Serve the steaks with a portion of the sauce poured over each.

This is our special recipe for Diane, devised after one satisfactory and many unsatisfactory restaurant samplings. Though it is more complicated than most Diane recipes, its taste more than compensates for the extra effort.

BRITTAINED BEEF

2 kg (4 lb) braising beef in a squarish or rounded piece
4 to 6 good-sized whole potatoes, peeled
2 cups plain flour plus a little water
2 tablespoons plain flour blended with 1 tablespoon butter

Marinade
1 medium-sized carrot
1 large onion
1 bottle good heavy red wine, such as burgundy
1 teaspoon thyme
2 teaspoons dry mustard powder
½ teaspoon salt
3 heaped teaspoons pickled pink peppercorns (or green ones)

1 clove
1 juniper berry — optional
1 bay leaf

Find a pot or casserole high enough to take the piece of meat and with sufficient room inside it to take the potatoes as well. We used the first cut next to the rump for this recipe, but much less expensive cuts can be substituted, provided they are neither gristly nor fatty inside. Brisket or blade work well.

Grate the carrot and the onion, carefully saving all the juices (so grate over a plate rather than a board). Mix the bottle of wine with the grated onion and carrot, the thyme, mustard powder, salt and about two-thirds of the peppercorns.

Press 1 clove, 1 juniper berry, half the bay leaf and half the remaining peppercorns into the bottom of the meat, then set it in the pot you intend to cook it in. Then press the other half of the bay leaf and the rest of the peppercorns into the top of the meat, and lift it off the bottom of the dish for a second to ensure the marinade has run underneath. If there is insufficient marinade to cover the top of the meat, add water. Put a lid on the pot and set it in the refrigerator for 48 hours.

At the end of this time remove the meat from the marinade, picking off all the peppercorns, bay leaf, clove and juniper berry from the surface and returning them to the marinade. Salt the outside of the meat.

Using a very small amount of clarified butter (or other lubricant), heat a frying-pan to a very high temperature and sear the meat very brown all over. Since it is a very large piece and is to cook slowly for a long time, searing won't hurt it.

Place the meat in its pot amid the marinade and push down the potatoes all around it. Make sure the bits in the marinade are evenly distributed around the meat, not all on the bottom.

Take the 2 cups of flour and mix with sufficient water to make a pliable, non-sticky dough. Shape the dough into a fairly thick rope. Put the rope on the rim of the pot so that it continues all the way around without a break and overlaps a bit where the two ends meet. Then put the lid on the pot, pressing it down slightly, forcing the dough to ooze a little outward. Squash the dough which has oozed out across the junction of pot and put the lid on to seal it. Never cut away the excess dough!

Place the pot in the oven at no more than 150°C (300°F) for 6 hours. When cooking with a dough-sealed pan, make sure your oven is not hotter than the thermostat, or the contents will boil briskly and break the seal.

At the end of the cooking period, break away the sealing crust (it tastes delicious!) and remove the meat. Slice it as thinly as you can, arranging the slices down the middle of a piping hot serving platter, with the potatoes around the edges. Cover the platter with foil and place in a warm oven to keep hot.

Strain the marinade. Taste it and see if it needs extra salt, which it well may do. Put the flour/butter paste into a small saucepan and add the marinade to it, stirring. Cook gently over low heat for about 5 minutes, stirring constantly, and never letting the sauce boil outright. Pour this over the meat slices and the potatoes and serve.

This quanitity will serve six people.

Though this dish is fairly complicated to prepare, its flavour is superb. Casseroling in a pot sealed with dough keeps every vestige of goodness and taste inside where it belongs, and ensures that the marinade does not evaporate, thus becoming too concentrated in flavour.

SUPERHOT CHICKEN

12 halves chicken breasts, skinned and boned (6 whole breasts)

Marinade
1 tablespoon lemon juice
2 teaspoons white vinegar
2 tablespoons ground ginger or 2 pieces root ginger, if available
1 teaspoon ground coriander
12 cardamom seeds (called pulses)
2 teaspoons mustard seeds
2 teaspoons dry mustard powder
6 cloves garlic
¼ teaspoon cayenne pepper
1 teaspoon salt
1 cup safflower oil

Combine the marinade ingredients in a blender and mix at high speed until smoothly puréed.

Rub the marinade well into the chicken pieces and pour the remaining mixture over the chicken in a dish. Cover and store in the refrigerator for a minimum of two days, as long as a week.

Fry, barbecue or grill the chicken pieces until brown and cooked through.

DILLED BEEF WITH ARTICHOKE HEARTS

1½kg (3lb) lean steak cut 2½cm (1in) thick
1 teaspoon salt
½ cup plain flour
500g (1lb) sliced mushrooms
3 tins or 3 packets frozen artichoke hearts or 200g (1lb) fresh
  ones
1 bottle red wine
1 tablespoon dill

Trim the fat off the meat and cut it into cubes. Mix the salt into the flour, roll the meat in it and then grey the meat in a frying pan. Tip the meat into a large saucepan.

Fry the mushrooms, as they will tend to be tough if cooked without frying first. Add to the meat in the pot.

Drain or thaw the artichokes and reserve the liquor. Place in the pot. (Fresh ones are wonderful but hard to come by. However, if they are fresh, add half a cup of water to the recipe.)

If there is any flour left over, mix it to a lumpless paste with some of the wine, then keep on adding liquid — wine, artichoke juice, water if needed. Pour over the contents of the pot. If you can be bothered with an extra step, take some of the liquid and use it to rinse out the frying-pan, as the drippings will make an excellent addition to the flavour of the dish.

Add the dill and stir well. Put a tight lid on the pot and simmer very gently for 2 hours.

Cool to room temperature, then place in the freezer for at least a week.

To serve, thaw and simmer gently for 1 hour.

Unless this dish is frozen and allowed to mature frozen, the dill does not mellow and the flavour is not what it should be.

This recipe makes a wonderful filling for a pastry-topped pie. If you do decide to make it into a pie, thaw and place cold in the pie dish, then cover with pastry. Bake at 220°C (425°F) for 20 minutes, then reduce the heat to 150°C (300°F) and bake for another 45 minutes.

SALTIMBOCCA ALLA ROMANA

6 very thin good-sized veal steaks
12 slices prosciutto (Parma ham)
salt

6 teaspoons minced fresh sage (or 3 teaspoons dried sage)
4 tablespoons marsala al'uovo
1 cup cream

Trim any tendon off the veal, then pound each steak with a
hammer until it is very thin indeed, though still holding well
together (it should then be large enough to divide into two
good-sized pieces per steak).

Sprinkle the surface of the steak lightly with salt, then place a
slice of prosciutto on top of it, and sprinkle liberally with sage.
Either fold the meat over double, or roll up. Secure with a
toothpick which can be easily removed after frying. Salt the
outside of each piece of meat lightly.

Heat a little clarified butter or other lubricant in a pan, and
thoroughly brown the veal pieces at high heat. Turn the heat
right down, remove any toothpicks, pour in a little water (2 to
4 tablespoons), cover tightly and simmer for 1 hour.

Remove the lid, evaporate the remaining water, add the
marsala and the cream and stir well.

Saltimbocca is best served with no accompaniment other
than a side dish of fresh green beans and a small plate of spaghetti with the following sauce:

1 medium-sized tin tomato paste (or 2 small tins)
6 large ripe fresh tomatoes, peeled and diced
2 tablespoons Italian herbs (or mixed herbs)
1 cup dry vermouth (or sweet vermouth)
2 teaspoons sugar if dry vermouth, 1 if sweet vermouth

It is an old trick of Italian cooks to add sugar to tomato sauce,
in order to cut its acidity. If you are sugar-conscious, peel a
potato and throw it in during the cooking, removing it afterwards.

Combine the ingredients and cook over slow heat uncovered
until the sauce is thick, usually for several hours.

Top each small plate of spaghetti with 2 heaped tablespoons of this sauce.

A special note on sage

*Saltimbocca and other Italian dishes taste so much better if
you use fresh sage. It isn't hard to grow your own sage. Just
buy a packet of sage seed and sprinkle it over the surface of a
prepared seed box or a sunny, well-turned spot of earth in the
garden. Don't cover the seed with earth, merely water well.
Once the sage is growing, it is hardy and thrives perennially,*

responding well to sun and frequent waterings.

Saltimbocca can be varied. To turn it into plain veal marsala, leave out the ham and sage. To turn it into veal cordon bleu, leave out the sage but top each slice of proscuitto with a slice of Gruyere cheese, omitting the marsala and halving the quantity of cream.

BEEF STROGANOFF

1½kg (3lb) lean steak, sliced very thinly
450g (1lb) small mushrooms
4 medium-sized onions
1 teaspoon salt
pepper
½ cup cream
¾ cup sour cream

Pound the steak with a meat hammer or mallet until it is well broken and extremely thin, then cut it into strips about 13mm (½in) wide and 10cm (4in) long. If you don't want to pound the meat, it is advisable to tenderise it with meat tenderiser, as this dish is cooked rapidly and this does tend to make the meat tough.

Cut any over-long stalks from the mushrooms and discard. Thinly slice the mushrooms to 6mm (¼in) thick.

Slice the onions to about the same thickness as the mushrooms.

Have a warm bowl in the oven in which to place the meat and onions after they are cooked in turn.

Sprinkle the meat liberally with salt (and pepper if you wish). Heat a big frying-pan to a high temperature, place a little clarified butter or other lubricant in it, and fry the meat quickly, stirring and turning to ensure it is brown on all sides. Place the meat in the bowl in the oven.

Brown the onions in the frying-pan, and add them to the meat to keep them warm.

Fry the mushrooms until tender.

Tip the meat and onions back into the pan with the mushrooms, heat them well through to make sure the contents are very hot, then turn off the heat. Stir in the fresh cream first, then the sour cream. Serve on noodles.

This is a very easy version of a very famous dish, and in our opinion not only one of the most authentic in taste, but the best in taste. Cooks (we hesitate to call them chefs!) do the most inexcusable things to stroganoff. It should not contain wine, nor vegetables other than mushrooms and onions. Nor should it swim in sauce. If you use sour cream on its own, unless you cool the meat mixture down to a point where it may not retain enough heat to be palatable when served, the sour cream will curdle. By adding fresh cream first to the hot ingredients, you will find the sour cream behaves angelically.

BEARNAISE BUTTER

1 cup chopped shallots (or spring onions)
2 teaspoons tarragon
1 teaspoon freshly ground black pepper
½ teaspoon salt
1 tablespoon tarragon vinegar
1 cup dry white vermouth
450g (1 lb) butter

Place the shallots, tarragon, pepper, salt, vinegar and vermouth in a blender, and purée them. Leave the butter in a warm place to grow soft but not melted.

Place the purée in a wide-bottomed saucepan, and boil down until there is very little liquid in the mixture, watching to see it doesn't burn when it gets towards the desired state. Cool.

Thoroughly beat the mixture into the butter. Fill a pastry bag and force the mixture through a large rose tube to make buds, or turn into small crocks, or divide into tablespoon-sized portions. Store wrapped in foil or in containers in the freezer until needed.

This is wonderful placed on top of grilled or fried steaks which are otherwise plain, in our opinion tastier even than sauce bearnaise, which is basically the same mixture as above with the addition of egg yolks, and much harder to make.

BERNAISE COOKING BUTTER

If you would like to cook with bearnaise butter also (see bearnaise chicken), make a quantity of bearnaise cooking butter at the same time as you make standard bearnaise mixture. Double the quantity of the ingredients for the blender and reduce by boiling in the same way. Halve when cool. Beat half into the

450g softened butter.

Take another 450g of butter and clarify it by melting gently over low heat and pouring off the clear golden liquid, leaving the white curdy residue in the bottom of the pan to be discarded. Beat the other half of the bearnaise mixture into the liquid portion of the butter and chill until set, then freeze for use later on.

BEARNAISE CHICKEN

8 halves chicken breasts, boned and skinned
4 tablespoons bearnaise cooking butter
1 egg (or 1 cup milk)
1 cup flour mixed with 1 teaspoon salt

Dip the chicken pieces in the egg (or milk) and then roll them in the flour, shaking off the excess.

Melt the bearnaise cooking butter in a frying-pan on high heat (because you have used clarified butter, it will not burn) and fry the chicken pieces until brown on both sides. Reduce heat and continue cooking gently until done.

SEASONED BUTTER FOR LAMB

450g (1 lb) butter, very soft but not melted
1 tablespoon rosemary
½ teaspoon salt
½ teaspoon freshly ground black pepper
2 teaspoons mustard powder
1 cup dry white vermouth

Place the rosemary, salt, pepper, mustard powder and vermouth in a blender and whisk at high speed until smooth and lump-free.

Tip the contents of the blender into a saucepan with a wide bottom and boil until the mixture is reduced to about 3 tablespoons. Cool.

Beat into the butter and prepare as for bearnaise butter for storage in the freezer until needed.

This is a wonderful accompaniment to grilled or fried lamb chops, also rack of lamb which is not otherwise treated than a simple roasting process.

CLAUDIE'S CASSEROLE

6 lamb leg chops (or other large lean chops)
3 medium-sized onions
3 medium-sized carrots
3 medium-sized potatoes
1 medium-sized turnip
1 teaspoon salt
freshly ground pepper
1 clove garlic (or ½ teaspoon garlic powder)
2 cups lukewarm water
½ teaspoon sage
½ teaspoon Italian herbs (or mixed herbs)
2 bay leaves
*440g (1lb) can of red, white, assorted or Lima beans to your
    taste.*

Trim away the fat from the chops, and take out any sharp or
splintered bones. Peel the onions, carrots, potatoes and turnip, then cut the potatoes into four pieces each, the carrots
into thick circles, the turnips into slivers, the onions into thick
rings. Each of these vegetables should be 2½cm (1 in) or more
thick when finished so they don't fall apart during cooking.

Heat a little clarified butter or other cooking lubricant in a
frying-pan.

Salt and pepper the chops well on each side, liberally sprinkling the garlic powder over them at this stage if you are using
garlic powder. If using the clove, crush it and throw it into the
pan while you fry the chops grey-brown on either side. Turn
them into a large casserole or Dutch oven, depending upon
whether you wish to cook in the oven or on top of the stove.

Put another tiny amount of the lubricant into the frying-
pan and lightly brown the onions. Turn them into the pot on
top of the meat.

Take the 2 cups of lukewarm water and tip them into the
frying-pan, stirring carefully to make sure all the good bits on
the bottom of the pan are loosened and incorporated into the
liquid. Pour on to the top of the chops and onions, taking care
the liquid isn't too hot.

Put the sage, Italian seasoning, and bay leaves in the pot,
then the other vegetables and the beans straight out of the can,
complete with their liquid. Top up if necessary with more
lukewarm water; the fluid should barely cover the top of the
vegetables.

Put the lid on very tightly, sealing with flour and water dough if necessary (see Brittained beef, page 74, for method).

If using a Dutch oven on top of the stove, cook at a bare simmer; if baking in a casserole, set the oven at 150°C (300°F).

Do not stir during cooking, but leave the contents in their layers, meat on the bottom, vegetables on the top.

Cooking time is a minimum of 3 hours.

Just before serving, taste the liquid to see if it needs more salt; if it does, then add extra salt to the thickener, which is 1½ tablespoons cornflour in a little cold water. Stir well so that the meat and vegetables become mixed and all the liquid is thickened.

Remove the bay leaves if you can find them. We never can!

It may sound unbearably plain and stodgy, but this to us is the greatest casserole dish in the world. It is genuine French home-cooking, and indicates that the French do not always use wine and cream for flavour.

Variations Use thin T-bone steaks instead of lamb chops. Vary the vegetables to suit your fancy — mushrooms, celery, parsnips, etc. However, if you use mushrooms, do fry them first, otherwise they will tend to be tough.

PORK SPARERIBS

1½ kg (3 lb) pork spareribs (or beef)
1 teaspoon ground ginger
1 clove garlic, crushed
1 small onion, finely diced
¼ cup honey
1 tablespoon Worcestershire sauce
1 cup tomato sauce
½ cup sweet red vermouth (or white)

Trim the ribs and arrange them side by side in a shallow pan.

Bake in a 180°C (350°F) oven for 1¼ hours, then remove the pan and pour off the fat.

Mix the ginger, garlic, onion and honey to a smooth paste with the Worcestershire sauce, add the tomato sauce gradually and then the vermouth.

Spoon this over the meat and bake for a further hour with the oven heat reduced to no more than 150°C (300°F). Baste frequently, and do watch that the food does not scorch or burn, as these sugary recipes have a tendency to catch quickly.

ROAST PUMPED LEG OF LAMB

2 kg (4 lb) leg of lamb, boned and pumped by the butcher
salt and pepper

Stuffing
1 cup dry breadcrumbs
1 small onion
½ teaspoon sage
¼ teaspoon oregano
¼ teaspoon thyme
½ teaspoon Italian herbs (or mixed herbs)
2 tablespoons soft butter
sufficient cream to make a moist but firm stuffing

Fill the cavity of the leg with the stuffing, and if necessary secure with skewers or twine.

Sprinkle salt and pepper lavishly over the outside of the meat, and place in a baking pan with a little lubricant to prevent the meat sticking.

Bake in a 160°C (320°F) oven for 2½ hours.

VEAL RAGOUT

1 kg (2 lb) lean stewing veal
1 teaspoon salt
pinch freshly ground black pepper
1 large onion, chopped finely
½ cup dry white vermouth
2 large ripe tomatoes, skinned and chopped
1 tablespoon sugar
1 large capsicum, cut into thin strips (or 2 small capsicums)

Trim the veal and cut into cubes about 2½ cm (1 in) square. Sprinkle salt and pepper over it.

In a pan, fry the veal until it is grey-brown, then add the onion and continue frying gently, stirring constantly.

Pour in the vermouth, cover the pan, and simmer for 5 minutes.

Remove the lid, add the tomatoes, sugar and capsicum. Cover very tightly and simmer for 1½ hours. If you prefer your capisicum crisp, stir it in just before serving.

BEEF OR VEAL GOULASH

2 kg (4 lb) lean steak cut 2½ cm (1 in) thick (or veal, similar)
2 kg (4 lb) potatoes
oil
2 teaspoons salt
1 cup plain flour
4 tablespoons sweet Hungarian paprika (or 3 tablespoons
*   ordinary paprika)*
1 teaspoon freshly ground black pepper (or ½ teaspoon
*   prepared pepper)*
4 medium-sized onions
1 small can tomato paste
1 cup dry white vermouth (if substituting sweet white
*   vermouth, then eliminate the tablespoon of sugar)*
2 cups warm water
1 tablespoon sugar
2 cups cream
1 cup sour cream

Peel the potatoes and cut into chunks 4 cm (1½ in) square.
Deep-fry the potato chunks in oil until crisp and brown on the
outside.

Cut the steak (or veal steak) into chunks about the same
size as the potatoes.

Mix the salt, flour, paprika and pepper together well and
roll the meat in it thoroughly.

In a pan, fry the meat until it is grey-brown.

Peel the onions and slice them tissue-thin.

Mix the tomato paste with the remains of the flour/paprika
mixture until smooth, then add the vermouth gradually to
avoid lumps. Add the water and stir in the sugar until dissolved.

Tip the finely sliced onion and the liquid into a pot with
the meat and potato cubes. Put a tight lid on the pot.

Cook for 3 hours very, very slowly, stirring about once
every hour (or half hour, if you are an anxious cook).

Before serving, stir in the cream, followed by the sour
cream, and mix well.

BUSH PORK CASSEROLE

1½ kg (3 lb) pork chops (or lamb neck, or leg chops)
½ teaspoon salt
½ cup plain flour

1 teaspoon Italian herbs (or mixed herbs)
2 medium-sized onions
2 tins red beans (or assorted)
1 cup tomato sauce
4 tablespoons Worcestershire sauce
1 tablespoon molasses
2 cups warm water

Cut the fat off the meat and roll in the flour mixed with the salt and herbs. Slice the onions into rings about 12mm (½in) thick.

If you wish, you can fry the meat and the onions first, though this is not necessary.

Take a large casserole (or Dutch oven), place a layer of meat on its bottom, then a layer of onion and beans. Fill up the pan in this way. (Reserve the juice from the beans.)

Mix together the tomato sauce, Worcestershire sauce, molasses, water and liquor from the beans, then pour over the contents of the casserole. Put a tight lid on the casserole.

Bake at 150°C (300°F) for 3 hours, or simmer on top of the stove for 3 hours.

HAM SHOULDER

1 kg (2 lb) rolled boned ham shoulder (or canned ham shoulder)
1 medium-sized can pineapple slices
salt
1 tablespoon prepared mustard, Australian or hot English to taste
2 tablespoons brown sugar

Drain the juice off the pineapple slices and reserve.

Place the meat in a pan (or small baking dish). Spread the prepared mustard over the outside of the meat and sprinkle a little salt over it. Sprinkle the brown sugar evenly on top of this. (Don't worry about the under-surface of the meat; it forms a nice contrast if it is not covered with the mustard/ sugar combination.) Place the pineapple slices evenly all over the outside, then pour the juice on top.

Bake at 150°C (300°F) for 2 hours. If you turn the oven up towards the end of baking to let the dish brown, watch carefully to see it doesn't burn.

ROAST DUCKLING WITH CHERRY STUFFING AND ORANGE-MANGO SAUCE

1½ kg (3 lb) duckling

Stuffing
1 cup stoned cherries — there are enough in a 425g can
2 cups breadcrumbs
½ teaspoon salt
1 cup cherry syrup
¼ cup orange juice
1 tablespoon Italian herbs (or mixed herbs)
½ cup onion, chopped
2 liberal tablespoons butter

Tear all the fat out of the duck's abdominal cavity, then wash the duck thoroughly inside and out. Our bird was home-grown and fed on spinach, so we were especially lucky; the bird was young and not too fatty, its skin fragile and thin. We prefer to cut out both the neck and the oil gland at the base of the tail, a purely personal taste; the neck we used to make stock for the orange-mango sauce. The above quantity may seem like a lot of stuffing, but we got every bit of it nicely tucked away inside.

To make the stuffing is very simple: just combine the ingredients in a large bowl and blend well together by using your hands, then start stuffing the bird.

Once the cavity is full, secure the openings with small skewers and place the bird in a good-sized roasting pan on a bed of refined beef dripping shavings (only 1 tablespoon in all).

Set the oven to 150°C (300°F) only, and bake for 1 hour.

At the end of this first hour, take the duck out and prick the skin to ensure crispness. At this time we distributed peeled potatoes, cut no more than 2½cm (1in) thick, around the duck in its dish, and returned it to the oven for a further 1½ hours at 160°C (320°F). This made a total cooking time of 2½ hours.

If you prefer a slightly under-done bird, cut the roasting time to 2 hours.

ORANGE-MANGO SAUCE

2/3 cup orange juice
1 cup of fresh or canned mango pulp

½ tablespoon butter
2 tablespoons cornflour
3 tablespoons duck stock
1 tablespoon cognac
pinch salt
2 teaspoons sugar
1 teaspoon fresh grated orange rind (or ¼ teaspoon dried orange rind)

Make a roux by melting the butter, adding the cornflour and stirring well, then trickle in the duck stock (made from the neck and giblets of the duck, well boiled), stirring constantly over low heat. When this is all in, add the orange juice and cognac less gradually, but stirring. Add the salt, sugar and orange rind and mango pulp. Cook for 5 minutes at a simmering boil. If this is too thick for your taste, thin it with more stock.

Serve with orange salad.

GRANDMA'S CURRY

1 kg (2 lb) blade (or other braising steak)
2 medium-sized onions
1 medium-sized tomato
1 large apple, eating rather than cooking
1 banana
2 teaspoons curry powder
¼ teaspoon salt
1 level tablespoon plain flour
½ cup raisins
2 cups water
1 tablespoon tomato sauce

Strip the fat off the meat and cut up the meat very small. Very finely dice the onions, tomato, apple and banana.

Mix together the curry powder, salt and flour and roll the meat in it. Lightly fry the meat, add the onions and fruit, including raisins, stir and fry for 5 minutes.

Stir in the water and tomato sauce, cover and simmer in the pan for 2 hours.

MEAT LOAF OR RISSOLES

750g (1½ lb) finely minced beef, lean rather than fatty
250g (½ lb) sausage mince
2 medium-sized onions, minced (or finely chopped)
4 slices crisp bacon, crumbled into small pieces
1 teaspoon salt
1 cup plain flour
2 teaspoons mixed herbs
1 egg
½ cup tomato sauce (or tomato purée)

Place the meats, onion, bacon, salt, flour, herbs in a large bowl and mix by hand — rather messy, but the only way to do it properly.

Lightly beat the egg, pour it into the bowl together with the tomato sauce, and work well through the other ingredients. If the mixture is too soggy, add more flour to gain the consistency you prefer.

Shape by hand into a loaf, place in a baking tin and bake in a slow oven for 2 hours.

We prefer to use flour rather than breadcrumbs because meat loaves made on breadcrumbs don't hold together well during baking. This mixture, if preferred, can be shaped into rissoles and dry-fried.

VENISON JUGGED

1 haunch venison
seasoned plain flour
450g (1 lb) butter
freshly ground black pepper
cayenne
1 lemon
1 onion
5 or 6 cloves
2 cups red wine
1 tablespoon walnut ketchup
earthenware crock with lid

Cut the meat into thin slices. Dredge each slice in the seasoned flour.

Melt a portion of the butter in a heavy-based pan and fry each slice until brown.

As each slice is fried, pack it into the earthenware crock, sprinkling each layer with freshly ground black pepper and cayenne, and salt (if you have not included the ingredients in the seasoned flour).

Allow sufficient room at the top of the jar to add the lemon, quartered and seeded, and the onion stuck with the cloves.

With pan scraps and the remainder of the butter, make a brown gravy using the remainder of the seasoned flour and more flour if needed. This gravy should not be too thick. Pour it over the meat in the crock until the meat is covered. Tie down the lid.

Place the crock in a boiler of water and boil for 3 hours, adding more boiling water to the boiler as needed.

When cooked, remove the lemon and onion and empty the contents of the crock into a large pan, add the wine and the walnut ketchup, shaking continuously over the heat until mixed and heated. Serve with snippets of toast and crab apple jelly.

This recipe has been adapted from an old colonial recipe for kangaroo jugged. In the early days of settlement in Australia, kangaroo was the most common meat seen on the tables of the colonists. The meat is very dark and contains little fat. In New Zealand venison is more readily available than in Australia.

CORNED SILVERSIDE

1 piece corned silverside, 1½—2 kg (2½—3½ lb)
1 heaped tablespoon raw sugar (or brown)
2 bay leaves
2 tablespoons peppercorns
1 medium-sized lemon cut into thick slices, with skin (or 1 tablespoon vinegar, or 2 cups red wine)

Weigh the piece of meat and allow 80 minutes per kg for cooking time.

Rinse the meat in cold water to remove any surface brine. Place in a deep pot and cover with cold water. Add sugar, bay leaves, peppercorns and lemon (or vinegar, or wine). Bring to simmering and allow to simmer gently for required time. When cooked a fork should pierce the meat easily.

Remove from liquid and allow to stand a few moments before carving.

Serve the silverside hot, sliced not too thinly and accompanied by boiled carrots, cabbage and whole boiled potatoes, onion sauce or horseradish sauce.

Silverside is the cut taken from the hindquarter above the leg cut (used as gravy beef) and the topside and round cuts. From a yearling this is often roasted, grilled or fried; but in the mature beast it is usually corned. Each butcher has his own favourite pickling mixture.

TRIPE AND ONIONS

1 kg (2 lb) honeycomb tripe
3 tablespoons butter
6 tablespoons plain flour
½ teaspoon nutmeg
2 cups milk
1 cup mild Cheddar cheese, grated
4 medium-sized onions, sliced thickly

Wash the tripe very well, drain and cut into bite-sized pieces. Place the pieces in a saucepan of very well salted water, put the lid on the pot, and simmer the tripe for 1 hour. Drain.

Melt the butter in a smaller saucepan, turn off the heat and gradually stir in the flour and nutmeg to form a paste. Add the milk a little at a time until a smooth, lump-free liquid results.

Turn on the heat again, and stir in half the grated cheese while the sauce heats. Add the onions and stir constantly until the sauce is thickened. If you prefer a saltier sauce, add salt to taste, but remember the tripe has been salted during boiling.

Place the tripe in a shallow dish and pour the sauce over it, then sprinkle the remaining grated cheese over the top.

Bake at 175°C (350°F) until the cheese topping is well browned.

Serves four to six people.

GEERTRUIDA'S NASI GORENG

3 cups long-grain rice
1½ kg (3 lb) lean pork
4 tablespoons soy sauce
4 cloves garlic, crushed (or finely chopped)
oil
1 large onion, finely sliced

2 stalks celery, chopped small
1 capsicum, sliced
5 shallots, trimmed and finely sliced
1 teaspoon sambal oelek
225g (½lb) peeled prawns
½ cabbage, shredded

Boil the rice for 12 minutes, then drain and spread to dry on a large platter (or tray).

Cut up the pork into cubes and marinate in the soy sauce and garlic for 5 hours, turning regularly.

Start the cooking process about 45 minutes before you intend to serve.

Heat a little oil in a large wok and fry the onions until golden brown, then add the pork and cook until the pork is quite soft.

Add the celery, capsicum and shallots, stirring constantly, after which stir in the sambal oelek.

Stir in the rice and prawns, and lastly add the cabbage. Do not add the cabbage more than 20 minutes before serving, or it will overcook.

Garnish before serving with strips of paper-thin omelette. For six to ten people, depending upon appetite.

4. SAUCES

This is a very short chapter as throughout the text we have usually given the method for making the sauce or gravy called for with a particular recipe. However, we do remember our own early attempts at sauce making, very confused by the French names and having no idea of the correct proportions of flour to liquid to fat to use; so in the following we give a few definitions and explain the basic techniques used. Once you master these, sauces will have lost their mystery.

Beurre manie is the smooth paste made by mixing butter and flour together, usually in equal quantities by weight. Away from the heat, small pinches of the *beurre manie* are whisked into whatever stock or soup you wish to thicken until there are no lumps. The mixture is then returned to the heat and stirred continually until it thickens.

Roux. The butter and flour are cooked together slowly for a few minutes. When the *roux* is cooked, the heated liquid is added while stirring briskly. This slow cooking of the butter and flour does two things — it changes the nature of the flour making it ready to absorb fluid, and takes away any raw flour taste.

Do you want a thick or a thin sauce?

	flour	liquid	fat or oil
thin sauce	1 tablespoon	1 cup	½ tablespoon
medium sauce	1½ tablespoons	1 cup	¾ tablespoon
thick sauce	2 tablespoons	1 cup	1 tablespoon
soufflé base	3 tablespoons	1 cup	1½ tablespoons

We have said flour and by this mean white wheaten flour, but you can use any other type of flour you like. Potato flour, cornflour (corn starch), arrowroot and rice flour make interesting variations to your sauces and add subtle flavours of their own.

Things that can go wrong when making sauces

Be sure that your liquid is very hot and the *roux* has bubbled for two minutes before combining the two. Use a heavy-based pot for sauce making; do not use aluminium pots as these tend to discolour white sauces. If you do get lumps, force the sauce through a fine sieve and simmer for another four or five minutes, or put the sauce in a blender. If the sauce is too thin, away from the heat beat in small pinches of *beurre manie*, and return to the boil for another few minutes, stirring continually. Thick sauce may be thinned by bringing it back to simmering point and beating in more liquid, one tablespoon at a time.

THE SAUCE FAMILIES

The white sauces: There are two main branches. *Béchamel* uses milk as the liquid, *velouté* is made with a white stock such as chicken or fish. Both use a butter and flour *roux* as the thickening agent.

Brown sauces are made from well flavoured brown stock and a *roux* that has been slowly cooked to a nut brown colour.

Hollandaise is the queen of the egg yolk and butter sauces.

Vinaigrette or French dressing is the leader of the oil and vinegar sauces.

Flavoured butters are just that – butter to which herbs and seasonings have been added.

SAUCE BÉCHAMEL OR BASIC WHITE SAUCE
These quantities will give you one cup of medium thickness or general purpose white sauce.

¾ tablespoon butter
1½ tablespoons flour
1 cup milk
⅛ teaspoon salt

You will need a small, heavy bottomed saucepan, a spatula (or spoon) and a wire whisk, and a second small pot in which to heat the milk.

In the saucepan melt the butter over a low heat, blend in the flour using the spatula and stir continually until the flour and butter bubble and froth. Cook for two minutes without browning. You now have a white *roux*.

At the same time bring the milk to the boil, and add the salt to the milk.

Remove the *roux* from the heat; wait until it has stopped bubbling and pour in all the hot milk. Beat strongly with the whisk to blend the liquid with the *roux* making sure no bits are stuck to the sides of the saucepan. Return to a moderate heat, whisk until it comes to the boil and boil for one minute, stirring continuously.

Your sauce is now ready for any additional flavourings.

SAUCE VELOUTÉ

Exactly as for *sauce béchamel*, except you use 1 cup of white stock instead of the milk.

These are your two basic white sauces and here are a few of the many things you can do with them.

Sauce Mornay

This is a cheese sauce. Bring 2 cups of medium *béchamel* or *velouté* to the boil and away from the heat beat in 50 grams (about 1½ozs) coarsely grated cheese until it has blended with the sauce. Do not be tempted to add too much cheese as the sauce will become stringy. Season with salt and pepper and a pinch of nutmeg. (We find old, matured cheese preferable to fresh chedder, the latter being inclined to become stringy when heated.)

Sauce aurore or tomato sauce

Beat 4 or 5 tablespoons of cooked tomato purée into 2 cups of simmering *béchamel* or *velouté* sauce. The more purée, the stronger the colour and flavour. Season with basil.

Herb flavoured sauces

Make a white sauce and before serving, stir in the finely chopped herb or herbs of your choice.

There are many, many more themes you can play with the white sauces either using your own imagination or following the recipes found in cookbooks more exotic than this one.

BASIC BROWN SAUCE

If you have the time and patience to follow the instructions for making the famed French *demi-glace*, do not let us deter you. But quite frankly, we do not have the time to spend up to four days making a sauce, and we do not know anyone who does. However, there is an easier method. You do need a well flavoured stock. If you have been simmering meats, save one or two cups of the liquid as this makes excellent stock after the fat has been removed. Otherwise use 3 or 4 beef cubes, but do take 20 minutes to improve the flavour as follows:

2 cups water
3 or 4 beef cubes
1 small onion finely chopped

1 small carrot finely chopped
parsley
bay leaf
thyme, pinch only
optional: 3 tablespoons red wine

Simmer for 20 to 30 minutes, strain through a fine sieve, discard the solids and you have a good stock that only requires thickening to become a brown sauce.

2 cups brown stock
1 heaped tablespoon arrowroot or cornflour

Blend the arrowroot or cornflour with 2 or 3 tablespoons of *cold* stock. Now beat in the remainder of the stock and simmer for 5 minutes. Taste and correct seasoning with pepper and salt.

HOLLANDAISE

This is the sauce that everyone loves and that frightens many cooks. The ingredients for the basic sauce are egg yolks, melted butter and lemon juice; the trick is to make the egg yolks absorb the butter without scrambling them. Remember what happens to egg yolks when they are heated? They gradually thicken and eventually solidify; therefore, temperature plays the most important part in the technique. An egg yolk will absorb between 70 and 80 grams of butter, but until you have gained a little experience do not attempt to use more than 50 grams of butter. You need the following tools and we suggest that you assemble these before you start:

1 small saucepan in which to melt the butter
1 double boiler: have the water simmering in the lower container and use the upper one to make the sauce. If you do not have a double boiler, a bowl sitting on top of a pot of simmering water serves well.
1 bowl of iced water, large enough to place the sauce pot in whenever necessary to lower the temperature
1 wire whisk

3 egg yolks
200g (½lb) butter
1 tablespoon lemon juice
1 tablespoon cold water
large pinch salt

Cut off two pieces of the butter, each about 15g (½oz) and set aside. Melt the remainder of the butter in the small pot and set aside.

In the upper pot of the double boiler or in the bowl beat the egg yolks, using the wire whisk, until they are sticky and thick. Add the lemon juice, cold water and salt and beat for another minute.

Add one piece of the unmelted butter, but don't beat it. Now place the pot in the boiler over simmering water and stir with the whisk until you have a smooth cream that is slowly thickening. This should take 1 or 2 minutes; if the sauce becomes lumpy or you think it is thickening too quickly, plunge the pot in the bowl of iced water to cool the yolks, beating all the time. Return to the boiler. Keep beating until the wires of the whisk hold the sauce as a light cream. Remove from the heat and beat in the second piece of cold butter. By removing from the heat you have stopped the cooking process.

Now add the melted butter at first only a drop at a time, whisking until you have a very heavy cream. Pour in the melted butter more rapidly. Discard the milky residue which will have settled at the bottom of the melted butter.

Season with salt and pepper and more lemon juice if necessary.

Do not worry if all the melted butter is not absorbed. This is your first attempt and you have made a hollandaise sauce to be proud of. It can be served as it is or you can add herbs, or one or two spoonfuls of purée such as tomato, asparagus, shell fish. If you want a very light sauce for soufflés or egg dishes, just before serving fold in two stiffly beaten egg whites.

With practice you will be able to make a good hollandaise sauce in 5 to 10 minutes. But there is an even quicker method if you have an electric liquidizer. One warning, if you do not have a liquidizer jar that does not splatter, use a cloth over the top — melted butter is hot and burns! This method does not allow the egg yolks to absorb as much butter as the previous technique, and the texture of the finished sauce is a little different; but it is still a good hollandaise and a good method for the busy cook.

Hollandaise sauce made in a liquidizer
3 egg yolks
100 to 125g (½lb) butter
1 tablespoon lemon juice

1 tablespoon cold water
¼ teaspoon salt
pinch of pepper

Put egg yolks, lemon juice, water, salt and pepper in the jar of the liquidizer.

Heat the butter until it is foaming hot. A small pot with a pouring lip is very handy for this.

Cover the jar, using a cloth if it does not have a lid, and blend at top speed for two seconds. Without stopping the machine, start adding the liquid butter, drop by drop. (Just ease the cloth up a little to allow you to drip in the melted butter.) When the sauce has become a thick cream, stop the blender; do not worry if you have not used all the butter, and be very careful not to use any of the milky residue. If you wish to add more butter — the liquidizer method uses only about half the usual quantity of butter — remove the sauce from the jar and in a bowl beat in by hand more melted butter, but very slowly, a drop at a time.

BÉARNAISE SAUCE

If *hollandaise* sauce frightens the new cook, *sauce béarnaise* terrifies even accomplished cooks! Yet it is only an *hollandaise* in which you replace the lemon juice with wine and vinegar and use shallots, pepper and tarragon for seasoning. You will need the same implements plus one more small pot.

4 tablespoons wine vinegar
4 tablespoons white wine
1 tablespoon chopped shallots or spring onions
1 tablespoon chopped fresh tarragon (½ tablespoon dried)
⅛ teaspoon pepper
pinch of salt
3 egg yolks
100 to 125g (½lb) melted butter
25 to 30g (1 oz) cold butter
2 tablespoons chopped tarragon or parsley.

In a small saucepan boil together the first six ingredients and reduce to 2 tablespoons. Set this aside to cool.

Now proceed as for *hollandaise*. Having beaten the egg yolks until thick and sticky, strain the cool wine and vinegar mixture and beat into the yolks. Add half the cold butter and proceed as for *hollandaise*. Finally, correct seasonings and beat in the freshly chopped tarragon or parsley.

MAYONNAISE

We usually think of mayonnaise as a type of salad dressing, but really it is only a cold sauce for cold dishes. Like *hollandaise*, it depends on inducing egg yolks to absorb fat and form a creamy suspension, but in mayonnaise we use oil in place of butter. It can be made by hand beating or with an electric blender.

Have everything, ingredients, bowls and tools, at room temperature. And remember that 1 egg yolk will absorb only 1 cup of oil at the most (do not try to use full quanitities of oil for your first few tries — you will still make a good mayonnaise.) The other point is that the oil must be added slowly, very, very slowly.

You will need:
1 large wire whisk
1 bowl large enough to accommodate the whisk
1 tablespoon wine vinegar or lemon juice
½ teaspoon salt
¼ teaspoon dry or prepared mustard
1 cup olive oil, or any salad oil you prefer
2 tablespoons boiling water

You must be certain that bowl and whisk are clean, dry and warm. If you do this, you will have no trouble with the mayonnaise failing to thicken.

In the bowl beat the egg yolks for 1 or 2 minutes until they are thick and sticky. Add the vinegar or lemon juice, salt and mustard and beat for another half minute. The yolks are now ready to take up the oil.

This is added drop by drop, *and you must not stop beating* until the sauce has begun to thicken. Keep a steady beating motion of about two strokes per second — it does not matter in what direction you beat, or if you change hands or direction — just keep beating. Every few seconds stop adding the oil and continue beating to be certain that all the oil is being absorbed by the yolks. After about half a cup of oil has been added, your sauce will have thickened into a very heavy cream, and now you can have a short rest. The remainder of the oil may be added more quickly, 1 to 2 tablespoons at a time. If the end result is too thick and heavy, add a few drops of lemon juice or vinegar and beat to thin out the sauce.

Now for a neat anti-curdling trick. Beat in the 2 tablespoons of boiling water before adjusting the seasonings.

If you are not going to use the mayonnaise immediately, it may be stored, but first scrape it into a smaller container and cover tightly to prevent the formation of a skin.

Remedy for a failed mayonnaise!

If the sauce has failed to thicken, or if the finished product begins to release its oil and curdle, all is not lost. In a clean, warm bowl add 1 teaspoon of prepared mustard and 1 table-spoon of the sauce. Beat with the clean whisk for a few seconds until they thicken and cream. Continue in this way, adding one or two teaspoons of sauce at a time, being sure that each addition is absorbed into the sauce before adding more.

Mayonnaise can also be made in an electric liquidizer, and this takes no culinary skill at all. Purists may shudder, but for people in a hurry it is most useful.

1 egg, whole
¼ teaspoon dry mustard
½ teaspoon salt
1 tablespoon lemon juice or wine vinegar
1 cup salad oil or olive oil (you may not need all of this)

Into the liquidizer jar, break the whole egg and add the mustard and salt. Cover and blend at top speed for 30 seconds. The resulting mixture will be thick and frothy. Pour in the lemon juice or vinegar and blend for a further 10 seconds.

Working with the jar uncovered and the blender at high speed, start adding the oil into the centre of the mixture, one drop at a time. This must be done very slowly; when about half the oil has been added, the sauce will begin to thicken. Continue adding the oil in a very slow stream of drop-lets until the sauce is too thick for the blades of the machine to whirl. Scrape into your serving dish and adjust the seasonings.

These are two ways of making a basic mayonnaise, and now you can add various seasonings: chopped herbs of all kinds, spoonfuls of purée, chopped sour pickles, anchovy pastes — the list is endless.

GELATINE MAYONNAISE (for coating cold dishes)

½ cup liquid
30g (1oz) gelatine
1 cup mayonnaise

For the liquid you can use a few tablespoons of stock plus a
good wine vinegar, lemon juice and water, wine and stock —
anything that will enhance the food which you wish to cover.
The flavour should not be so strong that it masks the flavours
of your dish.

In a small saucepan dissolve the gelatine in the liquid, stirring over a low heat until all granules have disappeared. Cool
the gelatine mixture.

Gently beat the gelatine mixture into the mayonnaise and
adjust the seasonings. Do not become alarmed when the sauce
thins out; it will gradually thicken as the gelatine sets. When it
has become stiff enough to handle easily with a spoon, coat
the cold food. Refrigerate for the final setting.

SAUCE TARTARE

This sauce, so popular with fish dishes, fits in at this juncture,
as it too is made with egg yolks and oil; but here we use hard
boiled eggs. The following is our favourite recipe. Do not
attempt to make it in the liquidizer as the mixture becomes too
thick and clogs the blades.

4 hard-boiled egg yolks
1¼ tablespoons prepared mustard
¼ teaspoon salt
1 cup oil
lemon juice or wine vinegar as required
3 tablespoons chopped sour pickles
4 tablespoons chopped capers
1 tablespoon of each of the following herbs, finely chopped
*   parsley, chives, tarragon.*

In a mixing bowl mash and pound the egg yolks, mustard and
salt until you have a very smooth paste. This must be absolutely smooth, without any hint of lumps, otherwise the egg
yolks will not absorb the oil.

Now, proceeding as for mayonnaise, beat in the oil drop by
drop until you have a thickened sauce; use lemon juice or
vinegar to thin the sauce if it becomes too thick and continue

with the addition of the oil until it is all absorbed.

Having chopped the pickles and capers, squeeze out any excess liquid by screwing them up in a cloth. Gradually beat them into the sauce and finally beat in the herbs. Correct the seasoning.

VINAIGRETTES (Oil and Vinegar Sauces)

A true French dressing is made with wine vinegar, olive oil, salt, pepper, and mustard if you like it. You can add sugar, curry, cheese, tomato and even Worcestershire sauce, but please do not call the resulting mixture French dressing. Fresh herbs in season are always used in a French dressing. There is always a question as to what is the correct proportion of oil to vinegar to use. Three parts of oil to one part of vinegar is the usual mixture, but do not hesitate to work out your own mixture to suit your own taste.

There are two ways of combining the oil and vinegar. You may place the oil, vinegar, pinch of salt, dry mustard in a jar with a screw-top lid and shake vigorously until all are blended. Or, using a bowl, dissolve the salt in the vinegar by beating; then beat in the dry mustard if you are using mustard; now add the oil, drop at a time, beating continuously until you have a nice emulsion of oil and vinegar.

Finally, adjust seasonings of salt and pepper, and stir in the freshly chopped herbs.

Lemon juice is often substituted for the wine vinegar and makes an excellent French dressing.

DILL SAUCE

Oil and vinegar (or lemon) dressing can be used as the base for a number of other sauces and salad dressings, and dill sauce is just one of these.

1 egg yolk
4 tablespoons sour cream
¼ cup vinaigrette
lemon juice to taste
2 tablespoons chopped fresh dill

In a bowl beat the cream and egg yolk until well blended. Beat in the vinaigrette drop by drop as though making a mayonnaise. Adjust seasonings, adding lemon juice if necessary and stir in the dill.

By changing the dill to any other fresh herb, it is easy to vary this sauce — parsley, chives, tarragon, chervil, burnet, sweet basil.

THE BUTTER SAUCES

There are both hot and cold butter sauces. They are simply butters that have been made to absorb the flavours of herbs or spices, and even wines. We will start with the cold butter sauce as this is very simple. Its success depends on creaming the butter thoroughly before any flavouring is added. It does not matter how you do this — in an electric beater, beat it with a wooden spoon, pound it in a bowl with a pestle — as long as you beat until the butter is creamed. It is easier to start with butter at room temperature, soft but not oily. When sufficiently creamed, beat in the herbs or flavouring. Here are some suggestions. 100g (¼lb) of butter will absorb easily the quantities given, but there is no reason why you cannot vary the amounts.

> *1 to 2 tablespoons prepared mustard*
> *2 tablespoons finely chopped herbs of your own choice*
> *1 to 3 cloves garlic, well mashed*
> *2 hard-boiled egg yolks finely mashed and sieved*
> * plus 1 tablespoon chopped chives*
> *anchovies or anchovy sauce and lemon juice*
> * (taste as you add to achieve the flavour you desire)*

The list is endless, just dependent on your imagination. If you want a sweet butter sauce, beat in castor sugar and vanilla essence or rose water.

You may use the butter in its soft creamy state or return it to the refrigerator and it will firm up and can then be used as cold butter for spreads, etc.

As we have already found out, when you melt butter it separates out to a small amount of solids in the bottom of the pan, a little milky liquid and the golden fat floating on the top. However, if you beat a milk acid into the butter some change, either chemical or physical or perhaps both, takes place and the liquids and solids remain suspended in the fat. The following is a very simple lemon butter that illustrates the technique.

LEMON BUTTER SAUCE

4 tablespoons lemon juice
pinch white pepper
100 to 125g (¼ lb) chilled butter cut into 8 to 10 pieces
1 wire whisk
1 pot large enough to accommodate the whisk

Boil down the lemon juice to about 1 tablespoon. Add the pepper. Remove the pot from the stove and without delay beat in 2 pieces of butter. Return to a very low heat and adding one piece of butter at a time, beat until you have used all the butter. You will have a thick creamy sauce.

If you do not serve the sauce immediately and wish to rewarm it later, when the time is ready beat in 2 to 3 tablespoons of very hot water or vegetable stock if you are serving the sauce with vegetables.

BROWN BUTTER SAUCE

You can also make a brown butter sauce. Use either ghee or clarified butter, otherwise your sauce will not be clear but rather speckled.

150g (6oz) ghee or clarified butter
3 tablespoons finely chopped parsley
4 tablespoons wine vinegar or lemon juice
pepper and salt as needed

Melt the butter over a moderate heat. It will crackle and froth at first, but as this stops the butter will turn brown. Maintain an even, low heat until you have achieved a nut-brown colour and then remove from the heat. Stir in the chopped parsley and pour into a sauce boat. Using the same pot, without washing it, reduce the vinegar or lemon juice to approximately one tablespoon. Stir this into the browned butter. Season to taste.

We have concentrated on French sauces in this chapter. This is because we like them; they are good basics on which you can build; they teach you the art of sauce making. Always remember that the purpose of the sauce is to enhance the food, not mask poor cooking.

Every country has its own sauces and you will find the recipes for these in the cookbooks dealing with that particular cuisine. Perhaps some day someone will collect the sauces of the world into one gigantic volume! That would be rather fun!

In the meantime, don't be afraid to try your own ideas. Here are a few odds and ends that may be useful.

● Granny Smith apples (a green cooking apple) stewed with chopped mint makes a delightful sauce for cold lamb.
● tomatoes, onions and green peppers simmered in butter with a touch of sugar and pepper and salt makes a good accompaniment to a meat pie.
● any ripe fruit can be puréed and used as the base for a fruit sauce; ripe plums are particularly good.

So here's to good sauce making!

5. VEGETABLES AND SALADS

VEGETABLES

If you have got this far in your reading of our jottings on grandma's cooking — and our own — you will undoubtedly have come to the conclusion that we have great respect for the recipes and methods of yesteryear. And you are right. But for some obscure reason a particularly horrifying tradition has continued. Why do some Australian and English cooks believe that vegetables are dangerous creatures that have to be killed by immersion in fiercely boiling salty water for at least half an hour, but usually for the whole hour, before they are fit for human consumption? You all know the result: a soggy mess of cabbage or spinach dumped on a plate along with a slurp of watery potato. So it is no surprise that some children hate cooked vegetables. Even though Jean grew up in a vegetarian household, she much preferred raw carrots and cauliflower to the cooked versions. And we both retain vivid memories of sitting at the kitchen table from 1 p.m. until 4 p.m. gagging over one serving of mashed pumpkin until all had finally disappeared. Mind you, Jean has eaten pumpkin ever since and now loves it; but over the years she has learnt many ways of cooking pumpkin, and even of camouflaging it for guests who do not usually eat this wonderful vegetable. (Col still hates pumpkin and is wary of Jean's deceptions.)

We are always surprised at the number of people who complain about the time it takes to prepare vegetables, and opt for canned or frozen products. We do not decry the use of either method for preserving vegetables, and freely use both, whether home-processed or bought from the supermarket. But when fresh vegetables are obtainable, these are the ones we prefer, and this is what this chapter is all about.

Any garden product should be washed thoroughly before it is used, even if it is from your backyard garden. You may not have used insecticides, but your neighbour may have, and remember that all sprays are carried far afield on wind currents. Leafy vegetables, such as cabbage, spinach, sprouts, endive, should be washed first in salted water. The salt upsets any beasties that may be in them and they will wriggle out. Then dunk the vegetables in cold fresh water. Shake the leaves gently, but don't try to dry off all the droplets of water because, as we explain later, this is your cooking medium.

We use a stiff bristled brush for cleaning root vegetables. A good scrub under the running tap is often all that is necessary if the carrots and potatoes are young. If you feel you must peel potatoes and parsnips, let the peeling be thin because there is lots of nourishment stored just under the skins. Swedes, however, do need to be peeled thickly, otherwise there is a bitterness from the skin that is released during cooking and permeates the flesh; this is particularly so if the swedes or turnips are at all old, and it is probably this reason that makes these vegetables less popular.

METHODS FOR COOKING VEGETABLES

Dry heat   There are two reasons for using water in the cooking of vegetables: dry grains such as rice, legumes such as dry peas and beans, need to replace their free water that has evaporated in the maturing and drying processes so that all the starch granules can be converted to sugars. Other kinds of vegetables need a heat-conducting medium, the temperature of which can be easily controlled, and water is the liquid of choice because in itself it is flavourless, and will not mask the delicate tastes of vegetables. (We will not enter the debates on the merits of various water sources. Suffice it to say, most bodies controlling water supplies do make every effort to provide clean water.)

However, many vegetable nutriments and flavours dissolve in water, particularly in hot water; and as it is not practical to save all the vegetable water to make soup, over the years we have all been guilty of pouring down the sink a lot of good food. Theoretically, then, dry heat should be better than wet heat when cooking vegetables. You are using dry heat when you bake things in the oven, and edible roots lend themselves to this method very well. They can be baked dry by placing on the oven shelves, or you can put them with a little fat or oil in a pan — the fat will give them a crispy crust on the outside, leaving the inner portions soft and floury. This pan is put into the oven, or over a very low steady heat on top of the stove.

Potatoes, pumpkin, carrots, parsnips can be done in the above way. These roots have a high water content, some of which will be converted to steam during the cooking process. If you want baked potatoes to be floury inside, prick their skins in a few places with a fork before you put them in the oven and some of this steam will escape. Depending on the size of the potatoes or other roasting vegetables, they take about three-quarters of an hour to cook in a moderate oven. To check whether they are cooked, put your hand in an oven mitt and squeeze gently; if they are soft, they are cooked. If you want crisp outer skins on the potatoes, start them in a hot oven for about 10 minutes and then lower the heat.

Roasted vegetables are the perfect accompaniment for a roast of beef or roast leg of lamb. Put the prepared vegetables in the same roasting dish as the meat. Or you can blanch them first in boiling water for 5 to 10 minutes and then put them with the meat, allowing approximately half an hour for cooking.

Wet heat   Because of their large surface areas in relation to their bulk and because of their fragility, much or all of the water content of leafy vegetables will evaporate if you try to bake them and you will be left with crumbly ash; so a liquid heat medium is used, usually water. However, there is no reason why you can't use stock of any kind if you prefer blended flavours. Temperature is the important point.

For some reason boiling seems to have some magical quality, and everything must be boiled. Boiling is a very high temperature — 100°C (212°F) — and we can find no scientific reason for cooking all vegetables at this high temperature. From the point of view of nutrition and flavour, we consider lower temperatures are better. Time of cooking is directly related to temperature, and a gentler heat and a slightly longer cooking time give the best final results. You must balance time and temperature — too low a temperature will leave longer time for the nutriments to be leached into the water. Strike a happy medium by simmering, that is, keep the pot just under boiling.

How much water do you need? This is where we disagree with grandma and with many of our contemporaries. We use as little water as possible. With vegetables such as spinach, silver beet, sorrel and lettuce, we wash the leaves under the tap but do not attempt to dry them. We add no water to the pot because there is enough water hanging in droplets on the leaves but we usually throw in a generous dab of butter or margarine. Ensure that the lid is tight and cook from 3 to 5 minutes, depending on the age of the leaves. All the water will have evaporated, the leaves will have kept their green colour, and if you have used butter you have your sauce. Vegetables such as green beans and peas do require more water as they take longer to cook. We barely cover them with water and simmer young green peas for 10 minutes and beans for about 20 minutes.

We also cook without salt. This began when we were cooking for a friend who was on a salt-free diet, and we found we liked our vegetables better when salt was added at the table.

All the root vegetables can be cooked in water and as they are robust compared to the leaves of lettuce and spinach, the action of the boiling water will not damage them to the same extent. But again time is important. They are cooked until the cellulose has softened and the starch granules have exploded and converted to sugars. In other words, until they are soft but not mushy and falling to pieces. A potato, for example, should still look like a potato when lifted from the pot.

Most root vegetables require 20 to 30 minutes, but beetroot and turnips take much longer, particularly if they are mature. Don't be tempted to prick beetroot with a fork to see if they are done because these holes will allow the rich purple juices to escape. When a beetroot is cooked, the skin comes away easily but the vegetable itself remains in good shape and still rather firm. It should be taken out of the boiling water and immediately plunged into very cold water. While they stay hot, they will continue to cook. (This applies to all vegetables, particularly the root ones which can retain the heat for a long time.) So unless they are to be eaten immediately, they should be refreshed in cold water and reheated when required (see the French method for cooking vegetables, page 109-110).

Swedes and turnips are very strongly flavoured and not to everybody's taste. If you peel them thickly and then dice them to 2½cm (1in) they cook more quickly, and some of the strong flavour will be leached into the cooking water. Because of their all-pervading taste, they should be cooked by themselves, unless it is a stew that is being made.

The French method   We all have friends and relatives who never arrive on time for a meal (these kind of people do not remain friends of the cook for long). However, when you fear this is going to happen, use the French method for cooking vegetables — blanching and refreshing.

To blanch anything, you put it into boiling water for a few minutes. The time varies for different foods, but they should be left in the boiling water until they are cooked to the crunchy stage, never longer. Remove from the heat at once, drain, and plunge into icy-cold water (under the running tap will do if your water supply is very cold). Leave the vegetables in the cold water until cooled right through (while they retain any heat, the cooking process will continue) and then drain and dry by gently patting the vegetables between the folds of an absorbent cloth or kitchen paper. Be careful not to press the juices out. They can now be held for up to an hour before reheating in butter.

Be generous with the butter and have it bubbling before you throw in the refreshed vegetables. (Clarified butter will not burn so readily.) Keep the pot or pan shaking over the heat for a few minutes until all the pieces are well coated in butter and heated right through. Serve immediately, using the butter as a sauce.

You can ring the changes at this reheating stage by using cream or sour cream instead of butter.

Frozen vegetables have been blanched and refreshed before freezing; therefore, after thawing all that is necessary is heating in butter.

Steaming   Cauliflower and broccoli are flower heads and as such, are delicate in structure. They can be cooked by gently simmering, but are ideal for steaming. Any vegetable can be cooked by this method, and you do not need a pressure-cooker for simple steaming. Steamers come in all shapes and sizes. Essentially they consist of a base pot to hold the boiling water and a container with holes in its bottom that sits snuggly on top of the base pot. This top container has a tightly fitted lid. The food to be cooked is placed in the top container, the one with holes in the bottom. Bring the water to the boil and when the steam is rising steadily put the second container on top of the first. Wait a few minutes for the steam to percolate through the holes in its base, and then ensure that the lid is tight. This method avoids much of the leaching of essential minerals and vitamins that takes place when you cook directly in water.

If there are divisions in the steamer, you can keep the various vegetables separated, and you can always add the faster cooking ones last.

There are also multi-storeyed steamers with several containers sitting one on top of the other, and the steam finds its way through the holes in each one. We know one ingenious lass who cooks her whole meal on one gas ring, starting with a steamed pudding in the bottom container (the one with the boiling water), potatoes and carrots in the first storey, greens in the second, and she has even been known to make her sauce in a pan on the top (this one does not have holes in the bottom)!

It does take a little longer to cook vegetables by this method, but they taste very good.

A pressure-cooker uses super-heated steam under pressure. This means that anything cooked in a pressure-cooker will take less time than ordinary cooking methods, very much less, and it is wise to follow the times given in the instructions when you purchase your cooker. The main drawback in using a pressure-cooker is that everything is given the same time, so leafy vegetables and fresh green peas should be cooked separately, otherwise when the root vegetables are cooked the greens will be mush. But a pressure-cooker is ideal for cooking beetroot which cooks in a fraction of the time taken by conventional methods, and does not lose so much of its colouring.

Braising   Try braising your vegetables. This takes much longer, but if you are not pressed for time, the end results are excellent. You need a fireproof casserole with a well-fitted lid. To braise celery or leeks, first wash them thoroughly to remove any soil or beasties; cut off the roots and the green tops (the latter can be dried and used for flavouring soup). Try to keep the celery in one piece. The vegetables should then be blanched, refreshed and dried. Celery and leeks require 10 minutes for blanching. Grease the casserole well with butter, not forgetting the lid, and place the whole stalk of celery or the leeks in the casserole. Pour over about ¼ cup of chicken stock and dot the vegetables liberally with butter, using at least 2 tablespoons. Put on the lid and cook in a moderately hot oven at about 180°C (340°F). The vegetables will take at least 1½ hours to bake at this temperature, and you will end up with a little too much moisture; so at the end of cooking, remove them from the oven and reduce the moisture to about half. Use this as your sauce to pour over the leeks or celery when they are served. During the baking process, the lid must fit tightly so that no steam escapes. Never be tempted to add more liquid, but you can baste with melted butter as often as you like.

If you make sure that the oven heat is below the boiling point of water — 100°C (212°F) — none of the water will turn into steam; it will take much longer, up to 2 hours, but you will have beautifully cooked vegetables. Try whole lettuce with young garden peas (a few still in their pods). The lettuce should not be blanched for longer than 3 minutes.

When you are uncertain as to what time the meal is to be served, this low temperature cooking is ideal, because you can turn up the heat and finish the cooking in steam. When a menu says *à la poele*, it means the vegetables have been cooked at below the boiling point of water and basted with melted butter.

THE POTATO

We want to make a strong plea on behalf of the potato. Spuds, taties, murphies, or what you will, these are one of our most versatile vegetables. There are numerous varieties that are obtainable all year round. They can be eaten at any time during their growth: as new potatoes no larger than walnuts or as mature potatoes each big enough for four people; they can be eaten at breakfast, lunch or dinner. You can bake them, boil them, fry them, make them into pancakes, use them in bread-making. But can you get a decent serving of potato in a restaurant? Why are potatoes unfashionable? And what makes restaurateurs think that a spoonful of boiled rice and a heap of watery spinach take the place of creamy mashed potatoes and green peas? Is it economics? Or is it snobbery arising from the phrase 'the common potato'?

We don't believe potatoes are common. They are plentiful and usually readily available, but not common in the derogatory sense. Since beginning work on this cookbook, we have sampled some of the so-called better-class restaurants of Sydney, but we have yet to be served a good potato. With some dishes we get chipped potatoes; but we like potatoes plain. Old-fashioned, if you like, but we do not believe we are alone in this preference.

The following are a few of the ways in which you can cook potatoes. There are dozens more. Whole books have been written in praise of potatoes and their uses. Jean once watched Mother Easthope assist her friend, Mrs Schowe, give a 3-hour cooking demonstration using nothing but potatoes, and they had by no means exhausted their ideas.

ROAST POTATOES

When roasting the Sunday joint, thinly peel several large potatoes and cut them into slices about 2½cm (1in) thick. Put them in the baking dish to surround the meat; half way through the cooking time, turn them over. They come out crisped and brown on the outside, and soft and floury inside — an essential accompaniment to a roast dinner.

POTATOES BAKED IN THEIR JACKETS

Do not peel. With a stiff brush, scrub the potatoes clean and, using a sharply pointed knife, remove any eyes. Dry-bake by placing them on the oven shelf. The time for cooking depends on the size of the potatoes and the temperature of your oven. If you want crusty outsides, start them off in a hot oven for 10 minutes, and then turn down the heat to moderate. Otherwise use a low to moderate temperature. To test whether they are done, put your hand in an oven mitt and squeeze them gently. If they are soft, they are cooked. A medium-sized potato takes about three-quarters of an hour in a moderately hot oven. Choose potatoes of the same size, preferably large, so that they will be cooked in the same time. To serve, make two cuts across one end, add a generous dab of butter, and if you want to decorate them, sprinkle chopped parsley or chives on the snowy white inside part that is showing. Always supply plenty of butter, or if you prefer, cream or sour cream. Add pepper and salt and you have food fit for a king.

BOILED POTATOES

Whether you peel the potatoes or not is a personal decision. Col always peels them; Jean seldom peels them. Have a pot with a well-fitting lid and use only enough water so that they do not boil dry. Medium-sized potatoes take about 20 minutes to cook in gently boiling water. But this time-factor can vary either way, not only with the size of the potatoes, but also the variety and whether they are new potatoes or old potatoes. If you are not sure, use a skewer: it should easily penetrate the centre of the potato. If you have not peeled the potatoes before cooking, this is easily done before serving. Insert a fork into one end and with a sharp knife break the skin and peel it off. Please yourself whether you salt the water -- half a teaspoon is ample for medium-sized potatoes. The boiled potatoes can be served as they are or you can turn them into mashed potatoes.

MASHED POTATOES

Having boiled and skinned the potatoes, return them to the dry pot and shake briskly over a low heat to dry off any excess moisture. Now mash with a potato masher, add butter generously and perhaps a very little milk. Beat the potatoes with a fork until light and fluffy. If you have not used salt during the cooking, add it now. But be careful, tasting as you go, because over-salted potatoes are just as unpalatable as those without salt. They are now ready to serve; or you can add a little chopped parsley or chives. Try creaming them with fresh cream instead of the butter, but it must be thick cream so that the mixture remains fluffy and not wet and sloppy.

DUCHESSE POTATOES

Duchesse potatoes are useful for all sorts of dishes, both for their flavour and for their appearance. Prepare as for boiled potatoes and mash thoroughly; or better still force the cooked potato through a sieve so that all lumps have been removed. Add 1 tablespoon of butter, a little milk (the exact quantity really depends on the variety of potato, but just enough to make them moist) and 1 egg for every 450g (1lb) of potato. Beat the potato well with a fork or whisk.

The mixture is now ready to put into a forcing-bag with a large star-nozzle and here you can use your imagination. Simple duchesse potatoes are heaped in pyramids on a baking sheet and baked in a hot oven at 220°C (425°F) until lightly browned; this takes about 10 minutes. But you can use duchesse potatoes to make nests into which you drop a raw egg before baking; you can garnish any meat or fish dish that requires potato as a complement; you can decorate the top of a shepherd's pie.

CROQUETTES

Boil the potatoes and mash thoroughly or force them through a sieve. They must be absolutely smooth and without lumps. For each 450g (1lb) of potatoes you use a generous tablespoon of butter and an egg and beat the mixture well with a fork (the same as for duchesse potatoes, but omitting the milk). With well-floured hands pinch up small pieces of the mixture and roll them into balls about the size of a large walnut. Brush the outsides with the beaten egg and coat with browned breadcrumbs.

The croquettes are now ready for frying. This is done the same way as for frying fish or making chipped potatoes. Heat the cooking oil in a deep saucepan with a heavy base. The croquettes are put into the wire basket and immersed in the hot oil. Do not fry too many at once (the same rules as for frying fish) because each time you put the croquettes into the hot oil the temperature is lowered and the more you put in the longer it takes for the oil to return to frying temperatures. The temperature should be 190—195°C (375—385°F). (To check your temperature if you do not have a thermometer, drop a few 2½cm (1in) cubes of bread into the hot oil; they should brown in 30 seconds.)

Because the potato is already cooked, the croquettes will only take 3 or 4 minutes to heat through and the outside to become golden brown. Tip them on to several layers of kitchen paper to absorb any excess fat, and keep them hot in the warming oven. They are less likely to burst during frying if you coat each croquette *twice* with the egg and the bread-crumbs.

Various herbs can be added to the potato mixture and don't think that mint and parsley are the only herbs to be used — try grated nutmeg, onion juice, finely chopped hard-boiled egg, small shrimps or prawns. With a little imagination, you can have everyone guessing.

The potatoes don't have to be shaped into balls; they can be small cylinders, cubes, cones. If time allows, chill the croquettes for an hour or so before frying; they will take a little longer to cook, but are less likely to fall apart.

CHIPPED POTATOES (as in fish 'n' chips)

Use old and large potatoes. Peel them thinly and then cut into chips which will be the length of the potato and between ½—1cm (¼—½in) thick.

There are two methods for preparing the chips for frying. If you are in a hurry, blanch and refresh the chips by placing them in boiling water for 3 minutes and then plunging them into ice-cold water. Or if you have the time, soak the prepared chips in cold water for at least half an hour (this removes some of the surface starch). In both cases, dry the chips thoroughly on kitchen paper.

Have your deep-frying pot one-third full of oil or fat. Never have it more than one-third full or you run the risk of overflowing the hot oil when you immerse the chips. The chips are put into the hot oil. The temperature should be 195°C (385°).

Cook the chips for about 5 minutes, keeping the basket moving to ensure even cooking. Now remove the basket from the oil, increase the temperature to 200°C (395°F) and return the basket to the pot. Fry the chips until they are golden brown. Remove from the hot oil, drain on kitchen paper, and serve very hot with salt. As with all other deep-frying, never crowd the basket. It is better to make the chips in several lots if you are frying a large quantity. After the first frying in the lower temperature, the chips can be held for any length of time. The last hotter frying is done just before serving. [To check the temperature of your cooking fat, 2½cm (1in) cubes of bread will brown in 60 seconds if the fat is 177—188°C (350—370°F), 40 seconds at 188—195°C (370—380°F), 20 seconds at 193—199°C (380—390°F).]

POTATOES FOR POTATO SALAD

Choose large, evenly shaped potatoes because they are easier to dice. Cook as for boiled potatoes. Peel while hot and then dice by cutting into slices, and then again at right-angles into strips, and finally into dice.

While the potatoes are cooking, prepare mayonnaise if you are making your own. If you used a cooked mayonnaise there are certain advantages. By adding it hot to the diced potatoes, they will continue to cook so you do not have to cook them until they are soft, and they are easier to handle when cutting into dice. If you have all your other ingredients ready — onion, celery, grated carrot, salad herbs — you can combine these while the potatoes are still hot, the mayonnaise will soak into the potatoes and you will not have tasteless lumps of cold potato sitting at the bottom of a sea of watery mayonnaise.

Old potatoes make better potato salad than new potatoes; and although leftover potatoes can be used, we prefer to cook potatoes specifically for the job.

Although we could continue with potatoes for many more pages, we will stop here. We do not know who first called potatoes 'humble', but we hope you are convinced that versatile is a better description.

JERUSALEM ARTICHOKES

These are not to be confused with the globe and crown artichokes; the latter are refined thistles and you eat the fleshy bases of the leaves surrounding the thistle-head and base of the flower after the choke or beard, actually the stamens of the thistle flower, has been removed. Jerusalem artichokes belong to the sunflower family (*Helianthus tuberosus* to be botanically correct) and the English in their own fashion have corrupted the Italian name of *Girazole articiccio*. It must be by the same logic that they call soup made from Jerusalem artichokes, Palestine soup!

The Jerusalem artichoke is an ugly-looking tuber that is said to have been brought from America to Europe in 1607. They are warty and knobbly and you never find two exactly alike. There are several varieties and the tubers range in colour from dirty white through red to purple, but they all taste the same — a little sweet, perhaps a little bit like the globe artichokes, and with a flavour all their own. In appearance, they are not unlike green ginger roots. You either like artichokes or you hate them.

First, they must be dug at the right time: too early and they are only fat roots, too late in the season and they have started to sprout for the next year's growth. The plants make an elegant garden subject, being members of the sunflower family; they grow to nearly 2½m (8 ft) in height, branch freely and have masses of bright yellow sunflowers about 5 to 8cm (2 to 3in) in diameter. When they are flowering they love plenty of water.

They make good floral arrangements and picking does not detract from the wealth of tubers. When the flower have died and the whole plant dies off, this is the time to dig. A healthy plant will yield at least half a bucket of tubers. Discard any small tubers and use only the large; you never manage to dig them all and next year you will have another crop without any further gardening. They need a good deal of scrubbing; usually Jean tips them on to the lawn and hoses them with a strong jet of water before attempting to scrub. Having got them reasonably free of dirt, give them a scrub but don't worry if you can't remove all the dirt because the skins are discarded after cooking.

The tubers are simmered in unsalted water until they are soft. Skinning them is rather a nuisance and fiddly. This is easier when they are still hot, so use heavy-duty rubber gloves to protect your fingers. Squeeze the tuber and the soft inside will squelch out. Discard the tough skins and force the pulp through a sieve to remove any lumps. You now have a thin purée which is the basis for a wonderful soup — Palestine soup.

PALESTINE SOUP

2 cups hot artichoke purée
1 cup thin white sauce
juice of 1 onion
salt and pepper

To the hot artichoke purée add the cup of white sauce and the onion juice; simmer gently for a few minutes and serve after seasoning with the salt and pepper.

Add herbs if you so desire, but the flavour of the artichokes is delicate and should not be drowned. Jean often omits the onion, and for a further variation, adds 2 cups of artichoke purée to 1 cup of potato soup. Delicious. But a warning: it is better than pea soup for causing flatulence, so do not serve Palestine soup if you are going on to a theatre party! It is a family dish, rather than a party dish.

The French call Jerusalem artichokes Topinambour *and have a delightful story to explain the name. When these ugly tubers were first brought to France from Massachusetts they were called* Poire de Terre, *probably because they looked a bit like an ugly potato. The following year the explorer Claude de Launay returned from Brazil with several members of the Topinambour tribe and put them on exhibition in Paris. Some smart lad rather unkindly likened these strangers to the* Poire de Terre, *and that vegetable has been called* Topinambour *ever since. We have not been able to determine whether the Topinambour tribe were ever called* Poire de Terre!

CARROTS

Carrots can be baked or boiled like any other root vegetable, but, when you can spare a few extra minutes at the stove, try glazing them.

GLAZED CARROTS

If the carrots are very small, young and tender, leave them whole; if they are more mature, either slice them evenly or cut them into juilienne strips. Cook them in the smallest possible quantity of water; it is best to use an open pan without a lid. When you become expert, you will correctly judge the quantity of water; but there is no reason why you cannot add a little more water if the pan is becoming dry before the carrots are cooked. Just make sure it is boiling water so that you don't drop the temperature of the cooking carrots. (To be quite honest, only skilled cooks who are glazing carrots every day judge the correct quantity of water at first.)

Juggle the cooking so that the carrots are cooked as the pan becomes almost, but not quite, dry. Now add a large lump of butter and 2 or 3 pinches (about 1 level teaspoon) of sugar. Keep the pan moving so the carrots are rolled in the gooey butter and sugar mixture. Don't let your pan become too hot, or the sugar will burn. Serve them immediately.

Swedes and turnips, and even onions, can be done in the same manner. We don't know why, but glazed carrots are called *carottes Vichy* on the menu, but glazed onions and glazed turnips are always *oignons glaces* and *navets glaces*.

PARSNIPS

Parsnips are not to everyone's taste. They emit quite a strong odour when being boiled, particularly if they are old and well matured. The thin, but tough skin should be peeled, and if the parsnips are at all old, the fibrous centre core should be removed. After this preliminary preparation they may be either boiled or baked. If using the boiling method, cook them until tender, drain and mash with butter, pepper and salt. To bake, you can put them around the roast with the potatoes, or they can be baked dry on the oven shelf.

PARSNIP SOUFFLÉ

boil sufficent parsnips to give 1 cup of mashed vegetable
2 tablespoons butter
1 tablespoon plain flour
½ cup milk
2 eggs
salt and pepper

Melt the butter, stir in the flour and gradually add the milk. Stirring continuously, bring the mixture to the boil and cook for 2 to 3 minutes. You will have a thin white sauce. Let it cool a little — it should feel warm to your fingertips.

Add the mashed parsnip, mixing thoroughly.

Separate the egg yolks from the whites and beat them well into the mixture. Use salt and pepper to taste.

Beat the egg whites until they are very stiff. Fold into the parsnip mixture as lightly as possible.

Turn the whole mixture into the prepared soufflé dish and bake in a moderate oven at 175°C (350°F) for about 30 minutes. Serve immediately.

A little grated nutmeg or ground ginger added to the mashed parsnips will give a subtle flavour to the soufflé. In fact, you can have your diners guessing, particularly if you do not mention the hated word 'parsnip'.

BEETROOT

Sometimes called beets, the tender, dark crimson flesh of beetroot has a sweet flavour (sugar-beets belong to the same family), and can be used hot or cold, as pickles or to make soup called borsch. They can be either baked or boiled, or grated and used raw. Be careful not to damage the roots or skin before you cook the beetroot, or they will 'bleed' and much of the rich colouring will be lost in the cooking water. Just wash off the dirt and trim the tops to within about 2½cm (in) of the fat root.

Beetroot take about 1½ to 2 hours in boiling water. When cooked, the skins are easily removed with the fingers but let them cool a little first. A pressure-cooker is useful for cooking beetroot; young medium-sized beets will cook in about 20 minutes.

When cooked, if you are going to serve them hot, slice or cut them into dice and add butter or hot white sauce. In Australia hot beetroot are seldom served, but they make an interesting and colourful addition to any hot dinner.

To prepare this vegetable for a cold dish, slice the beetroot and soak in either vinegar and sugar or lemon juice and sugar. Add a pinch of salt if you so desire.

There is really no comparison between home-cooked beetroot and the canned product. If you have your own garden, beetroot are easy to grow, and can be harvested at any stage of growth. When they are about the size of large cherries, thin out the rows and use these little beets for pickling. Boil in water — they only take about 20 minutes at this stage — and then drop them into your pickling solution. Aunt Janet Devery, who never wasted anything, always saved not only the gherkin jars but also the pickling liquid from the gherkins. The tiny beets were dropped into the jars, the liquid re-heated and poured over them and the jars resealed. They were then stored for at least two weeks or longer if she could find a safe hiding-place — and the pickled beetroots used in her salads.

GREEN BEANS

If you do not like green beans, and some people don't, try the following method of cooking them with ginger.

BEANS WITH GINGER

450g (1 lb) fresh green beans
3 or 4 pieces of ginger preserved in syrup — about
   2 tablespoons
just enough water to cover beans
¼ teaspoon coriander seed, crushed
2 tablespoons butter (or margarine)
2 tablespoons chives, chopped

Prepare the beans by washing, stringing if necessary, and breaking them in halves.

Finely chop the preserved ginger pieces. When they are chopped you should have approximately 2 tablespoons, but the exact quantity can be varied.

Bring to a rolling boil sufficent water to just cover the beans, and no more. Toss in the beans, ginger and coriander seed. Put the lid on, and simmer for 10 minutes.

Melt the butter (or margarine) in a pan.

Drain the beans — there should be very little water to drain. Toss the beans and chives in the melted butter and cook for another 5 minutes; keep the pan moving over the heat during this final cooking.

Serve.

Note   *If you are on a salt-free diet, this is a pleasant way of having beans.*

BRUSSELS SPROUTS

We like our Brussels sprouts braised in butter, and the preparation adds only a few minutes to the cooking time.

BRUSSELS SPROUTS BRAISED IN BUTTER

Having trimmed and washed the sprouts, boil them uncovered for 5 or 6 minutes. Using a fireproof casserole dish with a well-fitting lid, smear butter liberally over the inside of the dish. Drain the sprouts and place them, heads up, in the casserole; sprinkle with pepper and salt and add more melted butter. Cover the casserole with the lid and heat it on the top of the stove until the contents begin to sizzle. Now place the casserole in the oven at medium heat for 15 to 20 minutes, until the sprouts are tender. Serve immediately.

You can vary this basic recipe by adding a few braised chestnuts to the casserole; instead of the butter, use 2 cups of hot sauce mornay; replace some of the butter with boiling cream.

ASPARAGUS

We agree with the noted cook Julia Child that there is only one way to cook asparagus: by the French method. When the new season's bundles of green asparagus are displayed in the shops they are difficult to resist but how many disappointments have you had when you cooked them? Our first attempts were woeful: limp, grey-green sticks with inedible tough fibrous stalks.

It pays to take the time to peel the lower ends of the asparagus stalks, using a potato peeler. The stalks will cook in the same time as the tips, and all will be edible.

Tie the peeled stalks in bundles and drop them into a large pot of boiling, salted water. Boil them slowly until they are just tender and drain immediately. If you leave 1 or 2 stalks out of the bundles, it is a simple matter to remove 1 stalk and test for tenderness.

When cooked, the asparagus may be served as a hot vegetable with the main dish. It can be chilled and served with salads. You can add a white sauce and serve the asparagus on toast.

THE UBIQUITOUS CHOKO

During the 1930s, the years of the Great Depression, every backyard and some front yards sported their own choko vine. The vines covered fences, out-houses, fruit trees and if not controlled would invade Dad's prized tomato patch. The flowers were insignificant, but later in the season large, pear-shaped, green fruit weighed down the fragile vines and Mum had the job of disposing of them. First, you fed the family on choko until the vegetable could no longer be disguised and then the children were sent with full baskets to give to neighbours. Invariably the neighbours had their own fill of chokos. The stories of disposal of chokos took wondrous turns, even to selling them to fruit-canning factories where they were said to be mixed with pears!

Now Col and Jean have found that chokos are sold in fruit and vegetable shops and at unacceptable prices. However, they are a good food and can be used in many ways.

Originally chokos came from the Central Americas where they are known as *chayote* and in other countries are called Christophine. No one seems to know when they were introduced into Australia, but they do thrive here. If you have to dig out an old choko vine, do not discard the large tuberous formation from which the roots sprout; it is not only edible but flavoursome. It tastes something like a sweet potato and you prepare it in the same way.

If you are growing your own chokos, do pick them before they are fully grown and mature. The young fruit are more sweet and tender and cook quickly. Try cooking them in the same way as zucchini. Simmer gently for a few minutes until soft and serve with lashings of butter and pepper and salt.

CHOKO FRITTERS

several chokos
pepper and salt
2 eggs (or 3)
grated onion (or chopped chives)

We call these fritters for want of a better name. Coarsely grate several chokos and let them stand for a few minutes. They contain a lot of water and this needs to be drained off (tip it into the soup stockpot). Add pepper and salt, and bind with 2 or 3 lightly beaten eggs. Fry the chokos quickly in a hot pan.

You can make one large fritter filling the whole pan, or make small fritters from spoonfuls. A grated onion or chopped chives improves the flavour.

When chokos are old, the seed in the centre develops into an oval, flat capsule that can be slipped out of the coarse outer flesh. Discard the outer flesh and fry the seed quickly in butter. It has a nutty taste, quite different from the accepted choko blandness.

AVOCADO

The avocado is not a pear, so let us call it plain avocado, although it is certainly not a plain fruit. Its uses are varied. Don't think of the avocado as a pre-dinner appetiser only. It can be used in tossed salads, as the basis for a delicious mayonnaise, as a vegetable with the main course, as a subtle ingredient of a soup.

AVOCADO MAYONNAISE

1 ripe avocado
2 hard-boiled egg yolks
sugar
1 to 2 tablespoons lemon juice
cream
pepper and salt

We do not give exact measurements for the sugar; the amount depends on whether you prefer a slightly sweet salad dressing or an acid sour one.

Blend together the flesh of the avocado, the hard-boiled egg yolks and the sugar until you have a smooth paste. Into this paste mix the lemon juice; now add sufficient fresh cream to give the consistency you desire. Season with the pepper and salt. One tablespoon of freshly chopped chives goes well with this mayonnaise.

AVOCADO AS A VEGETABLE WITH THE MAIN COURSE

You need a hard, unripe avocado. With a sharp knife, cut rings of avocado flesh about 1cm (½in) thick, leaving the skin on the rings. As you cut the rings the seed will separate. Remove any of the brown husk that surrounds the seed and sometimes clings to the inner surface of the fleshy rings. The avocado contains a lot of oil so you do not need to oil the pan for the quick frying of the rings. Heat the pan and place the rings in the bottom. Turn after 2 to 3 minutes; the surfaces will brown and crisp and the flesh will be soft and meaty. Serve one or two rings along with the other vegetables.

AVOCADO DIP

Mash the ripe avocado flesh; season with pepper and salt. You can add lemon juice if you like, and to make it go further a few spoonfuls of thick cream. Jean is an avocado fan and prefers unadulterated avocado with just a touch of pepper and salt, although sometimes she adds a few teaspoons of freshly chopped herbs such as sweet basil, chives, marjoram.

PEAS

Not many of us have access to fresh garden peas which we can pick, pod and cook immediately. Here are two recipes for cooking the peas you buy at the greengrocer's which, with all due respect to your grocer, are a little tired, having been picked for several days. Both recipes work well with old, end-of-the-season peas that are still green but rather hard.

GREEN PEAS 1

In addition to the shelled peas, you will need:
2 tablespoons butter
1 tablespoon sugar
1 tablespoon fresh mint leaves, chopped
salt and pepper

Drop the peas into boiling water and boil uncovered for 10 minutes, that is, until the peas are almost tender, but still slightly firm. Drain off the water. Return the pot containing the peas to a low heat, rolling the peas around until all excess moisture has evaporated. In a heavy-bottomed saucepan, melt the butter and sugar; add the mint; roll the peas around in the melted butter until they are well coated; cover with the pot lid and cook over a very low heat for about 10 minutes, stirring or tossing occasionally and making sure the butter does not brown. Season with salt and pepper and tip into a hot vegetable dish. Serve immediately. For mature and end-of-the-season peas, this method works well.

GREEN PEAS 2

500g (1 lb) shelled mature peas (but they must be fresh)
3 tablespoons chopped spring onions (use the green leaves)
2 tablespoons sugar
1 head lettuce, shredded
2 tablespoons softened butter
salt and pepper
heavy-based pot

Into the pot put the peas, onions, sugar, shredded lettuce and softened butter. If the peas are very hard, use your hands to squeeze them and roughly bruise, at the same time mixing thoroughly with the other ingredients. Cover with cold water; bring rapidly to the boil; boil for 20 minutes. Now begin tasting; if the peas are not tender, continue to boil. You will probably need to add more water, but make sure this additional water is boiling so the cooking process is not hindered by a reduction in temperature. When the peas are tender, remove the lid, quickly boil away all remaining fluids; season with salt and pepper; serve immediately.

TO IMPROVE THE FLAVOUR OF TINNED AND FROZEN PEAS

The addition of butter, finely chopped chives, chopped mint, chicken stock, mushroom soup, either in combination or using only one of these, will greatly improve the flavour of tinned or frozen peas.

SALADS

This is proving the hardest section to write, not because we do not make tasty salads (Jean is noted for her inventiveness in this area), but because we seldom reproduce the same salad. Everything depends on what is available. So rather than give a collection of salad recipes, here are a few words of wisdom about making salads.

The most important part of salad-making is the use of fresh ingredients. Lettuce does not have to be a part of the salad; if lettuces are too expensive or if they are old and wilted, forget them; use young spinach leaves, watercress, tops from very young beetroot, or other young vegetables instead of leaves. Prepare the salad just before the meal, put it into the refrigerator to crisp and add the mayonnaise immediately before serving.

There is a frustrated artist living in all of us and salads provide a wonderful medium in which to work. First choose your plate carefully: a deep bowl for a tossed salad, a large platter for a colourful display. Prepare each item, that is, grate the carrots or cut them into strips, slice the onions and cucumbers, wedge the tomatoes. Having washed all the vegetables, plunge them into a bowl of iced water for a few minutes and then carefully dry them on kitchen paper; this will result in crisp ingredients. And then use your imagination when arranging the platter. Pretty pictures in magazines can provide guidelines, but don't slavishly follow them.

We give a handful of salad recipes only and leave the rest to your ingenuity.

TOSSED GREEN SALAD

1 lettuce
1 small bunch watercress
a few young spinach leaves
6 to 8 spring onions

Tear the lettuce leaves into pieces. Separate the stalks from the watercress. Tear the spinach leaves. Cut the spring onions into small pieces, using green tops as well as the bulbs. Toss all of these with French dressing.

This is a very quickly made, simple salad and goes well as a side salad to the main dish. You don't have to use lettuce, cress and spinach, but can use any fresh, young vegetable leaves; beetroot tops, young Brussels sprouts, a few young green pea pods.

CECIL'S THISTLE SALAD

When Jean offers this salad to her guests, she never gives it a name or tells of what it is made; but salad-lovers always come back for more.

Wander around your garden, paying particular attention to the unweeded corners, and you can find ingredients for an unusual salad: young green milk-thistle leaves, chick-weed, land cress, young nasturtium leaves, in fact use any leaves that your canary likes but make sure thay are very young leaves. To these add mustard and cress greens, a few leaves of summer or winter savory, fresh herbs such as sweet basil, borage (and include a few of the beautiful blue flowers), parsley, chives, dandelion leaves, sweet marjoram. You do not need to use all these and certainly if using the more strongly flavoured herbs, include only a few of the fresh leaves. With a sharp knife, chop all the leaves finely and toss together.

You may use a French dressing or toss the salad greens in a rich mayonnaise and let stand in the refrigerator for 10 to 15 minutes before serving.

WALDORF SALAD

This is the famous salad that is said to have been first created at the Waldorf—Astoria Hotel in New York. There are minor variations, you don't have to use lettuce leaves, watercress can be added, but this is the method we use. It is a good accompaniment to a main dish of pork or duck.

3 or 4 tart apples, preferably red-skinned
white heart of 1 head of celery
1 tablespoon caster sugar
2 tablespoons lemon juice
½ cup mayonnaise
1 cup walnut pieces, chopped
1 small lettuce — we like the curly leaves of
    mignonette lettuce

We often add a Granny Smith apple to the red-skinned apples, particularly if no tart red apples are available. The red skin is for appearance only.

Dissolve the sugar in the lemon juice. Core 1 apple and slice it very thinly across the core. Drop these slices into the lemon juice so they will not discolour. Dice the remaining apples (do not peel) and combine with the mayonnaise. Leave to stand for half an hour. This action does break some of the rules of salad-making, but the apples taste better if they have had time to absorb some of the mayonnaise.

Wash and dice the celery, chop the walnut pieces. Line a bowl with the lettuce leaves. Combine chopped apple and mayonnaise with the celery and walnuts and pile into a heap in the middle of the bowl. Use the apple slices to fill in the space between the heap of salad and the lettuce leaves, either in fancy patterns, if you have time, or overlapping against the pile of salad mixture.

MOURINJARIE SALAD

1 avocado
1 heart of celery
1 green capsicum
2 young carrots
1 cup cauliflower florets
2 tablespoons French dressing

Peel and dice the avocado. Cut the white heart of celery into bite-sized pieces. Seed the pepper and cut it into strips. Cut the carrots into julienne strips. Break the cauliflower into small florets, discarding any coarse stalks.

Toss the above in the serving bowl. Add the French dressing; toss again. Serve.

You can add freshly chopped chives or herbs to the French dressing for a change.

This is one of those salads made from bits and pieces in the vegetable basket. We had unexpected visitors for dinner one night and plenty of meat in the freezer, but because of a drought there was little in the garden. The salad must have been good as the diners had second helpings and one of the lads drained the juices from the bowl. We were told it had to be included in our cookbook and that it should be called Mourinjarie after the name of Jean's mountain retreat.

ORANGE SALAD (FOR FISH DISHES)

1 sweet navel orange
1 lemon
1 tablespoon salad oil
sugar
freshly ground black pepper
salt
1 large firm tomato
1 medium-sized white onion
1 green cucumber

In a salad bowl, combine the juice of the lemon, the oil, sugar, pepper and salt by briskly beating with a fork until the oil is emulsified with the lemon juice.

Thinly slice the orange, retaining the skin; slice the tomato, onion and cucumber and toss them together in the lemon and oil dressing.

This is one of the few salads that improves with standing, so it may be prepared up to 1 hour before serving and kept in the refrigerator. It makes a delicious side salad to be served with fish-based dishes, particularly oily fish such as sea mullet.

Here are two salad-dressings. The first is quickly made; the second will keep for a week under refrigeration.

QUICK SALAD DRESSING

2 egg yolks, hard-boiled
2 to 3 tablespoons sugar, depending on how sweet your tooth is
½ cup lemon juice
½ to ¼ cup cream, depending on thickness
pepper and salt

Mash the egg yolks and sugar together until the sugar has dissolved; add lemon juice and cream, mixing to an even consistency. Use pepper and salt to taste; add more sugar if required.

Variations   Add a few capers, mashed; finely chopped chives or ripe olives improve the flavour; in fact, any herb or seasoning you fancy can be added.

If you have no cream, use sweetened condensed milk, but do not add sugar. Cream cheese can be substituted for the cream.

COOKED SALAD DRESSING

½ cup cottage cheese
½ cup plain yoghurt
½ cup cream
½ cup lemon juice
1 to 2 tablespoons rice flour, depending on how thick you like your mayonnaise
3 teaspoons mashed capers and about 1 teaspoon of the liquor from the capers
sugar
salt
mustard

Mix together the first seven ingredients and gently heat until the mixture thickens, stirring continually. At first it will appear to become thinner as the heat melts the cheese and yoghurt, but keep stirring and the mayonnaise will thicken. Add sugar, salt and mustard to suit your own taste-buds.

Vinegar may be used instead of the lemon juice, or you can use a mixture of the two.

We prefer either a white wine vinegar or an apple cider vinegar in this recipe, and unless you really like a tangy mayonnaise use only half the quantity of vinegar.

While the mayonnaise is still hot, you can bottle and seal it, and it will keep well.

The use of rice flour instead of plain flour ensures that, if the mixture is too thick or too thin, more fluid or more rice flour can be added, without lumps forming.

6. PASTRY AND PASTRY DISHES

Most people avoid making their own pastry, particularly the fancy kinds — puff, flaky, choux. If it can't be obtained ready-frozen in the supermarket, they are not willing to use recipes that call for pastry. This is truly a great pity, as all pastries, but especially the fancy ones, are so delicious when homemade. It doesn't matter if your pies aren't as prettily finished because you made the pastry case yourself, the sheer pleasure of having done it yourself (plus the fact that you can vouch for the goodness and quality of the ingredients!) more than makes up for an unprofessional finish. Besides, with practice you will become expert at flutes, crimps, spirals, rosettes and the like.

Good pastry is not much more difficult to make than many more popular cooking projects. The trouble is twofold; first, people who *can* make good pastry tend to mask their efforts in mystery; second, descriptions in books of how to make puff pastry are so garbled and indistinct they are impossible to follow, while the few books we have seen which attempt to illustrate the process do so inadequately. In grandma's day, you learnt to make pastry by watching mother or auntie make pastry, but girls no longer serve an apprenticeship in mother's kitchen, and the old arts are slowly disappearing. Mother Easthope, for instance, never made pastry from a book description; she watched her Great Aunt Aggie.

Col was so discouraged by the recipe book instructions that she had never tried to make puff or flaky pastry. Luckily Jean speedily put her right; now both can produce puff or flaky pastry in under an hour.

Pastry has a great advantage over most other so-called difficult cooking feats; you don't have to use it the moment it's made. In fact, it is distinctly improved by living for 24 hours in the refrigerator, and it freezes without impairment of any kind. So it can be made whenever you have the time, and stored indefinitely.

To make your task easier, we intend to give you every help we can in this introduction. The basic rules are simple and easily followed, the special equipment minimal and very inexpensive.

1. Keep everything cold when you are making cold-preparation pastry. Make sure the kitchen is cool and the oven not in use. Keep your utensils cool and your ingredients cold.

2. Always make sure you sift together flour, salt and (if used) baking powder before you start.

3. Good pastry can be made without baking powder, but the addition of ⅛ of a teaspoon of baking powder will ensure the pastry isn't tough.

4. If making short pastry, or a puff where some of the shortening is added to the flour before any liquid, never rub the shortening into the flour between your hands, as this heats it up; use a pastry blender or French whisk or two knives, and cut it in.

5. Use as little fluid as possible; never finish with sticky dough.

6. Fold lightly, mix lightly; never knead as if you were making bread, and keep your hands out of it as much as you can.

7. Try to make pastry the day before you need it, so you can give it 24 hours in the refrigerator.

8. When rolling pastry out to use in the creation of an actual dish, make sure it hasn't warmed to room temperature.

9. Never grease your baking container or tray. Flour the outside of your pastry if you like, though it isn't necessary.

10. Make sure your oven is well up to the required temperature before you put your pastry in to bake.

11. Wait 10 minutes before you peek while you are baking.

12. Never bang the oven door!

13. Never keep the oven door open too long.

The object of all this carefulness is to ensure that the air in the pastry stays cold until it is baked, and that the shortening never fuses with the flour, as happens in cake-making for instance. If you do fuse shortening and flour, you end up with tough, indigestible pastry. We should hasten to add that hot-water pastries follow a different rule, but hot-water pastries are highly specialised: choux for éclairs, cream puffs, etc., and basic hot-water pastry for the 'lead pies' as grandma always called them — pork pies, Melton Mowbray pies, etc. With short pastry, the shortening lies all through the flour unmelted in small beads; in puff or flaky pastry, the shortening lies unmelted through the flour in distinct layers. The presence of these quite separate components ensures exquisite pastry, for upon cooking the shortening melts and expands into the surrounding flour.

A word on different kinds of shortening. The only one we dislike intensely is suet, a purely personal preference. Grandma, way out in the bush, often had no other shortening than meat dripping, usually lamb or beef, which she kept as free from impurities and strong flavours as possible. Dripping makes good short pastry, but we feel it isn't suitable for the puffy types. Lard (pork dripping) also makes excellent short pastry. Personally, we find any kind of meat dripping too strong in taste for us, but if you like the taste, away you go!

Traditionally, pastry ought to be made without the addition of baking powder or other rising ingredients. Pastry doesn't rise in the manner of cake or of bread. Its rising is a combination of the spreading expansion upon melting of the shortening beads or layers, and the expansion of the cold air contained in the pastry as it becomes heated during baking. This expansion of cold air and unmelted shortening shows you how important it is to work pastry cold, cold, *cold*. However, all the old family recipes we possess include ⅛ of a teaspoon of baking powder, which is nowhere near enough to produce rising, so what good does it do? we asked. But when we were testing we found to our surprise that the pastry was indeed better with that tiny bit of baking powder in it.

You will find our recipes contain lemon juice. It is an old grandma maxim 'to improve your pastry and aid digestion'. Certainly we couldn't prove that the addition of lemon juice spoiled our pastry in any way — not to mention that lemon juice is an old cure for fat indigestion! Perhaps it also helps improve the taste.

Our best two pastries contain egg yolk, which most definitely makes the dough easier to work with, less inclined to be sticky and more able to cope with large amounts of shortening. These two pastries rose better than the others, not by much, but sufficient to be quite noticeable.

Now to special tools. There are only four of them, and none is a major budget consideration; in fact, three of them sold for $5 or less, at least at the time of writing.

The first is a pastry blender or pastry cutter (not to be confused with a sharp wheel or shape used for cutting out). It looks a little like a sideways French whisk, and it is invaluable for mixing the shortening with the flour before adding any liquid, as it breaks the cold shortening up into beads quickly and well. You could also use a French whisk, provided you don't beat with it, but instead use it like a stabbing knife, in and out of the mixture; however, its handle and shape are not as comfortable as a true pastry blender's. You can also use two knives, one in each hand, or both in one hand.

The second tool is a rolling-pin which can be filled with iced water. This is a great asset; after we bought ours we wondered how we had ever existed without one, for it has plenty of weight as well as being cold. Just remember to put it back into the refrigerator between rollings-out.

The third item is a plastic pastry sheet. Spread this on a cool stretch of the counter and you will find your pastry is less likely to stick when being rolled, which in turn means you will need less flour on your rolling-out surface. Also, a plastic pastry sheet wipes perfectly clean with a piece of kitchen paper, so you don't have to wash in between a lot of rolls when making puff pastry. When you do wash it at the end of the day, however, we suggest you use the bathtub, unless you are lucky enough to possess a very large sink.

The fourth tool is the costliest, but an absolutely wonderful kitchen addition and well worth an investment of $30 or 50: A pair of best-quality kitchen scissors. They are a wonderful tool: you can trim the fat off meat with them, cut up meat, or just about anything else from foil to cabbage to celery. And cut your pastry, too. When we were making a dish with puff or flaky pastry even a very sharp knife pulled it during cutting, and it's impossible to use a wheel-cutter when the lid is on the pie and that is what you are trimming. But a good pair of scissors works like a dream.

Chill everything you can when making pastry, including your mixing bowl and pastry sheet. If you're resting puff pastry in the refrigerator between rolls, wrap it up in the pastry sheet and stick it in the refrigerator, sheet and all. Also remember to return your rolling-pin to the refrigerator.

Try not to put your hands in a pastry mixture, as they warm the shortening, though towards the end of adding liquid you may find hands are the only sensible implement. But if so, don't be long!

Choose the working surface which is coldest – formica is colder than wood, but marble is colder than either. (How many people are lucky enough to have a slab of marble in the kitchen?)

Never use soft butter or other shortening unless the recipe calls for it, even though it is temptingly easy to work with it soft.

Water or other liquid added to pastry must be ice-cold! If you are going to err, err on the side of dryness when adding liquid. Experience is the only teacher. What you want is a ball of dough which isn't crumbling into bits but isn't clinging stickily to your hands. Add your liquid a small trickle at a time, and make sure it is well absorbed before you add another trickle.

Never over-flour your working surface, for the more flour on it, the more extra flour you will work into your dough as you roll it. This is important when you're making a puffy pastry, since it is rolled so many times the extra flour incorporated mounts up alarmingly.

Work pastry quickly, which comes with practice. The

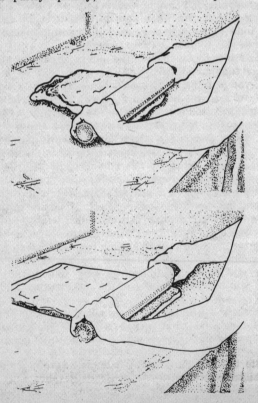

quicker it is finished the colder it will be, and the less likely the shortening is to melt.

When making puff pastry, shave a slab of really cold butter or margarine into thin flakes — not so thin they can be seen through, but no thicker than a cent. The thinner each layer of butter is, the more you'll be able to get into your pastry, and with less effort rolling out. Never spread lumps or slabs of butter on the dough. If you do use flakes, we suggest that you use two slabs of butter and shave only half of each one, for as the slab wears down it becomes very dipped in the middle and takes longer to shave; time is important where coldness is important.

Though we keep saying you should have a light hand with pastry, you will find when making puff or flaky pastry that the more butter you get into it, the harder it becomes to roll out. Indeed, at the end the only way you can roll it is with sheer brute strength. However, it doesn't seem to matter at this late stage, since our pastries did all they were supposed to do, and sometimes more.

If you're making puff or flaky pastry and you feel you can't work any more butter into it, but you haven't yet reached the amount stipulated in the recipe, *stop*. There is no reason why you should spoil your pastry just to adhere blindly to a recipe. So much depends on the kind of flour, and on your own working technique. We usually found that we got about ⅞ of the stipulated amount into our pastry. The danger-point occurs when the pastry sticks to the lightly floured sheet as it is lifted away, and you see a layer of butter underneath where it has torn away.

Make pastry a day ahead when you can, for it does best after 24 hours in the refrigerator. It also freezes beautifully, so it can be stored indefinitely — never throw the leftover scraps away, put them in the freezer and one day you'll find you've enough scraps to make a pie with.

In the final rolling-out when actually making a pie or some other goody, make sure the pastry hasn't been standing at room temperature, but is still cold. Use the iced-water rolling-pin and you'll find your pastry handles better even at this final stage. Puff or flaky pastry should be rolled out very thin, 3mm (⅛ in) or less if you can; short pastry is usually rolled a little thicker than this, as it doesn't have quite the same flexibility. Remember too that all pastries, but especially the puffy ones, have a tendency to shrink a little after rolling, so make sure when you cut something to size you've not cut it too small.

Never grease your baking container or sheet; there is more than enough shortening in the pastry itself to prevent sticking during baking. However, if you are making something like Cornish pasties or sausage rolls, which sit directly on a baking sheet, glaze them before you put them on the sheet and make sure the glaze doesn't run on to the naked sheet, or their bottoms are more likely to burn — not to mention that the sheet will be hard to clean afterwards.

Grandma says you must never, never open the oven door during the first 10 minutes of baking, or you'll wind up with flat pastry. This makes sense since the cold air in the pastry will be happiest expanding at a stable, unchanging oven temperature. Also, make sure your oven is at the required heat before you put your creation in to cook, and *never bang the oven door!*

Pastry should be baked in a hot oven, 220—230°C (425—450°F) at least for the first 10 minutes; if the item is one requiring a fairly long baking time, then the oven can be reduced to 175°C (350°F). However, the quicker the cooking process, the better the pastry will be, for in a hot oven the starch globules in the flour burst almost immediately and take up the melting shortening. So if you're making a deep pie with a filling, put in the filling piping hot just before topping and baking: this reduces the cooking time and enables you to use a hotter oven; it also starts the pastry cooking from the inside as it begins cooking on the outside.

DEFINITIONS

Short pastry   This is a solid pastry which doesn't separate into layers on baking. All the shortening is cut into the dry flour before any liquid is added. It is used for pies, flans, and other items which require a solid yet crumbly pastry.

Hot-water pastry   This is a very solid and elastic pastry (it can be shaped around a jar, for instance), somewhat nearer in texture to a bread dough without yeast. It is kept warm all the time it is being made. The shortening is melted and added to the liquid, brought to the boil and added to the flour all at once. It is then kneaded. Hot-water pastry is used for the tall, straight-sided pies which are filled with pork or other meat in aspic and eaten either hot or cold.

Quick puff pastry This is a rich pastry, quicker and easier to make than true puff pastry, but it doesn't rise and layer as well, and is used only for items not requiring shaping: pie tops, for instance. The shortening is cut into the flour dry instead of being laid on the dough during rolling, but it is rolled a number of times and kept very cold during making.

Puff pastry This is the lightest and richest of pastries, and is beautifully layered. The shortening (preferably all or mostly butter) is spread thinly on the dough while you are rolling it, then folded, rolled again, spread again, etc. It is kept very cold during making, and is used for fancy pies and toppings, as well as for pasties, vol-au-vents, Napoleons, and so on.

Flaky pastry This is a slightly stronger-textured pastry than true puff, but it is rich and many-layered, though the layers themselves are not as discrete. The shortening is in less proportion to flour than in true puff, but it is rolled out and spread in the same way, not as many times. It isn't kept as cold during making, and is used for pies, tarts and flans.

Choux pastry This is a very soft, light pastry, which can be piped into shapes before baking, and after baking is thin, crisp and airy. The shortening is melted in hot liquid before being added to the flour, and it contains a lot of egg. It is used in the making of éclairs, cream puffs, profiteroles and savoury aigrettes.

There has always been a great debate as to what exactly is the difference between a pie, a tart, and a flan. We thought for the fun of it that we would contribute our mite to the controversy, and have braced ourselves for bales of letters of indignant refutation.

Pie A dish which may or may not have a pastry bottom, but always has a pastry top.

Tart A dish which always has a pastry bottom, but never has a solid pastry top, though it may have strips of decorative pastry across its open top.

Flan A dish in which the pastry case is baked ahead of time; the filling isn't cooked after it is put into the case.

HOW TO ROLL AND BUTTER PUFF OR FLAKY PASTRY

When your dough is neither crumbly nor sticky, turn it on to a sparsely floured, cool pastry sheet, and with your rolling-pin full of iced water, roll the dough into a rectangular shape about twice as long as it is wide, with the long axis facing you.

Try to imagine the shape as consisting of three equal-sized parts which we'll call thirds; if you find this difficult, lightly draw a knife across the dough to make two faint lines which will visually divide the pastry into thirds. We will call them the third closest to you, the middle third, and the third farthest away from you.

It's better to get into a routine, and always butter the same two-thirds. We always butter the middle third and the third farthest away, leaving the third closest to us unbuttered. Use a thin layer of butter only; we like to cut it off a cold slab in nice big flakes and lay them side by side on the dough. If you're a precise kind of person, you can flake your butter ahead of time, put the flakes on cold plates and refrigerate them until a plate is needed, but in the long run it doesn't save much time, only keeps the butter colder.

Remember when laying your butter flakes on the dough to leave a 1 cm (½ in) margin of clear pastry along the sides, to prevent butter oozing out the ends when you're rolling. Butter the middle third and the third farthest away, then lever the edge of the third closest to you (the unbuttered third) off the pastry sheet and fold this third over the middle third so it covers this middle third as completely as possible. Then lever the far edge of the pastry away from the sheet and fold the third farthest away over the top of the first two. You will now have a neat, rather brick-shaped slab of pastry.

Press together its edges with the rolling pin to prevent butter oozing out, then pick up the slab and turn it sideways so its shorter edges are facing you. Roll it out to the same size and shape as the last time. Butter the middle and the farthest-away thirds, fold the unbuttered third closest to you over the middle third, then the third farthest away over the top of these. Press the edges together with the rolling-pin, pick up the slab and turn it sideways, and begin the cycle again.

Three such rolls and butters is sufficient for flaky pastry; for true puff, keep doing it as long as you can.

It sounds like a lot of work, but once you have practised, it isn't bad at all. We hope the illustrations will explain the steps more clearly than words can, and that between the two you will not have any trouble understanding exactly what you have to do. Good luck, and may you become the best pastry-cook in your neighbourhood!

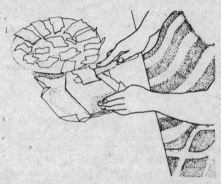

Flaking butter — to illustrate the technique and thickness.

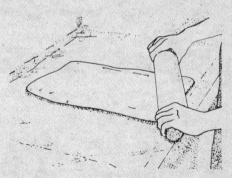

The pastry slab rolled out, about twice as long as it is wide.

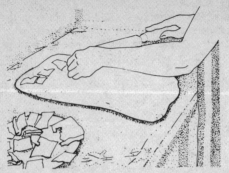

Beginning to lay butter flakes on the third that is farthest away.

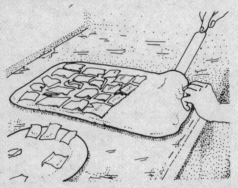

Butter flakes laid over the middle third and the third that is farthest away.

Beginning to fold the unbuttered, closest, third over the middle third.

The closest third folded over the middle third.

Folding the farthest-away third over the top of the other two.

The folding is finished and the pastry is now wider than it is long.

Lifting the slab to begin turning it sideways.

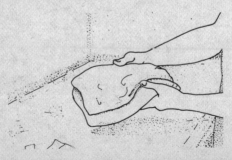

Turning the slab sideways.

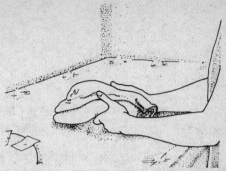

The slab is now laid down sideways, and is longer than it is wide.

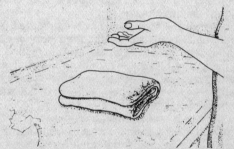

Make sure the open ends are well pressed down so that butter doesn't ooze out when you begin rolling again.

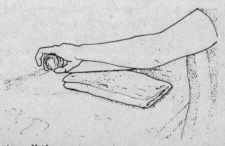

Beginning to roll the pastry again.

SHORT PASTRY

4 cups plain flour
½ teaspoon salt
⅛ teaspoon baking powder
2 egg yolks
2 cups iced water
2 tablespoons lemon juice
225 g (½ lb) cold butter (margarine or other shortening)

Sift together the flour, salt and baking powder, and place in a large chilled bowl.

Put the iced water, egg yolks and lemon juice in a cold jug, and beat them lightly to mix well.

Add the butter (or other shortening) to the flour in small amounts, making sure it is cold, and cut it into tiny particles with the pastry blender, two knives or a French whisk stabbed in and out of the mixture.

Only after all the shortening has been reduced to particles the size of small beads among the flour do you start adding liquid. Add it in small trickles, and mix it with a big blunt fork or the pastry blender — try not to use your hands until you must. You may not need the entire quantity of water stipulated, so be sure that you've got one trickle well into the mixture before you add another.

When the dough is of the right consistency, neither crumbly nor too sticky, quickly form it into a ball, and either store it in the refrigerator or freezer, or roll it out for use.

This is sufficient to make the top and bottom crusts of a pie 25 cm (10 in) in diameter.

This is a magnificent short pastry, especially when made on all butter. Since it is no more difficult to make than any other, we haven't thought it necessary to give an alternative recipe for short pastry. The egg yolk seems to render it easy to roll and handle, and improves the flavour. You can turn this same short pastry into the quickest puff; make it as we direct, then roll it out and fold it up three separate times, just as if you were making puff pastry, but without buttering it.

MEDIUM-QUICK PUFF PASTRY

3 cups plain flour
½ teaspoon salt
⅛ teaspoon baking powder
450g (1lb) butter (or margarine)
1 cup iced water
2 teaspoons lemon juice

Sift together the flour, salt and baking powder, and place in a large chilled bowl.

Divide the butter in half, and cut one of the halves into the flour before adding any liquid, as with short pastry.

Combine the iced water and lemon juice, and add it in trickles to the dry flour/butter mixture. You will probably need less than the cup of fluid, so be very careful not to add too much liquid at once. When the dough is neither crumbly nor sticky, pat it into a ball and turn it on to a lightly floured pastry sheet.

Divide the remaining butter into halves.

Now proceed as if you were making puff pastry, rolling the dough into a rectangle about twice as long as it is wide, and lightly draw two lines on it to divide it into three equal sections.

Spread half of the butter over the middle third of the pastry and the third farthest away from you, leaving the third closest to you unbuttered. Fold it as in puff pastry, press the edges down with the rolling-pin, lift the slab and turn it sideways, then roll it out to the same shape and size it was in the beginning.

Use the other half of the shortening to spread on the middle and farthest-away thirds, fold, press the edges down, turn sideways and roll.

This is sufficient for the shell and top of a pie that is 20cm (8in) in diameter.

FLAKY PASTRY

4 cups plain flour
½ teaspoon salt
2 teaspoons baking powder
2 teaspoons lemon juice
2 cups iced water
225g (½lb) butter
125g (¼lb) margarine

Combine and sift the flour, salt and baking powder, and place in a large bowl.

Add the lemon juice to the iced water and stir, then add the fluid in trickles to the flour, turning it with a large fork or spoon rather than your hands, at least until near the end of the mixing process. When the dough is neither crumbly not sticky, turn it out on to the pastry sheet, roll it up and place it in the refrigerator to chill for a while.

In this interval, cream together the butter and margarine until it is smoothly mixed and spreadable, but not runny. If you like, chill it for a little after the creaming is finished.

Take the dough out of the refrigerator, roll it out into a rectangle about twice as long as it is wide, and spread a layer of the shortening about 6mm (¼in) thick on the middle third and the third farthest away from you, as in puff pastry. Fold, press down the edges, turn it sideways, roll out again, and proceed until all the shortening (or as much as you dare) has been used.

Store it in the refrigerator or freezer until you want it. This quantity is sufficient to make the top and shell of a pie that is 25 cm (10 in) in diameter.

This is a queer, hybrid recipe which looks as if it shouldn't work; it probably does only because of the large amount of baking powder in it. However, we are not purists, only concerned with whether a recipe works well. This one works better than well; it makes a gorgeous, properly flaky pastry which looks and feels different from puff, yet tastes delicious and slices without breaking apart. Because it isn't worked as cold as the other recipes we have given, it doesn't handle as easily as the others.

RICH PUFF PASTRY

4 cups plain flour
½ teaspoon salt
⅛ teaspoon baking powder
2 cups iced water
2 egg yolks
2 tablepoons lemon juice
450g (1 lb) cold butter

Sift the flour, salt and baking powder together, and place in a large chilled bowl.

Combine the wet ingredients (water, egg yolks and lemon juice) in a jug, beating lightly with a fork to mix well, but not produce bubbles. Make sure the end result is still very cold; if the eggs and the lemon are taken directly from the refigerator, they will not raise the temperature of the water.

Trickle small amounts of the liquid into the flour, mixing it gently with a large fork or spoon; try not to use your hands until you can't possibly mix any other way, but then proceed very gingerly. When the dough has stopped looking and feeling crumbly, but isn't wet enough to stick to your hands, form it into a ball and put it out on a sparsely floured pastry sheet.

Using a rolling-pin filled with iced water, roll the dough into an oblong about twice as long as it is wide, with the long axis facing you. Take the slab of cold butter and shave thin pieces off it with a knife, then lay the pieces side by side on the middle third and the third farthest away from you, making sure you have left a 1cm (½in) margin around the edges. The third closest to you remains unbuttered, and is folded over the top of the middle third. You then fold the third farthest away over the top of these two, ending up with a neat, compact slab of dough. Press the edges down to seal the butter inside, lift it off the sheet and turn it sideways, then roll it out again to the same shape and size it was before. Put on more flakes of butter, fold, press the edges, turn sideways, roll out again, etc., until you have used up as much of the butter as you dare.

So long as the rolling-pin stays icy and the pastry feels cold to the touch you can continue rolling out, buttering, folding and rolling out again, but if the pastry starts to stick to the sheet in spite of the bit of flour, it is time to put it in the refrigerator for a rest. Just roll up the dough in the sheet and put it in, sheet and all. Put the rolling-pin in, too.

You should be able to get all the butter into this particular pastry without the underside breaking open to show the butter inside as you lift it off the sheet, which is the sign to stop. However, if it does occur, stop.

You will also find that as the pastry gets more and more butter into it, it becomes harder and harder to roll out; you have to put all your strength behind the rolling-pin. Don't worry. Hard usage at this stage doesn't seem to hurt the pastry at all. We've never seen one rise better than this one does.

Whenever we have made this pastry, we've found that if everything is kept really cold, it is only necessary to rest the dough once, half way through the buttering; then we have given it at least 20 minutes in the refrigerator.

This quantity is sufficient to make the top and bottom of a pie that is 25 cm (10 in) in diameter.

If you want to impress those who will eat your efforts, this is the pastry to make. It is absolutely gorgeous. You can use it to make anything from Napoleons to a steak-and-kidney pie.

CHOUX PASTRY

*125 g (¼ lb) butter
1 cup boiling water
1 cup plain flour
4 large eggs
½ teaspoon baking powder*

Put the butter in a heavy-bottomed saucepan and pour the boiling water over it. Turn on the heat and bring the mixture to the boil again.

When the butter is dissolved and while it is still boiling, add all the flour at once. Let the saucepan stay on the heat and for 5 minutes keep pushing the ball of dough around with a large spoon, and breaking it up; it is too solid to stir. This is to make sure the flour is thoroughly cooked, but if you don't keep pushing it around and breaking it up, it will catch on the bottom and burn — an asbestos mat will help.

At the end of the 5 minutes, remove the mixture from heat, turn the dough into a large bowl (belonging to your mixer if you have one), and let it cool.

When it is quite cool, break in an egg and beat well. Do the same to the other 3 eggs, beating each one very well before adding another. After the last egg is in, continue to beat for another 10 minutes. An electric beater makes the task less arduous, but if you have to beat by hand, lift the mixture up on the beater with each stroke so you get the air under it.

During the last part of the beating, add the baking powder and make sure it is well distributed.

Drop teaspoons of the mixture on an ungreased baking tray, or put the mixture in a large pastry forcing bag with a plain nozzle (or none at all) and squeeze out teaspoon-sized bits. If you produce thin peaks or tendrils on them, pat the tendrils down or they will burn before the rest of the puff is cooked.

For éclairs, you must use a pastry bag; squeeze a long cylinder of mixture out, like putting toothpaste on a brush, and if you can't seem to make the mixture stop when you want it to, cut the end with a knife. Each one should be about 12 cm (5 in) long.

A small teaspoon of mixture makes a profiterole-sized puff, a large teaspoon a cream puff. Make sure you leave plenty of vacant space around each one on the baking tray, they rise and spread enormously. A 30 by 45 cm (12 in by 18 in) baking tray will hold nine large or sixteen small puffs, or six éclairs. The mixture doesn't deteriorate, so you can bake a few at a time.

Bake at 220°C (425°F) for 30 to 40 minutes. Don't peek until they have been in for 15 minutes. Take them out when they are medium-brown on the thinner bits.

This makes about sixteen large puffs or twelve éclairs.

HOT-WATER PASTRY FOR RAISED PIES

4 cups plain flour
1 teaspoon salt
⅛ teaspoon baking powder
125 g (¼ lb) lard
½ cup water
1 teaspoon lemon juice

Sift the flour, salt and baking powder, and place them in a large bowl. This time you will be working warm, so don't bother looking for a kitchen cool-spot.

Put the lard in a saucepan and melt it, add the water and bring to the boil.

Immediately pour the boiling liquid into the flour, and mix them quickly with a spoon until they form a dough. If the dough is too sticky, add more flour.

Turn the dough on to a board and knead it until it is smooth, not cracked.

Keep the pastry warm while you are working with it, so hands are the approved tool.

SAVOURY PASTRY DISHES

If for no other reason, we felt obliged to include a proper pastry section in our book because pastry is such an important component of the Australian National Dish. Gourmetic snobs insist there is no true Australian cuisine, that our dishes are mostly British in origin and remain fairly indistinguishable from the current British versions.

But what about the meat pie, we ask? You see it now in English supermarkets, but you never did before the droves of Australians started appearing in the U.K. on two-year working holidays. We think the meat pie is genuinely, absolutely dinky-di Australian, and we think it is delicious, especially when homemade.

Just what *is* a meat pie? By definition it consists of a shell which can be either short or flaky pastry, a filling of minced steak in gravy, and a top of flaky or puff pastry. It can be either round or oval (one commercially produced pie is marketed as 'Australia's only square pie'), and it measures about 12 cm (4½ in) in diameter. It is eaten hot, usually with tomato sauce.

There are some pie devotees who insist that in a good pie the gravy must dribble down the chin while being eaten, but there is an equally vociferous school which says a good meat pie must be so stuffed with meat it is incapable of dribbling. Perhaps its chief appeal when compared to other dishes is its smallness, the way it can be held in the hand and eaten without such niceties as a plate or a knife and fork. Consequently, it is eaten both as a snack and as a meal, at the table or while standing up. It appears everywhere; in the home, for Saturday lunch, Friday-night tea or Sunday-night tea; outside the home it is sold from stalls at the horse races, the dog races, football, cricket, on the beaches, from school tuckshops and downtown luncheon take-aways — in short, just about anywhere Australians gather en masse.

Why not try making them instead of buying them? We have included recipes for the dinkum-Aussie plain, the steak and mushroom, and the steak and kidney varieties. We favour the steak and mushroom one, but you can try all three, or whichever appeals to you most of all.

Each of the following fillings makes a minimum of ten meat pies. The recipe for putting the pies together is given after the fillings.

GOOD OLD AUSSIE PLAIN PIES

1 kg (2 lb) beefsteak, coarsely minced
1 cup finely chopped onions
2 bay leaves
¼ teaspoon mixed herbs
½ teaspoon salt
pepper
⅔ cup of lukewarm water
2 tablespoons plain flour (or cornflour)
a little cold water
Parisian essence (or gravy browning)

Melt as small an amount of butter or other cooking fat or oil as you can get away with in the bottom of a large saucepan or Dutch oven, throw in the onions and brown them.

Add the minced steak plus the bay leaves, herbs, salt and a good grind of pepper; reduce the heat enough to grey the meat rather than brown it, as meat which is going to be stewed is more tender if it is greyed than browned.

When the meat looks well greyed, add sufficient lukewarm water to almost cover the contents of the pot. Use lukewarm water because it doesn't shock the meat the way cold or hot water does, and the contents come quickly and gently to the simmer.

Reduce the heat, put the lid on, and watch carefully that the meat never more than barely simmers. Put your pot on an asbestos mat if your range won't heat low enough. Never let the meat boil outright, for this toughens even the best cut.

Stew at a simmer for at least 30 minutes, though it doesn't matter if it cooks longer; we prefer to leave it on for 1 hour.

Five minutes before you turn the heat off, mix 2 teaspoons of flour (or cornflour) with a little cold water until it is free from lumps, then thicken the gravy by pouring it in and stirring well until the contents return to a simmer. If you like, you can add a small amount of Parisian essence or gravy browning to the thickening mixture; this will make the meat darker in colour.

STEAK AND MUSHROOM PIES

1 kg (2 lb) beefsteak, coarsely minced
450 g (1 lb) mushrooms, stalks and all (4 cups), diced
2 bay leaves
½ teaspoon salt
pepper
⅔ cup of lukewarm water
2 tablespoons plain flour (or cornflour)
a little cold water

Melt a very little butter or other cooking fat or oil in the bottom of a large saucepan or Dutch oven, throw in the mushrooms and fry them briskly until they are well reduced in size and a dark brown liquor has oozed from them.

Add the minced steak, plus the bay leaves, salt and pepper, reduce the heat and grey the meat, don't brown it.

Add sufficient lukewarm water to almost cover the meat; don't add hot or cold water, it makes the meat tougher. Bring the contents to a gentle simmer for at least 30 minutes, preferably an hour — never permit it to boil.

Five minutes before you turn the heat off, thicken the gravy with 2 tablespoons of flour (or cornflour) dissolved lump-free in a little cold water; it isn't necessary to add gravy browning to this filling, because the mushrooms darken it beautifully.

STEAK AND KIDNEY PIES

1 kg (2 lb) beefsteak, coarsely minced
4 lamb's kidneys, all strings removed, finely diced
¼ cup onion, diced
½ teaspoon salt
pepper
1 teaspoon sage
1 teaspoon thyme
⅔ cup lukewarm water
2 tablespoons plain flour (or cornflour)
a little cold water
Parisian essence (or gravy browning)

Melt a very little butter or other cooking fat or oil in the bottom of a large saucepan or Dutch oven, throw in the onions and brown them, then throw in the kidneys and cook them fairly quickly to a grey colour, stirring all the time and holding your nose (we think more people would like kidney if they didn't smell it while it cooked.)

Reduce the heat a little, add the minced steak and grey it well; remember that browning it will increase the chance of ending up with tough meat. Add the salt, pepper, sage and thyme at some stage of the greying process. We recommend a high amount of herb with kidney, it definitely improves the flavour.

When the meat is greyed and the herbs have been stirred in, add the lukewarm water so that it almost covers the contents of the pot. Don't add water which is too cold or too hot, you'll increase your chance of toughening the meat again.

Reduce the heat, put the lid on, and cook very gently at no more than a simmer for a minimum of 30 minutes, but preferably 1 hour.

Five minutes before you turn off the heat, thicken the mixture with 2 tablespoons of plain flour or cornflour dissolved without lumps in a little cold water. Stir it in vigorously and keep stirring until the meat returns to a simmer. We think steak and kidney shouldn't be browned, but if you wish add a little Parisian essence or gravy browning.

HOW TO PUT MEAT PIES TOGETHER

You need:
rolling space plus extra work space
a pastry sheet if you have one
a rolling pin, preferably an iced-water model
a baking tray
at least 5 or 6 meat pie tins, 10—12 cm (4—5 in) wide
a pastry brush
kitchen scissors if you have them
a sharp knife with a sharp point
2 slabs of puff or flaky pastry, kept cold
the hot meat filling of your choice
½ cup milk with 1 egg yolk beaten in it
a little plain flour

Be organised before you actually begin to make your pies, or you will wind up in an awful muddle. A batch of small things is always harder to assemble than one big dish, especially when, as with pies, the assembling consists of several different actions.

Make sure your oven is up to full heat by the time you are

ready to bake. However, this means a warm kitchen, and while we appreciate that you may not have much space at your command, try to assemble the pies as far from the oven as you can.

Important   Know your oven. Does it have a hot spot? If it does, make sure you don't put your baking tray full of pies on the level where the hot spot is, or you will burn your pies (and anything else you cook).

Assemble only as many pies as your baking tray will hold at any one time; since the filling is added hot, you can't leave extra pies sitting waiting to be baked for the whole length of time it takes to bake the first lot. We did ours five or six at a time.

Keep your pastry in the refrigerator until you are ready to use it. Take one slab out and divide it into two — one piece should be a bit bigger than the other. Put the smaller piece back in the refrigerator, and use the bigger piece to make five or six pie bottoms. It should do the quantity nicely.

Roll it out very thinly (about 3 mm — ⅛ in is thick enough) on a tray slightly better floured than you would have it during pastry-making; you will not be incorporating much flour into the pastry at this stage.

If your pie tin is, say, 12cm (5in) across, and 2½cm (1in) deep, you will need to have a piece of pastry 18cm (7in) across to cover it. Since this pastry tends to shrink a bit, add about an extra 1cm (½in) to be sure. (Nothing is more maddening than finding the pastry is too small. You can trim the excess away.)

When you put the pastry into the tin, make sure it doesn't have air bubbles underneath; lift a corner up, gently press the bottom, and ease out any air before replacing the corner.

Proper pie tins have a lip all around, but if you haven't been lucky enough to find them and are using aluminium foil ones, which have little or no lip, let a small margin of pastry overlap the foil edges. Foil does not conduct heat as efficiently as tin does, so the cooking time will be longer.

Trim any excess pastry away with scissors or a very sharp knife.

Immediately brush the rim of the pastry with egg and milk, or plain milk, or even water. If you do it now, it will be nicely tacky by the time you put on the lid.

Take the smaller piece of pastry out of the refrigerator, roll it out, and divide it into lid-sized pieces, allowing for shrinkage.

Some flaky pastry dough rolled out to make the bottoms of the pie shells.

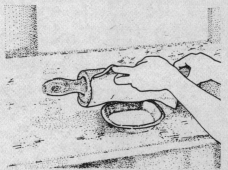

A pie bottom being turned into its tin.

The bottom has to be eased down well in the tin and air bubbles released.

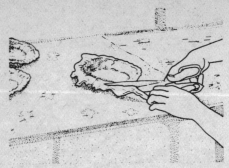

The pie bottom is in the tin and the edges are being trimmed.

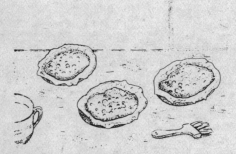

The hot meat filling in the prepared shells.

The edges have been glazed and the lids are being fitted.

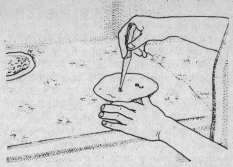

Cutting good nostrils in the lid so that the pie can breathe.

A tray of pies ready to go into the oven, and some cooked pies.

Meat pies with their inevitable accompaniment, tomato sauce.

If your pie tin is 12cm (5in) wide, make your lids 14cm (5½in) wide and you will be safe.

Ladle hot meat filling into a shell, but don't fill it to overflowing, have the level of the meat a little below the top. Put a pastry lid on, press the edges together firmly if you are using proper pie tins, or pinch the edges together if you are using foil tins. Trim away the excess with scissors or a sharp knife. Using a pointed sharp knife, cut two nostrils into the lid, opening them up well so the pie can breathe during its cooking. Pies which can't breathe properly split their seams.

Go to the next shell, fill it with meat, put a lid on, press or pinch the edges together, trim it, and cut nostrils in the lid. When you have made as many pies as you can bake at once, stop. Take the egg and milk and brush it over the lid of each pie to give it a nice gloss.

Put the pies on the baking tray, and put them in the oven at 225°C (425°F). They will take from 20 to 30 minutes to cook.

While one batch is baking, if you want to make more you can start them, but remember to check the progress of the pies in the oven, so that you will not be finished the second batch before the first is ready to come out.

When you take the pies out of the oven, turn them out of their tins and cool them on a wire rack (or eat them straight away). If you heat them later, make sure you do so in a much cooler oven, about 150°C (300°F).

This recipe makes approximately 10 to 12 pies. If your family have small appetites, cut the quantities in half. Incidentally, pies freeze well.

EGG AND BACON PIE

puff (or flaky) pastry, about half a slab
6 long rashers streaky bacon, rind removed
4 large eggs
1 cup cream
1 cup milk
pepper
small pinch herbs if you wish
¼—½ teaspoon salt, depending on the bacon
25 cm (10 in) pie tin
½ cup grated cheese

Fry the bacon rashers until nicely browned and crisping up,

but don't let them get crumble-crisp. Drain on paper.

Break the eggs into a bowl, add the milk and cream, give it a surface speckle of pepper and a small pinch of herbs if you wish. Add the salt, but be careful about how much because bacon can be salty itself. Beat until the mixture is blended well and has just a few bubbles on top.

Roll the pastry out as thinly as you can; 3 mm (⅛ in) thick doesn't seem much, but will make a very sturdy shell which will not break apart when you turn the pie out of its tin.

Lift the pastry carefully and put it into the ungreased tin. Decorate the edges if you like, twisting thin strips of pastry into spirals and pressing them at intervals on to a wetted margin — milk or water will do. However, the pastry itself layers so well that decoration is rather superfluous.

Cut the bacon into bits about 2½ cm (1 in) long and scatter them over the bottom of the pastry shell, then pour the egg mixture on top.

Bake the pie at 210°C (400°F), and wait 20 minutes before you peek. When you do peek, open the oven door sufficiently to sprinkle the grated cheese over the top of the pie; you will notice that the filling isn't set but wobbles when you move the dish. So close the oven door gently, turn the temperature down to 175°C (350°F), and bake the pie for a further 20 to 25 minutes. By this time the pie will have risen well, set well, and be a light brown on top.

When you take it out of the oven, lever it out of its tin and cool it on a wire rack; it can be eaten hot or cold.

CORNISH PASTIES (AND VARIATIONS THEREON)

On the following page you will find the instructions for putting together fillings and pastry for ten to twelve pasties. Each of the following fillings will fill about six pasties. If you choose one filling only, double its ingredients.

TRUE PASTY FILLING

2 tablespoons carrot, grated
2 tablespoons potato, grated
2 tablespoons onion, finely diced
2 tablespoons fresh small peas (or canned)
1 tablespoon rich beef stock
small pinch salt if the stock isn't too salty

Mix them together in a small bowl.

MUSHROOM PASTIES

2 tablespoons mushrooms, finely diced
2 tablespoons potato, grated
2 tablespoons onion, finely diced
2 tablespoons fresh small peas (or canned)
1 tablespoon rich beef stock
salt as needed

Mix them together in a small bowl.

BACON AND CABBAGE PASTIES

4 tablespoons fried bacon, crumbled
4 tablespoons cabbage, finely diced

Mix them together in a small bowl.

HOW TO PUT PASTIES TOGETHER

rolling-out space and extra working space
a pastry sheet if you have one
a rolling-pin, preferably an iced-water model
a baking sheet
a pastry brush
kitchen scissors if you have them
a sharp knife with a sharp point
1 slab of puff (or flaky) pastry
the filling or fillings of your choice
½ cup of milk with 1 egg yolk beaten into it
a little plain flour

The first thing is, if you have chosen to use only one filling, double its ingredients.

There are two kinds of pasty you can make; triangular ones, or ridge-backed oval ones. We suggest you make half of each shape, at least until you decide which you prefer.

For the triangular turnover ones, roll out the pastry thinly and cut it into squares about 15 by 15 cm (6 by 6 in). Brush all around the margins with egg and milk (or plain milk, or water), then put about a small tablespoon of filling to one side of the middle, making sure it doesn't spill into the wetted margin.

Lift the far corner, and put the unfilled side over the filled side, so you have a triangle instead of a square. Press the edges down well, then carefully cut one nostril in the top, making sure it is well opened. Brush the pastry with egg and milk glaze, and leave it to drain off excess fluid before you put it on the ungreased baking tray, or you will have glaze trickling on to the naked baking tray and it will burn.

To make the ridge-backed oval ones, roll out the pastry thinly and cut it into circles 15 cm (6 in) in diameter. Brush all around the edges with glaze liquid.

Put a small tablespoon of the filling mixture on the centre of the pastry circle. Then lift two opposite edges of the pastry and pinch them together firmly, making sure the ends you have made aren't going to come unglued and leak filling liquid.

Start pinching the rest of the edges together, working upwards on each side until your hands meet on top of the pastry. Cut a well-opened nostril on either side of the top of the ridge, then paint the surface of the pasty with glaze. Leave it to make sure excess glaze liquid has all run off before you put it on the baking tray.

Bake them one tray-load at a time in a 210°C (400°F) oven, and watch them carefully to make sure their bottoms don't burn as they get towards the end of their time. They will only take 15 to 20 minutes to bake. The raw vegetable filling will have cooked beautifully inside the pastry. After you have taken them out, turn them on to a wire rack to cool, or eat them hot. They are best eaten hot, so if you are going to eat them later, warm them in a 150°C (300°F) oven for 20 minutes. They freeze well.

This recipe makes ten to twelve pasties.

STEAK AND KIDNEY PIE

750g (1½ lb) round (or topside) steak, cut 2½ cm (1 in) thick
4 lamb's kidneys
2 smallish onions, diced
1 teaspoon sage
1 teaspoon thyme
1 cup lukewarm water
½ teaspoon salt, or to your taste
pepper
1 slab puff (or flaky) pastry, kept cold
25 cm (10 in) pie dish, with a good wide rim

Cut the fat off the steak and then cut it into 2½cm (1in) cubes. Roll the cubes in flour until they are well covered.

Don't use ox, calf or pig kidneys! Lamb's kidneys have no offensive smell of urine, and their flavour is more delicate. We are convinced that a lot of people dislike kidney because they have been served big-beast kidney, or else have been served lamb's kidney not well seasoned. The flavour is peculiar, and goes splendidly with lots of thyme and sage.

Take the lamb's kidneys, slice them in halves, then cut out all the strings. Slice the kidneys into small pieces.

Melt a little butter or other cooking fat or oil in a large saucepan or Dutch oven, throw in the onions and fry until they are browned. Then add the steak cubes and fry them, turning frequently until they are well greyed. Don't brown them, it makes them tough.

When the meat is greyed, add the kidneys and fry a little longer, stirring. Turn the heat right down, and add enough lukewarm water to almost cover the meat.

Add the herbs and a grind or sprinkle of pepper. Add the salt, tasting the liquid as you salt it to make sure it isn't too salty.

Put the lid on, and cook the meat at a bare simmer for 1 hour. Do make sure it doesn't boil outright because that will toughen the meat.

Unearth your pastry-making tools. Divide the slab of pastry into two but make one piece bigger than the other. Put the smaller piece back in the refrigerator, and use the bigger piece to make the bottom of the pie.

Roll the pastry on a lightly floured sheet 3mm (⅛ in) thick or less; even at this thinness, your pie will turn out of its case and hold together well.

Make sure your pastry when rolled is big enough to line the dish properly, then lift it and put it in the dish. Remove any air bubbles lurking underneath it by lifting a corner away from the side of the dish and gently pressing the bottom until the air escapes. Trim the edges, then brush the edges wet with milk, egg and milk, or water.

Take the smaller piece of pastry out of the refrigerator and roll it out to make the top; make sure you allow for slight shrinkage. When the top is ready to go on, you can fill your pie.

Big pies like this tend to sink in the middle when baking, so use a stemless egg-cup or one of those china gadets called a pie-raiser.

Place your egg-cup upsidedown in the centre of the shell, but don't press it in or you will fracture the bottom of the pastry. (Do the same with a pie-raiser.) Then fill your shell with hot steak and kidney, to about 5 mm (¼ in) below the top. Lift the rolled-out lid up on your roller, and slip it on to the pie. If you're using a pie-raiser, cut the pastry around its chimney immediately and let the lid subside on to the pie-raiser's shoulders.

Press the edges down with your thumb evenly all around the pie, and trim off the excess. If you have got any pastry over, you can decorate the pie, twisting thin strips into spirals and sticking them all around the pie edges with a little glazing mixture. Cut leaf shapes out of the dough and arrange them in a little cluster at intervals on the lid.

If you have a pie-raiser you don't have to cut nostrils to let the pie breathe; it does so through the pie-raiser's chimney. But otherwise cut two big nostrils in the lid near its centre. Glaze the top if you wish.

Bake in a 210°C (400°F) oven for 30 to 40 minutes, or until the top is browned and the pastry has risen into high layers.

This is sufficient for four to six people.

RAISED MUTTON PIE

450 g (1 lb) mutton (or lamb), fat-free and diced small
1 cup onion, finely chopped
1 teaspoon curry powder
½ teaspoon salt
pinch pepper
1 recipe quantity of freshly made, warm hot-water pastry
1 cup jellied stock

Cut off a quarter of the pastry dough, wrap it in foil and leave it to one side, but keep it warm.

Use the remaining pastry dough to make the shell of the pie. Roll it out to about 6 mm (¼ in) thick and mould it in one piece, bottom and sides without a join. The best way to do this is around a large jar or plastic container; if you have a small cake tin with very high sides, you can put the pastry inside it and mould. The diameter of the pie should be about 12—15 mm (5—6 in), and its sides should be almost as high as that. You can mould this pastry into a case using just your hands, for it is plastic and obedient, but the shape will not be as symmetrical or polished.

When you've finished making the case (it will stand up on its own), cut a piece of stiff brown paper almost as wide as the sides of the case, and pin it around the sides; this will help the pie keep its shape without sagging during baking. Stand the case to one side and prepare the filling.

Mix the diced mutton (or lamb) with the chopped onion, the curry powder, the salt and pepper. If you don't care for curry, you can substitute a teaspoon of your favourite mutton herb, or mixed herbs.

Tightly pack the meat mixture into the pie case, pressing some of it well down inside before adding more. The pie can be filled level with its top, as this is an uncooked filling and will shrink during baking. Also, this pastry doesn't rise very much.

Take the quarter of pastry you reserved earlier, and use it to make a lid. Roll it out about 5 cm (¼ in) thick, and just a little larger than the pie case. Damp the margins of the pie case with a little milk or water, then put the lid on and pinch the edges together. Cut a hole about the size of a cent in the middle of the lid.

This pastry moulds beautifully, so you can go mad decorating it. Flute or fan or crenellate the edges, make leaves and rosettes and curls for the centre.

Brush the pie top with milk to glaze it.

Place it in a 220°C (425°F) oven for 20 minutes, then have a look at it, close the door and reduce the oven heat to 150°C (300°F). Bake at this low heat for a further 1½ hours.

Take the pie out of the oven and let it cool on a wire rack for 30 minutes; it will still be warm, but not hot. Take the cup of warmed jelly stock and pour it carefully in through the hole in the lid centre. When liquid fills the hole and doesn't subside, all the spaces inside the pie are filled, and you can stop pouring. When the pie is quite cold, the stock will set to an aspic.

The pie is usually eaten cold, but is good hot, too. Heat it in a cool oven at 150°C (300°F) for 30 minutes.

You can substitute any kind of meat for this mutton filling. Veal and ham, pork, chicken. Just make sure your chosen alternative filling is fat-free and cut up small. You can also put hard-boiled eggs among the meat, or alternate layers of meat and layers of breadcrumb stuffing mixture flavoured with herbs.

SAUSAGE ROLLS

1 kg (2 lb) sausage mince
1 slab puff pastry (or flaky)
egg and milk for glazing
a little plain flour

Divide the slab of pastry into four fairly equal portions, put three back into the refrigerator, and use the fourth as the pastry envelopes for your first batch of sausage rolls. It is easier to roll out the cold puff pastry when you have a small amount of it.

Roll out the quarter-slab to 3mm (⅛ in) thick, even thinner if you have the will to persist. Try to make the shape of your piece of pastry as rectangular as you can, for this will save wastage.

Take your scissors if you have them, otherwise a sharp knife, and cut the pastry into strips 10cm (4in) wide; we got four strips each 10cm (4in) wide from ours, and each strip we cut into halves.

Take your pastry brush and put glaze mixture on each end of the separate strips.

Pluck enough of the sausage mince off the main mass to make into a fairly neat cylinder 10mm (4in) long and about 2½cm (1in) in diameter. Place the cylinder of sausage mince towards one end of one piece of pastry; choose the more irregular-shaped end, then you will have the neater, cut end on the outside of the sausage roll.

With the mince in place, roll it in the pastry piece and turn it so that the loose end is underneath, then press down gently and make sure the edge of the pastry is stuck down. Don't try to pinch the ends of the roll together, the ends should be left open, with the mince just about level with the pastry, not poking out.

Paint the top of each roll with a little egg and milk glaze, and put the rolls on kitchen paper to allow any excess glaze to drain off before putting the rolls on a baking tray.

A standard 30 by 45cm (12 by 18in) baking tray will hold eight rolls comfortably — you must leave plenty of space around each one. Put the baking tray on top of another baking tray so the bottoms won't burn. (We would like to know why manufacturers of baking trays don't make them thicker!) Don't grease the baking tray.

Bake in a 220°C (425°F) oven for about 25 minutes, or until the outsides of the rolls are well browned; you can peek after they have been in 10 minutes, but don't reduce the oven's heat.

This recipe makes between 24 and 30 sausage rolls; they are eaten hot, but if you want to serve them later, heat them in a cool oven at 150°C (300°F) oven for 20 minutes. They freeze well.

If you like, you can make sausage rolls with thick frankfurters instead of sausage mince, but they aren't nearly as tasty, and it seems a shame to waste puff pastry on frankfurters.

A special note about all the savoury pies and snacks! We have given recipes which call for puff or flaky pastry, but if you prefer short pastry there is no reason why you can't substitute it. The quantities will be exactly the same.

However, deep pies with a lot of filling made on short pastry may not stand up as well to being turned out of their tins, so be extra-careful if you do turn them out; otherwise leave them in their tins.

DESSERT PIES AND TARTS

When most cooks make sweet pies or tarts they tend to use short pastry, probably because they are frightened of making puff pastry. Yet most sweet pies and tarts ought to be puff, so we have stipulated puff or flaky pastry in our recipes. But they can as easily be made on short pastry, and the quantity of pastry will be much the same.

We are including several recipes, but it is in this section that your imagination can run riot. Invent your own fillings.

Fruit, for instance, makes wonderful fillings for pies, and jams for tarts.

The list of fruit is long: blackberries, raspberries, strawberries, gooseberries, rhubarb, apples, quinces, peaches, plums, nectarines.

You can do two things with fruit fillings; you can stew the fruit before putting it in its case, or you can put the fruit in the case raw, thinly sliced.

GUIDE FOR STEWING FRUIT

2 cups ripe and sweet fruit, peeled, cored, stoned, etc.,
2 tablespoons water (if the fruit is ripe and juicy there is no
*   need to add water)*
1 tablespoon sugar (if the fruit is tart, 2 tablespoons)

Stew the mixture on very gentle simmer for 20 minutes, and add it piping hot to the pastry case.

Raw fruit makes an excellent pie. Peel it, stone it, core it, whatever needs to be done, then slice it very thinly and lay the slices directly on the pastry. If the fruit is very juicy, drain the slices on kitchen paper first or you will have soggy pastry, especially if you are using short pastry. Then sprinkle the fruit with a little sugar (and cinnamon or nutmeg or ground clove or whatever spice you fancy with the particular kind of fruit. For a change, try spicing apple with clove instead of cinnamon).

If you are putting a lid on the pie, remember to cut well-opened nostrils in it so that it can breathe comfortably during cooking.

If you want to make a flan, and add your filling to a pre-cooked case, bake the flan case with a piece of foil tucked well over it, and the top of the foil filled with beans, rice, crusts of bread or pasta pieces.

Pastry ought to be the perfect foil for a sweet filling, so please don't sweeten your pastry by adding sugar to it when you are making it. The addition of sugar makes pastry flat, heavy and indigestible.

If your family has a sweet tooth, brush the pie lid with egg and milk glaze the moment it comes out of the oven, then sprinkle it well with white or brown sugar before the glaze coating dries.

APPLE STRUDEL

1 slab puff pastry or flaky pastry but do not substitute short
4 tart apples, peeled, cored, and thinly sliced
2 tablespoons brown sugar
1 cup sultanas (or small raisins, preferably golden)
ground cinnamon (or cloves)
milk and egg glaze

Roll out the pastry thinly; its final shape should be oblong, about 25 cm (10 in) wide and as long as possible, or about

45 cm (18 in).

Leave a 2½ cm (1 in) margin all around, and lay slices of apple over the pastry, then scatter the sultanas evenly over the apple — not too many, you should see the apple in between them. Sprinkle with sugar and cinnamon (or cloves), then press them gently into the pastry, not so hard that you force them through the other side.

Lift the pastry margin closest to you, and fold it over the top of some of the apple-surfaced pastry, about 10 cm (4 in) wide is enough. Fold it again, and again, as you would roll it up if you wanted a round finished product instead of a slab. The pastry slab will get wider as you keep on folding. Try to finish with the last pastry fold on the top, or otherwise turn it over. Stick it down with a little egg and milk, and both ends also.

Transfer the slab to a baking tray (ungreased), and with a very sharp knife slice the slab every 2 cm (1 in) or so, but not all the way through, only about half through.

Put the baking tray on top of another baking tray to prevent the bottom burning, and slide both trays into the oven at 210°C (400°F). Bake for 30 minutes at this temperature, open the oven door and see how it is progressing, then close the door and reduce the heat to 160°C (325°F). Continue to cook it for a further 20 minutes, or longer if you feel the middle isn't yet done.

When you take out the strudel, brush it immediately with egg and milk glaze, and sprinkle white sugar over the glaze before it dries. Leave the strudel on a wire rack to cool.

MACADAMIA BAKEWELL TART

½ slab of short (or flaky) pastry
3 large tablespoons butter
3 tablespoons sugar
3 eggs
1 cup breadcrumbs
1 cup ground macadamia nuts (or ground almonds)
4 tablespoons raspberry jam
25 cm (10 in) pie tin

Roll out the pastry and line the tin; decorate it if you like with flutes and spiral strips of pastry.

Cream the butter and sugar together, and beat the eggs well in a separate bowl. Gradually add the egg mixture to the creamed butter and sugar, and beat together well. Lightly stir in the breadcrumbs and the ground macadamias; if the mixture is too thick to spoon out and spread, thin it with a little milk.

Spread the bottom of the pastry with raspberry jam, then spoon the macadamia mixture on top of the jam, and even it out. If you like, press a few glacé cherries into the top.

Bake the tart in a 220°C (425°F) oven for 20 minutes, open the door to check that everything is all right, close it and reduce the heat to 160°C (325°F) for a further 20 minutes, or until the filling is firm and lightly browned.

CUSTARD TART

½ slab of short (or flaky) pastry
4 large eggs
1 cup cream
1 cup milk with a vanilla bean soaked in it if you have one
2 tablespoons sugar
½ teaspoon vanilla essence if you have no vanilla bean
grated nutmeg
25 cm (10 in) pie tin

Roll out the pastry and line the tin; decorate the edges with flutes or spirals if you like but this is one tart you can't criss-cross with pastry strips.

Beat together the eggs, cream, milk (without vanilla bean), sugar and vanilla essence if you are using it until they're well mixed and have a few bubbles on top.

Pour the mixture into the pastry case and sprinkle the top with nutmeg if you wish.

Bake at 220°C (425°F) for 20 minutes, open the oven door to check, close it and reduce the heat to 175°F (350°F) for a further 20 minutes, by which time the custard should be lightly browned on top, and well set.

CHRISTMAS MINCE PIES

2 cups large plump raisins
1 cup currants
½ cup glacé cherries
4 tablespoons orange marmalade
4 tablespoons brandy (or rum)
1 slab short (or puff) pastry
1 tray flat-bottomed patty-cake containers

Make the mince several days beforehand if you can, and store it tightly covered until you need it. If you have a blender, put the raisins and cherries through it, otherwise you can use a meat grinder, or chop them finely with a sharp knife. There is no need to mince the currants. Combine the raisins, currants, cherries, marmalade and liquor together, and mix well.

Divide the pastry slab into two pieces, one larger than the other, and put the smaller piece back in the refrigerator. Use the larger piece to make the pie bottoms. Roll it out thinly and line each patty-tin with it, leaving enough pastry round the edges of each one to use as a lid margin when trimming. Brush these margins with egg and milk or plain milk, though it is worth making egg and milk glaze so that it can be brushed on the lid afterwards.

Spoon the mincemeat into the shells, and don't over-fill them.

Roll out the smaller piece of the pastry slab, and use it for the pie lids. Pinch the margins together well before trimming, and cut nostrils in each pie.

Bake at 220°C (425°F) for about 30 minutes, or until the tops are nicely browned. If you put the patty-cake tray on a baking tray it will ensure that the bottoms don't brown faster than the tops.

When the pies come out of the oven, brush their tops immediately with egg and milk, and sprinkle white sugar on them before the glaze dries. Turn them on to wire racks to cool, then store them in tightly lidded containers until Christmas. They keep splendidly.

TREACLE TART

½ slab of short (or flaky) pastry
4 tablespoons treacle (or golden syrup)
juice of 1 lemon
rind of 1 lemon grated, no white pith in it
4 tablespoons breadcrumbs
25 cm (10 in) pie tin

Roll out the pastry and line the tin; decorate the edges with flutes or spirals, and save some pastry cut into thin strips.

Measure out the treacle (or golden syrup) using an oiled spoon so it is a true measure, and put it in an oiled saucepan. Add the lemon juice, lemon rind and breadcrumbs, and warm it gently, stirring.

Pour the mixture into the pastry shell, then make a lattice-work of pastry across the top with pastry strips.

Bake in a 220°C (425°F) oven for 30 minutes, or until the pastry is golden brown.

SAINT HONORE CAKE

This is the very king of all desserts; a mixture of choux pastry puffs coated with toffee, and two different fresh whipped creams, one flavoured with rum and one with chocolate. It looks magnificent, piled like a little alp on its dish, and it tastes even better. Not only that, but once you have mastered toffee-making, it is one of the easiest and most failure-resistant concoctions imaginable.

Make a full quantity of the choux pastry recipe, and form it into cream-puff shapes on the baking tray. Make the puff three different sizes (a pastry bag makes it easier) — little ones, medium ones and big ones, at least six of each. Leave them on a wire rack to cool, and make the toffee.

1. Toffee
2 cups white sugar
⅔ cup water

Read the pudding chapter for the ins and outs of toffee-making. The syrup must be boiled to the crunchy stage, which means a dark amber, very viscous liquid free of any taint of burning.

On a counter-top or table spread a large piece of aluminium foil, 45 cm (18 in) wide and about 75 cm (30 in) long. Smear the foil with butter, margarine or soft white vegetable shortening (not oil, it taints the food), and arrange the choux puffs on it with lots of vacant space around each one. A cool spot is better than a warm one.

Take the saucepan of boiling toffee off the stove and trickle the toffee over the tops of the puffs; if you do it slowly enough to control the stream, you will have more than enough toffee to coat them all. Don't worry about the toffee which runs off the puffs and pools on the foil because it will be used too.

Leave the puffs and their toffee-coating to cool; if your kitchen isn't too humid, you can get this far as early as the evening before you want the finished cake, but you will have to leave them where they are, undisturbed.

2. Whipped cream
6 cups cream
1 envelope unflavoured gelatine
3 tablespoons granulated sugar
1 teaspoon rum essence (or 1 tablespoon rum)
2 teaspoons chocolate drinking powder

Divide the cream into two lots, 4 cups in the first, 2 cups in the second. Use mixer bowls if you have an electric mixer.

Take the gelatine and put it in a small metal or heatproof jug, pour in ¼ cup boiling water, and sit the jug in a pan of boiling water. Stir the gelatine until it is all dissolved, then cool it.

Put the 4 cups of cream to beat on a slow mixer speed (or do it by hand; you have more control at the end), and slowly add 2 tablespoons granulated sugar; never use powdered sugar, it spoils the creamy taste. Add about two-thirds of the gelatine, and the rum essence (or rum). Beat it until it is stiff, but be careful it doesn't get to the butter stage. Chill it.

Beat the 2 cups of cream at a slow speed. Add the 1 tablespoon of sugar that is left, and the remiaining gelatine. Then gradually add the 2 teaspoons powdered drinking chocolate. Beat the mixture until it is stiff, but watch it doesn't turn into butter. Chill it. Also chill a large plate or dish.

Using a wide rubber spatula or a large spoon, ladle a thick base of rum-flavoured cream on to the chilled plate.

Lever the six or eight largest puffs off the foil, and try to get their spilled toffee edges to come with them; break them apart if the toffee has run together, and if the toffee overflow breaks off the puffs, save it.

Press these largest puffs gently into the cream base, pointing their toffee overflows outward. Then spoon chocolate cream between them, and put a big dollop of rum cream on top of them. Lever six or eight smaller puffs off the foil, trying to retain their overflowed toffee edges, and press them gently into the rum cream on top of the first layer. Point their overflow edges outward. Fill the spaces between them with chocolate cream, then put more rum cream on top of them. Keep building your miniature mountain of cream and toffee puffs until it thins to a peak. Take the broken-off toffee overflows, and stick them into the cream up the sides.

FRENCH PASTRIES

1 slab rich puff pastry
2 cups icing sugar
½ cup or 1 small can (125g) fruit pulp, passion-fruit or mango
  if possible
egg and milk glaze

Roll out the pastry slab into a rectangle about 15 cm (6 in) wide and 30 cm (12 in) long.

Paint the whole exposed surface with egg and milk glaze, and leave it until it becomes a little tacky, then roll up the 15 cm (6 in) side, so that you have a fat cylinder 30 cm (12 in) long. Wrap it very tightly in foil or cling-wrap so it can't unroll, and put it into the refrigerator for a rest.

When the pastry roll is cold and well stuck together, take the sharpest knife you own and slice it into rounds 12 mm (½ in) thick. You are working with the pastry layers the wrong way up for the first time in this recipe, so your rounds won't rise in height at all, they're cross-sections through the layers. However, they will spread sideways enormously, so allow plenty of room for each round on the baking tray.

Slice only as many rounds as you need to fill the baking tray; it isn't necessary to grease the tray.

Place the baking tray on top of another one to prevent burning, and bake in a 220°C (425°F) oven for 10 to 15 minutes, until nicely browned.

Turn the pastries on to a wire rack and allow them to get quite cold.

Mix the icing sugar with the fruit pulp, so that it makes a runny icing, and spread the icing liberally on each pastry. Let the icing dry thoroughly before you try to stack them one on top of another for storage.

The recipe makes about twenty-four pastries.

7. BREAD

We are always surprised at the number of good cooks who frankly admit they have never made bread. For us, bread-making is therapeutic. If you are angry, all your pent-up emotions are satisfied in punching down the dough (Mother Easthope made her best bread when the children had driven her to distraction). When you want to sit and dream, watching the yeast perform its miracle of rising the loaves is soothing; first as the yeast is working and later as the bread is baking the changing smells titillate not only your olfactory nerves but also the neighbours' (they always find an excuse to drop in just as you are lifting the bread from the oven). Finally, the sight, the smell, the feel of the finished product is one of the most satisfying experiences in a cook's life.

The bread recipes we are giving are simple, straightforward breads for cooks who have never made bread; however, even experienced bakers might enjoy these, as they are particularly good and tasty. But first take the time to read the basic principles of breadmaking which follow. Once you understand these and have mastered the simple techniques involved, you will lose your fear of making bread. Then, after the third or fourth successful batch of bread, buy yourself a big book on bread-making and have fun with more sophisticated recipes.

THE BASIC PRINCIPLES

Gluten is a protein that has the property, when wet, of stretching and forming an elastic network. Flour made from the wheat grain has the best protein for making bread, but the strength and quantity of the gluten varies, not only with the variety of grain from which the flour is made, but with the season during which the wheat was grown and even the locale in which it was grown. You have probably noticed that bread recipes do not give exact amounts of flour; this is because of the variations in amount and quality of the gluten. However, these days flour millers blend their wheats before milling so the quality of the flour will be consistent. We suggest you stay with the same brand of flour so that the ratio of flour to water for your mixes will not need to be varied very much.

Yeast is a living plant which, with moisture, food (sugar) and the correct temperature, produces carbon dioxide. The bubbles of gas are entrapped in the gluten mesh, causing the dough to rise, or to use the professional term, the bread is leavened. Yeast works best at body temperatures, around the 37°C (97°F) mark on the thermometer. For your first ventures with bread-making it is wise to use a thermometer; if too cold the yeast action is sluggish, if too hot the yeast is killed.

Yeast is readily available in several forms, but for bread-making 'compressed yeast' or 'active dry yeast' are the easiest to use. If you do not bake bread regularly, the active dry yeast is the better buy: when packaged in air-tight sachets its shelf-life is about twelve months. East sachet holds sufficient dry yeast to make two 450g (1lb) loaves. (Always check with the instructions supplied with the product as to the quantities of yeast to flour, but a rule of thumb is 7g of active dry yeast equals 28g of compressed yeast, or ¼oz dry yeast is evivalent to 1oz of compressed yeast.)

Still talking about yeast, it is a wise precaution to prove the yeast before you add it to the flour. Having measured the quantity of water you require for the dough, take from this measured amount about half a cup and in this cup dissolve the yeast and half the sugar requirements. The water must be lukewarm, i.e., body temperature. Stand this mixture in a warm place and after a few minutes the yeast should begin to work; the top becomes quite frothy if the yeast is alive. If nothing happens after 10 minutes, abandon the project, for the yeast is dead — either it was no good before you began, or the water was too hot and killed it. If the latter, try again.

The liquids usually used in bread-making are water and/or milk. All water breads have heavier, crisper crusts, for example, French bread; milk breads have a velvety texture and softer crusts. For special flavours other liquids are used such as buttermilk, fruit juices. However, whatever variant you use, water is the best medium for dissolving the yeast when you are proving it.

Salt and sugar are added for flavour. For tasty bread you need a little of each. By using honey, brown sugar, molasses or other sugar syrups you can vary the flavour, but always remember, if using liquid sugars, that you must reduce the other liquid (milk or water) by an equal amount.

Eggs and powdered milk are sometimes added, both for special flavours and to enrich the bread. Eggs make the bread tender and a golden colour, but again pay attention to the overall quantity of fluid — beat the eggs lightly and let their volume replace an equal amount of fluid. The powdered milk is sifted with the flour, or you may prefer to dissolve it in the water. Either way works, but remember to save half a cup of water for dissolving the yeast.

Shortening is sometimes added to the bread mix, either as oil, melted butter or melted margarine. This is an optional addition but it does improve the keeping qualities of the finished loaves.

THE TECHNIQUES USED IN BREAD-MAKING

Bread is not pastry. It is not fragile. When the recipe says 'punch down the dough', it means *punch down the dough*. You punch the dough to break up and release any large air bubbles; if your finished product is full of holes, you probably did not punch the dough down hard enough. This is one cooking process where being heavy-handed doesn't matter.

The action of beating is performed at the beginning, after you have added the yeast and water, but not all the flour, so the mixture is thin and is referred to as 'the wet sponge'. Good bakers say it should be beaten with 300 strokes of a wooden spoon; that is, about 10 to 15 minutes allowing for one or two rests, because it is hard work. If you have a *powerful* electric mixer, by all means use it, but on slow speed and for 3 to 5 minutes. The beating action brings the gluten out of the flour and when you lift your beating instrument, the sponge should feel elastic and hang down. Beat until the sponge is smooth throughout. Then gradually beat in more flour until the sponge is dry enough to work with your hands. We are now ready to knead.

By kneading the dough you work it into a plastic mass. *The Shorter Oxford Dictionary* defines 'to knead' as 'to mix and work up into a homogeneous plastic mass, by drawing out, folding over and pressing together.' The best implements with which to perform this action are your hands. Smear a light coat of cooking oil over them, lightly flour them, and go to work in the same vigorous fashion as potters mix and model their clay.

Use the heels of the hands to work the mass and the fingers to fold it towards you. As you work, make quarter turns of the lump of dough to keep it a rounded mass; shaping is done at the end of the kneading process. Keep the kneading board well floured and also the surface of the dough. As the flour is kneaded in, add more flour to both the board and the dough until the dough is no longer sticky. The final dough should be satiny and smooth.

If you get tired, have a rest; nothing will spoil. If you are

After the first rising, poking the fingers hard into the dough.

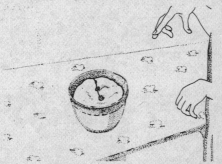

The indentations, sharp and clear, left after the fingers have been poked into the dough.

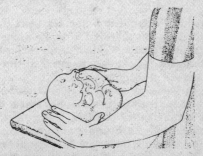

Beginning to knead the dough.

Kneading the dough and pushing the heels of the hand hard into the dough.

The dough set to rise in its tins for the second time. The bread rolls are in lined catfood tins, which have been sterilised.

interrupted for longer than 5 minutes, place the dough in the refrigerator (not the freezer). When you come back to the kneading, the warmth of your hands will quickly raise the temperature and you will feel the elasticity return to the dough.

Some of the more powerful electric mixers have a dough mixing and kneading attachment which is very efficient but we never use ours because it takes all the fun out of bread-making.

We have already mentioned temperature in connection with yeast. Temperature is important throughout the bread-making process. Start your bread after the kitchen is warm and don't decide to make puff pastry while you are waiting for the dough to rise; one or other, or both, will be failures because of the wrong temperature. Knead the dough on a wooden bench or a large board you keep especially for this purpose; the wood holds the warmth of the dough and a little flouring will stop it from sticking. Never use a marble slab; it is too cold.

If the temperature is stable, the bread dough will rise slowly and steadily. In farmhouse kitchens with fuel stoves there was never any problem in finding an appropriately warm place away from draughts. The modern tiled and stainless-steel kitchen does pose a few problems, but we have found several spots that work. One spot is on top of the refrigerator at the back, where the hot air rises from the dispersion plates, has a very constant temperature. Another is inside a sunny window. In the winter the fireplace hearth can be used, but do not get the bowl too close to the fire or the cooking process will begin before the dough has properly risen. Wherever you put the rising dough, *avoid draughts*. An even 27°C (80°F) is ideal. Don't worry if the temperature is a little lower, it will only take longer for the dough to double in size, if the air is warmer than this, the dough will rise more quickly but you will have a very open texture in the finished loaf.

What kind of tin should bread be baked in? You can use anything you like. There are the traditional oblong deep tins; if you want a round loaf, use a round cake tin, but be sure it is deep enough to allow for the increase in bulk of your loaf. For the small herb loaves, we have found the small lined tins in which a certain brand of tunafish-for-cats is packed are perfect. When they become scarred, the cat is given a fish diet until we have enough tins again. Teflon-lined bread tins produce beautifully crusted breads. There is probably no sound scientific reason for this tip, but it works; like old teapots and tea-making, old and tried bread tins bake the best loaves. We never allow anyone to use our bread tins for any other purpose.

Oven temperatures. Heat the oven to 220°C (425°F). When the bread is put in the oven the dough will continue to rise for a short time as the air and gas bubbles expand, but the yeast action will be quickly stopped by the heat. After about 10 to 15 minutes, the crust will have formed and begun to brown; lower the oven to between 190°C and 200°C (375°F and 400°F) and complete the cooking. Depending on the size of the loaves, this will be about 35 to 40 minutes for total cooking time. Rolls and buns will take less time because they are smaller and therefore heat through more quickly. Always use the middle shelf of the oven, and do not try to cook other foods at the same time.

When the loaves are cooked, they will pull away from the sides of the cooking tins. To double-check whether the bread is cooked, remove one loaf from its tin; the sides should be a golden brown, and it should sound hollow when you tap it. If the bread is not cooked, return to its tin, lower the heat of the oven further and cook for a further 5 to 10 minutes.

Tip the cooked loaves out of their tins and stand them up-sidedown on a wire rack to cool. This is to allow the steam to escape from the bread as it cools and so prevent the middle of your loaf from becoming soggy. When the loaves, buns or rolls are cool, store them in an air-tight container.

Glazing the tops of the loaves gives them a professional appearance. For plain breads, lightly brush milk over the loaf before you put it in the oven. But you can be venturesome and try any glazes you have used on such things as pastries. Beat together egg yolk and a little milk, and for sweet breads add a little brown sugar. For spicy breads, a sprinkle of cinnamon (or ground ginger) may be added to the glaze. If it is an orange-flavoured bread, add a sprinkle of finely ground orange rind (no white pith). The glaze for buns is applied after the buns are cooked but before they have cooled; this is to prevent the sugar's burning. And of course, this warning applies whenever using sugar in a glaze — do not use a sugar glaze if cooking in a very hot oven.

There are stages during the working of the dough when you can stop and hold up the process. As bread-making requires warmth, you can stop the yeast action by wrapping the bread in air-tight aluminium foil or plastic bags and putting it into the refrigerator. Do not wrap it too tightly because even though the temperature is reduced, a little working of the yeast will continue. Remember at what stage you were at when you resume. The warmth of your hands will rapidly start the yeast action.

As long as the room temperature is not too high, you can let the dough rise overnight. This makes a good bread of fine texture. Because the action of the yeast is slow, the carbon dioxide bubbles are small, and you never get holes in the bread. However, we would not suggest you do this during mid summer in Sydney. We tried it once before there was an air-conditioner in the kitchen. The yeast worked actively, too actively, all night and in the morning the kitchen had become the set of a science fiction movie with malevolent-looking dough creeping across the floor. The early morning weather report informed us that 'Sydney had had one of its hottest nights on record, with temperatures never dropping below 90°.'

THE STORAGE OF BREAD

To store your baked loaves, first allow them to cool right through then wrap in air-tight plastic or aluminium foil; the bread may then be stored in the bread cupboard, the refrigerator, or if for longer periods it may be frozen in the freezer. To use frozen bread, thaw in its wrappers at room temperature for 2 to 3 hours depending on the size of the loaf; remove the wrappings and allow air to circulate by placing the loaf on a wire rack. To crisp the crusts, place the bread in a moderate oven for a few minutes. If you are in a hurry, place the aluminium-wrapped frozen loaf in a moderate oven at 190°C (375°F) for about 20 minutes. Unwrap for the last 5 minutes to crisp the crusts.

Home-made bread keeps extremely well, and remains fresh much longer than the average Australian white loaf. However, if you are watching your figure make half quantities, because the chief danger from home-made bread is that most of it is eaten hot from the oven!

If you plan to bake bread once a week, we suggest you add a little shortening to the basic mixture — about 1 tablespoon of butter (or cooking oil). If using butter, melt it and add to the water. The oil may be dribbled in when you are adding the water to the flour. The shortening helps keep the bread moist and fresh.

By now you will be eager to make your first batch of bread. The first recipe is for plain white bread. It is simple and straight-forward, and all the other recipes are based on the methods used here. If you prefer wholemeal bread to white, we still recommend that your first attempt be with white bread. You are more likely to be successful because the gluten is easier to work from the plain white flour.

PLAIN WHITE BREAD

To make two ½ kg (1 lb) loaves you will need:
8 cups plain white flour
2½ cups warm water
1 sachet active dry yeast, 7g (¼oz)

1 tablespoon sugar
2 teaspoons salt

1. Prove the yeast. Using half a cup of the warm water, dissolve the yeast and half the sugar. Stand aside in a warm place.
2. While the yeast is proving, sift together 4 cups of the flour, the salt and the remaining sugar.
3. Sift the remaining 4 cups of flour into a separate bowl.
4. By this time the yeast should be working. Make a well in the centre of the larger amount of flour and pour in the yeast. Gradually add the water and mix until you have a wet sponge.
5. Now beat. The end result after 10 to 15 minutes should be smooth but elastic when you lift the beating spoon. If you think the mix is too wet, sprinkle in more flour from the reserve bowl.
6. Gradually add more of the flour and using one hand (remember to oil and flour the hand!) work the mixture into a soft dough.
7. Turn out the dough on to the floured board (use flour from the reserve, as this flour will be worked into the dough) and begin kneading. As it is kneaded in, add more flour to the board and the surface of the dough until it is no longer sticky. The final dough should be satiny and smooth.
8. Put the lump of dough into a greased bowl; lightly grease the top of the dough; cover loosely with a cloth and set in a warm place to rise until it is approximately doubled in size. This will take about 1½ to 2 hours, depending on the temperature of your warm place.
9. To test whether the dough has risen sufficiently, insert two fingers into the dough; the indentations should remain. Punch down the dough in the bowl, squeezing out the large gas bubbles and shape it into a ball again.
10. Turn the dough ball on to the floured board. Grasp the centre of the ball and squeeze and tear it into two portions. These are your two loaves.
11. Return one of the loaves to the bowl. Knead the other for 10 minutes and mould it into the shape you require — round for a cottage loaf, oval for the traditional bread shape. Repeat with the other loaf.
12. Put the shaped loaves into greased bread tins (or on trays), cover loosely and again let them rise until almost doubled.
13. Bake in a hot oven at 220°C (425°F). Open the oven after about 15 minutes; if the loaves are browning, lower the

temperature to about 190°C (375°F) and complete baking. Thirty-five to 40 minutes after putting the bread in the oven, the loaves should be pulling away from the sides of the tins. Turn out one loaf and test; are the crusts golden brown and does it sound hollow? Yes! The bread is cooked. Cool them on a wire rack. And don't you feel pleased with yourself!

Note After beating the wet sponge to smoothness, some cooks set the mixture aside to rise for half an hour. If you have the time to do this, it does improve the texture of the bread; it is stronger and less likely to crumble when cut. After this first rising, proceed directly with Step 6.

So you have baked your first loaf of bread and you want to try some variations. Here are some simple things you can do, working from the basic recipe for white bread

MILK BREAD

Instead of 2½ cups of water, use ½ cup of water to dissolve the yeast and 2 cups of milk for mixing the dough. However, always scald and then cool the milk before adding it to the flour. (To scald milk, heat it to just below boiling point, and cool rapidly; skim off any skin that forms on the top.) Milk is a wonderful medium for growing the kinds of bacteria which attack and kill yeast. Despite pasteurization, allowing milk to stand in the kitchen until it has reached body temperature is enough to make it unsuitable for bread-making.

Equally good is the addition of 4 or 5 tablespoons of full-cream powdered milk instead of dairy milk. The powdered milk may be either sifted with the flour or dissolved in 2 of the cups of water.

EGG-ENRICHED BREAD

Lightly beat 2 eggs, measure their volume and make the appropriate adjustment in the liquid content of the mixture. The beaten eggs are added when you are adding the water to make the wet sponge.

HERB BREAD

You can make several kinds from the one mix. When you come to the step where you are dividing the dough to go into the bread tins for baking, divide it into as many pieces as the number of herbs you wish to use. To each add 1 teaspoon or more of the given herb; the exact quantity depends on the strength of flavour you like. Work the herb into the dough as you are shaping it to go into the baking tins.

We usually make clover leaf loaves for the herb bread. For one clover leaf, roll balls of dough about 2½cm (1in) in diameter and put three of these balls in one small tin — they should just touch so that as each ball rises it fuses gently with its neighbour. (This is where the fish tins come in handy!) Or you can make small bun shapes and cook them on a baking sheet, being sure to allow sufficient room between each one for expansion during the final rising and the baking process.

Suggested herbs that can be used: marjoram, oregano, sage, mixed herbs, sweet basil, dill weed, savory, powdered garlic (this latter makes superb garlic bread). In fact, any kind of herb or spice you like. The herbs can be dried or fresh, it doesn't matter. These are fun to experiment with, but always make a note of the mixtures of herbs and the quantities that you have used, because you will want to remember them for special occasions.

SWEET BREAD

Dried fruits and nuts are used for these. The dried fruits have a high sugar-content in themselves, so do not be tempted to add more sugar to the basic recipe, unless your family has a very sweet tooth. Allow about 1 cup of fruit or fruit and nuts to 8 cups of flour. When you become expert, you can try working in more fruit, but there is a limit to how much fruit the mix will hold. Work the fruit into your dough when you are shaping the loaves. If you flour the fruit first, use flour from the measured quantity or the dough will become too dry, and at this stage it is too late to add more moisture.

WHOLEMEAL BREAD AND BREAD USING OTHER GRAINS

Full wholemeal (as opposed to plain white flour) makes a heavy loaf that for some people is quite unpalatable. For your first attempt at wholemeal bread, substitute 1 cup of wholemeal for 1 cup of the plain white flour. If this is to your liking, in the next batch increase the proportion. You will quckly find a combination of wholemeal and plain white flour that suits your requirements. The dough will take a little longer to rise than with white bread; and it does not double its size; so be prepared for smaller, heavier loaves.

The same rule goes for the addition of flours made from grains other than wheat. The gluten content and the gluten quality of other grains differ from wheat flour, but another member of the Easthope clan has given us this tip. If you are using flour made from grains such as rye where the gluten content is low, replace 1 cup of the flour with 1 cup of gluten flour. Gluten flour is made from wheat flour after the starch has been washed away, and is obtainable from health-food stores or any other food outlet that supplies special diabetic foods — gluten flour has no carbohydrate content, so it is useful if you are slimming.

The rising times for all these flour combinations are longer (2 hours instead of 1½ hours), and these darker-coloured breads do not double in bulk when they rise; however, the test with two fingers into the top of the risen dough still applies. Because the loaves are smaller, use smaller bread tins. Baking times and temperatures are much the same. But by this stage you will have gone out and bought yourself a book devoted to bread-making alone!

BREAD ROLLS

When we want to serve hot bread rolls either before or with the first course, we use the following recipe. The dough rises quickly because double the quantity of yeast is used. You can start the dough earlier in the day, and after the second rising hold the uncooked rolls in the refrigerator until about 30 minutes before the dinner. This is a great advantage if the meal is delayed because the bread rolls will not be spoilt.

1 sachet active dry yeast, 7g (¼oz)
1 tablespoon sugar
¾ cup warm water
1 egg
1 tablespoon butter
4 cups plain white flour
1 tablespoon powdered milk
1 teaspoon salt

1.   Using a middle-sized mixing bowl, dissolve the yeast and sugar in the warm water, and stand in a warm place to prove

the yeast.

2.   Lightly beat the egg and stir it into the yeast mixture.

3.   Melt the butter but do not have it too hot; stir this into the mix.

4.   Sift together the flour, powdered milk and salt, and gradually add to the liquids in the bowl until you have a stiff batter. It should be smooth; a few beats with the stirring spoon helps.

5.   Leaving the dough in the mixing bowl, set aside and leave until it has doubled in size.

6.   Punch down the dough and knead into twelve balls, and pop one ball into each of the twelve greased patty tins.

7.   Now check the time. Under normal rising conditions with the temperature about 27°C (80°F), the dough will rise to the top of the tins in about 20 to 30 minutes. They will take another 15 minutes to cook.

You can slow up the yeast action by putting the rolls straight into the refrigerator, or you can let them rise for 10 to 15 minutes and then hold them. However, keep an eye on them because the yeast will continue to work although slowly and the dough will rise. On removal from the refrigerator, the rolls will take about 10 minutes to return to room temperature before they are put in the heated oven.

8.   Bake at 200°C (400°F) for 15 minutes, or until the tops are lightly browned.

9.   Turn out of the tins and serve immediately with loads of butter.

With a little imagination you can work all kinds of variations on this theme. The recipe makes good herb rolls. Instead of forming into rolls, after the dough has risen the first time, roll out the dough into a circle. Spread this lightly with butter and then divide the circle into segments by cutting diagonals across it at even distances apart. Starting with the curved outer edge of the segment roll up the dough finishing with the point. Set these on a baking sheet to rise, and cook as for the plain rolls. This is an easy way to make garlic bread; just sprinkle the ground garlic powder over the buttered surface before rolling up the segments.

BASIC SWEET BREAD

Our neighbours state that this is the best bread we make. For some unknown reason we let our heads go when making it and make all sorts of changes: fruit and nut bread, spicy rolls and even doughnuts. This is the basic recipe, and then we will give you some of our more successful experiments.

2 packets of active dry yeast, 14g (½oz)
1 tablespoon sugar
2½ cups warm water
8 cups plain white flour
3 teaspoons salt
pinch of saffron (or carotene) — optional
3 eggs
¾ cup wheat germ
2 tablespoons shortening, either butter or oil

This will make two good-sized loaves, or several smaller ones.
1.   Dissolve the yeast and sugar in ½ cup of the warm water, and set aside in a warm place to prove.
2.   Sift together 4 cups of flour, the salt and the saffron.
3.   Sift the remaining 4 cups of flour into a reserve bowl.
4.   Making a well in the centre of the first bowl of flour, add the now-frothing yeast mixture, 1 cup of water and the eggs. Beat well until smooth; this will be a very wet sponge because of the eggs but don't worry. Set it aside in a warm place to rise for 30 minutes.
5.   Now add the wheat germ, the shortening, the second cup of water, beating well.
6.   Add sufficient of the reserve flour (the second 4 cups) to make a dough that can be handled easily. Knead for 15 to 20 minutes and set aside to rise until it has doubled in size.
7.   Punch down the dough, knead a few minutes and shape your loaves.
8.   Put the loaves into greased tins and again set aside to rise until doubled in size.
9.   Bake at 200°C (400°F) for 15 minutes; then lower to 170°C (350°F) for 30 minutes or until the bread draws away from the sides of the tins.
10. Remove from the tins when cooked and cool on a wire rack before storing.

Now for some of our variations.
   After the second rising (end of Step 6), punch down the dough and knead into a ball. Divide the ball in two equal pieces and, kneading, work each piece into a square about 6mm (¼in) thick; use the rolling-pin if you need to. Coat

each square with a thick spread of butter and here we allow for our differing tastes.

Col's square is covered with juicy raisins, but Jean's is more exotic. First she sprinkles the butter with brown sugar and then adds raisins, chopped nuts (any variety that happens to be in the cupboard but macadamias are her favourite), chopped preserved ginger, cinnamon and a sprinkle of grated orange rind.

Now start from one corner and roll up the square like a sponge roll. Carefully lift this roll on to a baking sheet and curve it into a circle. With a sharp knife make slashes about 2½cm (1in) apart through the upper layers of the roll but do not cut right through to the bottom or the fillings will run out. Set aside to rise and bake as for the plain bread.

For doughnuts we roll out a portion of the dough to 6mm (¼in) thickness; then cut with a doughnut cutter. (If you do not have a doughnut cutter, use a large cookie cutter and then cut a hole in the middle of each circle with a small cutter — use the centre bits to knead into more doughnuts.) Let the doughnuts rise until double in size and then fry in deep hot oil. Drain on absorbent kitchen paper and sprinkle with sugar (or cinnamon). An easy way to coat the doughnuts with the sugar is to drop them into a strong paper bag containing the mixture of sugar and cinnamon and shake the bag.

Some tips for baking bread.

1.   Always add the salt to the flour, *not* to the yeast. Salt dramatically slows the action of yeast, but when sifted through the flour this action is greatly tempered; in fact, it is almost negligible.

2.   If the day is very dry with little moisture in the air, cover the rising bread with a damp cloth. This prevents drying and crusting of the top of the dough. The light coating of oil used on the dough serves the same purpose.

3.   Never use tight plastic wrapping paper to cover the rising dough. This will stop the dough from expanding because the air in the top of the bowl has nowhere to go. Use a light cloth thrown over the bowl; this is sufficient to stop the top crusting and to keep out any flying beasties. Nothing will stop children from poking their fingers into the rising dough! Don't be too hard on them; it is a big temptation.

4.   Extra yeast will make the dough rise more quickly, but punch and knead it thoroughly to express the large gas bubbles or the finished loaves will be full of holes. If you are using

coarsely ground wholemeal flour, we recommend additional yeast.

5.　To wash the utensils used in the dough preparation, first soak them in *cold* water. Hot water will begin to cook the flour. When finished with a tool, drop it into a bowl of cold water before the air has a chance of drying the dough into a hard clay-like mass.

6.　We will not enter the argument as to whether bread tins should be greased or floured. We use a thin coating of cooking oil and get nice golden brown crusts. If you use teflon-lined bread tins, there is no argument.

PULLED BREAD

Make your usual white bread mix and bake it for *half* the usual time. Remove the loaves from the oven and turn them out of their tins. Now tear the half-cooked bread into chunks, being careful to leave the edges ragged — do not attempt to mould the pieces into clean shapes, but rather tear them with your hands. Do not use a knife to cut the chunks. Spread these pieces out on a shallow baking dish and return them to the oven to complete the cooking process.

The resultant bread consists of golden chunks of crisp bread that are the perfect accompaniment for party spreads, and if they are small for dips. They are certainly a change from the eternal wafers and crackers.

We often serve them, hot from the oven, with bowls of thick pea soup. Daubed with chunks of homemade butter, and eaten sitting before an open log fire, you have the beginning of a pleasant winter's evening.

8. PUDDINGS

Fancy puddings, or puddings which require some time and effort in their preparation, have fallen sadly out of favour in household kitchens. The home puddings now popular are all of the quickly-throw-together-variety; icecream, store-bought, with syrup topping, also store-bought. Quick-mix vanilla or butterscotch or chocolate puddings, store-bought and beaten with a little milk; canned fruit with store-bought spray-can cream; fresh strawberries in season as a sop to good health and diet.

When we were children, puddings were varied and fascinating, and mother didn't repeat herself once in a month of daily puddings. Some were hot, some were cold; some were boiled, some were baked, some were steamed; some were dry, some were laced with sauce. A simple pudding then was custard sauce with bananas sliced into it, or last night's leftover pudding drowned in freshly made custard sauce.

We don't exhort you to return to the days when puddings were an everyday addition to the dinner menu; what we do suggest is that occasionally, perhaps once a week, you try some of the wonderful assortment of old-fashioned puddings included here.

Once you have grasped the underlying principles that govern one particular type of pudding, you can branch out on your own, and substitute all sorts of brilliant additions for the ones we suggest.

Taking puddings in their various categories, we will go through the types, explain what a type consists of, and how to make it. After that we will include an assortment of recipes which we hope will cover some of the main variations on each type. And after that, you're on your own.

Boiled puddings   This is the category into which the traditional Christmas pudding fits. Boiled puddings contain ingredients which require a very long, slow cooking.

Steamed puddings   Like a boiled pudding, these are wrapped in something and submerged in boiling water, but unlike boiled puddings, that something is heavy, made of ceramic or metal, and completely shields the pudding from the water. Steamed puddings have a very spongy, light, cake-like consistency.

Baked puddings These might be called the egg puddings, for here one finds all the traditional custards, rices and rice substitutes (sago, tapioca, semolina). However, this category also contains the fruit puddings baked with tops of cake or crumbs.

Creamed puddings These are the saucy puddings, which are really made on a basis of a white sauce, suitably sweetened, of course. They include creamed rices, creamed sagos, and custard sauces.

Shivery puddings These must be served chilled, and include all the various things one can do with flavoured gelatine, and chilled custards or white sauces.

Icecreams This category speaks for itself. Icecream has been with us for many decades, thanks to the old home churn, and we still feel that home-made icecreams are the best.

Tarts and pies We have treated this category in a special section devoted to pastry.

Boiled puddings are not high favourites of ours, and when we do make them, we refuse to incorporate suet, traditionally inseparable from a boiled pudding. We don't like suet; not particularly for health reasons, but for taste reasons, and the groaning heavy texture it adds that other shortenings do not.

If you have never made a steamed pudding, you must obtain the right kind of material for wrapping it in before you start. Once the pudding is made, the mixture is deposited, packed as closely together as possible, into the middle of a huge square, a metre (yard) on every side. The material is always unbleached calico (American: unbleached muslin), which has strong cotton fibres closely woven together, so that the mixture doesn't leak through during boiling. Never, never substitute a synthetic, non-cotton material! Synthetic fibres are non-porous, and do not permit the passage of fluids. In boiling a pudding, it is necessary to have porous material around it, even though it must be closely woven and strong.

Perhaps the chief reason we don't like boiled puddings much (including Christmas pudding) is that no matter what you do, the very outside of the pudding will be watery, a sort of semi-solid, greyish, gluey crust. Christmas pudding which is steamed is much nicer, though not orthodox.

Before depositing the pudding on the cloth, sprinkle the cloth well with flour all over the central area where it will actually touch the pudding mixture. After the pudding mix-

ture is packed on the cloth's centre, the cloth is gathered up
tightly around it, and tied strongly with string wound round
and round the neck of material just above the pudding top.
Boiled puddings don't rise, so you don't have to have much
slack.

Once wrapped and tied, the pudding is placed in a large pot
of gently boiling water, and is boiled for about 6 to 8 hours. It
is unwrapped after the cooking, placed on a dish, and served
accompanied by some sort of sauce, and a liquor-blended
sweet butter.

Grandma usually made four or five Christmas puddings —
some to be eaten by the numerous children, grandchildren and
other relatives who always turned up for Christmas dinner, and
the remainder to be sent to those families who could not come
home. So several weeks before Christmas, the laundry copper
was scrubbed and scoured, because there was never an iron pot
made large enough to hold them all; and someone was delegated
to keep the fire burning under the copper for the 5 or 6 hours
it took to cook them. Steamed puddings always remind us of
Alice in Wonderland and treacle. Perhaps that's why we love
treacle; the word, the taste, the concept. We can never think of
treacle without thinking of the Dormouse, nor for that matter
can we think about large teapots without thinking of the
Dormouse.

Treacle pudding seems to us to be the most famous of all
British puddings, just as treacle tart is of British tarts. They
are the two which one never sees duplicated on a supermarket
shelf by some large manufacturer.

As with all other steamed puddings, treacle pudding is made
like a thick, almost doughy cake mixture, which is then
pushed into a greased container, tightly lidded, and cooked
in a closed pot with boiling water half way up its sides. In
British countries you can buy the aluminium basin called
steamed pudding basins; they are distinguished from all other
basins by having a close-fitting lid which is clipped at three
equidistant points around the edge with curved snaps, so that
the inside of the basin is never unsealed during cooking. An
ordinary pottery-ceramic basin can be substituted, provided it
has a very distinct rim which juts out from the main sides of
the basin, and therefore enables you to tie a string firmly
around it just under the rim's edge. You can thus fill the
basin with mixture, cover it firmly with two layers of aluminium foil, a layer of pudding-cloth material, or two layers
of heavy unwaxed paper; this paper is then tied down firmly

under the rim with string, and to stop the string slipping off down the sloping basin sides, another piece of string is tied from one side of the rim to the other, over the top, and looped through the string round the rim. The drawings show you how to do this very clearly.

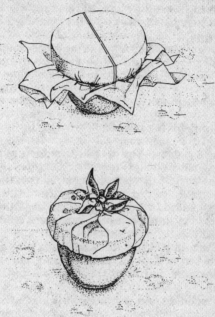

When the basin is sealed, it is placed into an already boiling saucepan of water; the water must reach half way up the sides of the basin, so you have to measure this before starting to heat the water, or you'll scald yourself doing it at the last moment. Never put a steamed pudding into water which isn't already boiling, and never let the water go off the boil, for you must keep up a steady supply of steam inside the saucepan. Once the pudding is in, you must ensure that the lid is tight, so that as little steam as possible escapes, and the pressure is higher inside. Check at half-hour intervals that the water hasn't boiled too low, and if it has, replenish it from a kettle of boiling water, never water which isn't already boiling, or you'll stop steam production in your pudding saucepan.

How long you steam a pudding depends upon its size. The middle-sized pudding basin, which holds 6 cups of liquid, feeds four to six persons comfortably, and takes about 90 minutes to steam itself cooked. We have a beautiful little pottery-ceramic basin in the fat blue-and-white stripes of Cornish pottery, and it is exactly the same size as our middle pudding basin; it has a nicely jutting-out rim on it, and does a steamed pudding equally as well as the proper container.

Your pudding basin should be about two-thirds full, never more, of mixture. If you have too much mixture, leave some of it out — never over-fill the basin, because the mixture rises, and has nowhere to go except into the boiling water of the pot. Ugh! Our recipe for steamed pudding basic mixture exactly two-thirds fills this middle-sized basin.

Steamed puddings come in endless varieties, even aside from treacle pudding. You can add ingredients to the mixture, or, if what you're adding is very thick and gooey, you can plop it in the bottom of the steaming basin, and put the mixture in on top. Treacle, golden syrup, heavy chocolate sauces, and jams are all added in this way, so that when the pudding is turned out, the softened jam or syrup runs gently down the pudding sides.

Most steamed puddings, because they are dry and cakey in nature, are served with a hot runny sauce poured over each helping; the most popular of these sauces is custard, of which more later.

Baked puddings are absolutely delicious, too. In variety they are amazing, and you can use all sorts of things you might not have realised you could.

The standard favourites, caramel custard (creme Caramel or *creme renversée au caramel*) and rice pudding, have so many equally delicious companions that you can bake puddings galore without repeating yourself. As a child, Col's favourite was something called apple sponge, the recipe for which is given in this chapter.

The most difficult thing about most baked puddings is the baking itself, for puddings are both fragile and sweet, and do best with a long, slow cooking process. For that reason, the most delicate of them are baked in a dish which sits in another dish of hot water, and the oven temperature is adjusted so that the dish of hot water steams, but never boils. When this is the chosen method of cooking, we have often found that recipe books give most unrealistic baking times, such as 30 to 40 minutes; they will actually take much longer than that unless they are in a very shallow dish, and therefore are not very thick.

Grain puddings, such as rice, tapioca, sago and semolina, are easy and quick to make. There are some simple rules governing their composition. To every 2 cups of milk you use 6 tablespoons of sago or tapioca; for semolina use 2 tablespoons, for rice use 4 tablespoons. To make it easier, here is a little table.

Rice	4 tablespoons per 2 cups milk, no soaking first
Sago	6 tablespoons per 2 cups milk, soak in water 2 hours first.
Tapioca	6 tablespoons per 2 cups milk, soak in water overnight.
Semolina	2 tablespoons per 2 cups milk, no soaking first

The grain, having been soaked or not, as directed, is scattered on the bottom of a baking dish or casserole, the milk poured on top with the sugar dissolved in it, and preferably a couple of eggs beaten into it as well. The top is then sprinkled with cinnamon or nutmeg or both, and the pudding is baked standing in a dish of simmering hot water (don't have the oven temperature so high the water boils!) until a knife thrust deeply into its middle comes out clean and not sticky, about an hour later.

Creamed puddings are usually grain/milk puddings, and the same rules apply as for baking them, the amount of grain to the amount of milk, that is. Rice must be boiled or soaked for 10 minutes in water first, however. With all of the grains, just throw them into the milk and boil them very gently until cooked, in the top of a double boiler.

The equipment for making puddings is minimal. A steaming basin, whether it be a basin sold for that purpose with clipped lid attached, or a basin with a rim you can tie a lid over yourself; a deep dish with sloping sides for baked puddings; a tall straight-sided round dish, made of a clear plastic or glass, for 'shivery' puddings that have various layers to display; a pudding cloth, if you want to boil puddings; and an old cotton stocking, if you want to boil your jam roly-poly.

BASIC STEAMED PUDDINGS

3 tablespoons butter
3 tablespoons sugar
2 eggs
4 tablespoons milk
1 cup plain flour
2 teaspoons baking powder

Cream the butter and sugar, then break in the first egg and beat well. Add the second egg and beat well. Add the milk and beat well.

Sift the flour and baking powder together, then add it gradually to the mixture, stirring well.

At the end, the mixture will be very stiff and quite unpourable, though not so stiff as a dough.

Grease your pudding steamer or pottery basin well, and turn the mixture into it.

This mixture fits perfectly in a medium-sized steamer or basin which holds six cups of fluid when filled to the brim or near it — check the size of your basin by doing this if you have any doubts.

If you are using a basin instead of a steamer, tie it as shown in the drawing on page 195.

Put the basin or steamer in a large saucepan of boiling water; the level of water must be half way up the sides of the basin. Put a tight lid on the saucepan, and steam for 1½ hours. Never let the water go off the boil, and replenish it if necessary. Once the pudding is in the saucepan, do not move it or disturb it in any way.

A pudding of this size feeds four to six people.

What we have given you is only the basic recipe. It is tasty just as it is, if it is served with chocolate rum sauce or custard sauce. (The recipe for each sauce is given at the end of the chapter.)

However, with this recipe you can do many things, and turn your basic into a number of variations, some of them quite famous.

TREACLE PUDDING

Grease the steamer or basin, put 4 tablespoons of treacle (or golden syrup) in the bottom then put the pudding mixture on top. Don't worry if the syrup wells up and over the pudding mixture. Steam the pudding as usual.

SPOTTED DICK OR SPOTTED DOG

To the mixture, add 1 cup of raisins (puffed muscatels), and steam the pudding as usual.

MARMALADE PUDDING

Grease the steamer or basin, put 4 tablespoons marmalade jam in the bottom, and put the pudding mixture on top.

COLLEGE PUDDING

Grease the steamer or basin, put 4 tablespoons raspberry (or strawberry) jam in the bottom, and put the pudding mixture on top of it.

DATE PUDDING

To the mixture add 1 cup chopped dates and steam the pudding as usual.

GOLDEN PUDDING

Grease the steamer or basin, then put 4 tablespoons apricot jam on the bottom, then put the mixture on top.

HONITON PUDDING

To the mixture, add 1 tablespoon lemon juice and 1 tablespoon grated lemon rind (or 1 teaspoon dried powdered lemon rind).

Note   Most of these puddings are served with custard sauce, or a sweet white sauce.

To serve a steamed pudding, turn it on to a plate upside-down, so that if a heavy syrup (or jam) has been put on the bottom of the mould, it then trickles down the pudding's sides.

This recipe for basic pudding is an excellent one, and gives you a pudding of splendid texture. So whatever things you put in it or under it, don't fiddle with the basic recipe itself. The amounts of ingredients given for the basic recipe are just right.

CHRISTMAS PUDDING

4 cups raisins (puffed muscatels)
6 cups sultanas (raisins)
½ cup chopped almonds
4 tablespoons chopped orange peel (orange citron)
4 tablespoons chopped lemon peel (lemon citron)
1 cup glacé cherries, chopped
2 cups brandy
450g (1 lb) butter
1 cup dark brown sugar
8 large eggs
1 cup apple purée (or apple sauce)
½ cup orange juice
6 cups fresh soft breadcrumbs
2 cups plain flour
2 tablespoons ground ginger
2 tablespoons cinnamon
2 tablespoons nutmeg
2 tablespoons allspice
1 teaspoon curry powder
1 teaspoon salt
1 teaspoon baking powder

Chop the fruit and almonds and orange and lemon peel, dust lightly with a little flour, and put in a basin overnight with the brandy poured over them.

Cream the butter and sugar, then beat in the eggs one by one, getting each one well absorbed before breaking in another. The mixture will look very curdled by the time the last egg is added, but this is quite normal for rich dark cakes and puddings, and as the flour is added the curdling disappears.

To the creamed butter/sugar with eggs beaten in, add the apple purée and beat well, then the orange juice and beat well.

To the liquid mixture, add the breadcrumbs a cup at a time, mixing well.

Sift the flour together with the spices, salt and baking powder, then stand the mixture aside in a basin.

To the liquid and breadcrumbs, add 2 cups of the soaked fruit, stirring well.

Add ½ cup of the flour, stirring well.

Add 2 more cups of the fruit, then ½ cup of the flour, and continue in this way until all the fruit and flour has been incorporated.

You may find that it is impossible towards the end to mix with any other implement than your hands, so do use your hands.

Make sure that you put into the pudding all the liquid that might have run out of the fruit as it soaked overnight. You don't want to lose the brandy!

Spread the pudding cloth, sprinkle it with flour except for the outer margins, then pile the pudding mixture in its centre. Tie it up tightly and well with string.

Place the mixture tied in its cloth in a very large pot of boiling water, put the lid on the pot, and boil the pudding for 8 hours. As the water evaporates replenish it with more boiling water — never add water which isn't boiling, and never let your pudding go off the boil.

It is best to make the pudding at least two weeks before Christmas, to permit it to mature.

You can add small silver coins to the mixture which is traditional for Christmas. But make certain they are silver coins, and do not use any of the modern Australian five and ten cent pieces which are amalgams of metals other than silver.

The pudding is served with brandy butter and hot custard (see end of chapter).

PLUM DUFF

225g (½lb) butter
1 cup hot water
1 cup white sugar
2 eggs
2 cups plain flour
½ teaspoon baking powder
pinch salt
1 teaspoon cinnamon
2 cups raisins (puffed muscatels)
2 cups sultanas (raisins)

Melt the butter in a saucepan with the hot water, and leave to cool.

When it is cool, add the sugar and stir, then add the eggs, which should be beaten together first separately.

Sift the flour together with the baking powder, salt and cinnamon.

Add a cup of the fruit and then a ½ cup of the flour to the

liquid mixture, and keep adding fruit and flour alternately until they are used up.

Spread out the pudding cloth, sprinkle it well with flour in the middle area, then put the mixture in the middle, and tie the cloth tightly with string or tape.

Place in a large pot of water which is already boiling, put the lid on and boil the pudding for 4 hours, making sure the water doesn't evaporate or go off the boil.

Serve hot, with hot custard (page 222) or a custard of your own making.

APPLE OR QUINCE DUMPLINGS

half a recipe quantity of short pastry (see pastry page 146)
4 medium-sized apples (or quinces)
4 tablespoons sugar (or honey)

Peel the apples (or quinces), and dig out the cores without boring quite all the way through. Fill each cavity with a tablespoon of sugar (or honey).

Divide the pastry into four, roll each piece out to about 6mm (¼in) thick, and wrap an apple (or quince) in it, brushing the edges with milk and pinching together very well.

Take four pieces of unbleached calico (U.S. muslin), sprinkle the middle area of each with flour, then wrap an apple or quince dumpling up in it, and tie securely.

Boil in a large pot of water for 2 hours, with the lid on.

Serve with custard or sweet white sauce.

FLUFFY GINGER PUDDING

1 tablespoon butter
2 tablespoons golden syrup (or maple syrup, or treacle)
1 teaspoon bicarbonate of soda
½ cup warm milk
½ teaspoon ground ginger
1 cup self-raising flour

Beat the butter and golden syrup to a cream.

Add the soda to the milk and then pour this into the cream mixture.

Sift the ground ginger with the flour and fold them into the mixture.

Put the mixture into a greased pudding steamer and steam for 1 hour.

Maple syrup may be used in place of the golden syrup; or if you like a darker, stronger-flavoured pudding, use treacle. The quantity of ginger may also be varied to suit your own taste.

Serve with a hot sweet white or custard sauce, or with ice-cream.

JAM ROLY-POLY

This famous pudding is included in the pudding chapter rather than in the pastry section because the pastry section was becoming rather long, and this is a true pudding; it can be boiled, steamed or baked.

Jean knew a little boy who used occasionally to win a lot of marbles from his friends by betting that on that day his mother would serve jam roly-poly for pudding. He was never wrong, but how he was always right remained a mystery for a long time. It was only when he grew up that he divulged his secret: 'When there was jam roly-poly, Mum only had one stocking on!'

His family was obviously one where jam roly-poly was boiled, and traditionally it was boiled in a ladies' cotton stocking!

1 recipe quantity of short pastry (see page 146)
1 jar raspberry jam
1 baking dish, large pudding steamer, or ladies' cotton stocking

Roll the pastry to about 6cm (¼in) thick, and spread it thickly with raspberry jam.

How you roll it up depends upon the size and shape of your cooking container.

If you use a dish for baking in the oven, fold the pastry over and over on itself into the same shape as the dish. Always grease your dish well with white vegetable shortening before you put the roly-poly in it.

If you use a large pudding steamer or basin, fold or roll the pastry as near to the shape of your basin as you can, then stuff it in and push it down evenly. Again, make sure your steamer or basin is well greased beforehand.

It you want to boil the pudding, roll the pastry into a cylinder about the same thickness as Mum's leg, and then push it into the cotton stocking, and tie the stocking at each end just where the pastry ends. (If you are fastidious you can make a cylinder from your pudding cloth.) Put it in a large pot of boiling water and boil for 2 hours.

For baking, bake at 185°C (375°F) for 1 hour.

For steaming, steam for 2 hours.

Serve with custard sauce.

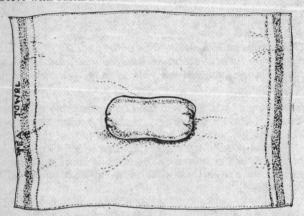

The roly-poly pudding in its cloth.

The pudding pastry wrapped in the cloth and pinned.

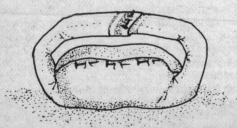

The ends of the cloth brought together to form a handle.

BREAD-AND-BUTTER CUSTARD

900g (2lb) loaf white bread, preferably unsliced and square
450g (½lb) soft butter
2 cups raisins (puffed muscatels)
8 large eggs
2 cups cream
2 cups milk
4 tablespoons white sugar
1 teaspoon vanilla essence
1 teaspoon grated or ground nutmeg (omit if you don't like it)
rectangular dish 20cm by 30cm (8in by 12in), such as for
  lasagna

Slice the bread about 1cm (½in) thick, and butter each slice
lavishly on one side only, then cut into fingers about 2½cm
(1in) wide.

Lay the fingers of bread butter side up all over the bottom
of the dish, then spread the raisins over their buttered tops.
Lay as many of the rest of the bread fingers as you can on top
of the raisin layer, buttered sides downwards.

In the large bowl of an electric mixer (otherwise, use a
rotary or French whisk and a large bowl) put the eggs, cream,
milk, sugar and vanilla. Beat vigorously for 10 minutes.

Carefully pour the custard mixture over the top of the
bread slices, in a thin stream that doesn't move the bread
slices. As the dish begins to fill, the uppermost slices of bread
will rise and float; this is normal and highly desirable.

Lavishly sprinkle the top of the custard with nutmeg.

Put the dish into another larger one, and fill the larger one
with boiling water, as close to the top as you can, bearing in
mind getting it into the (heated) oven. If you have the kind of
oven which is big enough to allow you to add the boiling (or
very hot) water when the dish is actually inside the oven, then
please do.

Have the oven temperature set to 160°C (325°F), and
regulate it so that the water surrounding the custard dish simmers, but never boils vigorously.

Bake for 1 hour, or until a knife thrust into the middle
comes out clean. The bread on top should have begun to
brown and crisp up a little.

Serve hot or cold — though we think it is best hot.

This is a superb party or dinner pudding, yet among connoisseurs it seems to be heartily despised. If you offered us a choice between bread-and-butter custard and zabaglione, we know which we would take! This is a fairly large custard, which will feed about ten people, but we decided to make it a large recipe because it's great as a leftover, chilled.

BAKED RICE PUDDING

4 tablespoons rice, long-grained
2 cups milk
2 tablespoons caster sugar (or superfine sugar)
2 eggs
1 cup raisins (puffed muscatels)

Put the rice, milk and 1 tablespoon of the sugar into the top of a double boiler, and cook the mixture for 2 hours, by which time the rice should be soft and fluffy, and most of the milk absorbed.

Separate the whites from the yolks of the eggs, and beat the yolks sufficiently to break them up and turn them creamy.

Let the rice-and-milk mixture cool to lukewarm, then stir in the egg yolks, and the raisins.

Put the rice mixture on the bottom of a square casserole dish 15 cm (6 in) square, which has been greased with white vegetable shortening.

Beat the egg whites with the other tablespoon of sugar until they are stiff enough to stand in peaks. Tip it on top of the rice mixture and spread it evenly.

Bake at 160°C (325°F) for about 25 to 30 minutes, or until the meringue topping is lightly browned.

CREAMED RICE PUDDING

4 tablespoons rice
1 cup milk
1 cup cream
3 tablespoons caster (or superfine) sugar — more if you wish
4 beaten eggs
1 teaspoon cinnamon
1 teaspoon nutmeg

Put the rice, milk and cream into the top of a double boiler, and stir in the sugar. Put the lid on the pot and cook for 2 hours.

At the end of the 2 hours, take the lid off, give the rice a stir, and then add the beaten eggs, stirring again.

Put the cinnamon in a heap on one side of the pudding, and the nutmeg on the other. Fold the spices through the rice without mixing them thoroughly, and serve the pudding hot with extra cream if you like.

LEMON SAGO

6 tablespoons sago
2 cups water
2 tablespoons golden syrup (or honey)
1 tablespoon moist brown sugar
1 lemon — juice plus grated yellow of rind

Soak the sago overnight, then wash it well, add it to the 2 cups of water and boil until clear, stirring frequently.

When the sago has cleared (that is, become transparent), add the syrup, sugar, lemon juice and the outside yellow of the rind grated thinly.

Cook the mixture gently at a simmer for 10 minutes.

Turn it into a jelly mould, chill and serve cold with cream or custard.

This was always a favourite pudding with the early settlers, particularly the children. Frequently, it was the only pudding, because sago was nearly always on the pantry shelf and you could always find lemons — either from your own lemon tree or from a bush lemon tree. The so-called bush lemons are not indigenous to Australia although you can find them in many out-of-the-way places. They are the descendants of the first lemons brought to Australia, and where you find a wild lemon tree you will find the foundations of an old bush hut. The lemons themselves are not handsome; they are knobbly fruit of varying size and shape, but are juicy and have thick rind ideal for grating. When Jean found two old trees near her wild mountain retreat, Mother Easthope became ecstatic and made lemon cheese.

However, when we wanted a recipe for lemon sago we had problems. Apparently this delightful dessert is not made these days. And then in the same week two recipes turned up. Our thanks to Mrs Marjorie Easthope and to Mrs Grace Cameron.

GRANDMA STONE'S BAKED APPLES AND RICE

4 large green Granny Smith apples
4 tablespoons uncooked rice
½ cup boiling water
salt
3 cups milk
½ cup cream
1 lemon
seedless black-currant jelly
12 Chinese dates
sugar

Cover the rice with the boiling water, add a pinch of salt, and cook it over a low heat until the water is absorbed.

Add the milk and cream, stirring steadily. Lower the heat and cook slowly, stirring occasionally.

Meanwhile, grate the lemon rind to obtain 2 teaspoons of fresh rind. Squeeze the lemon.

Peel the apples, roll on the lemon juice to prevent browning and discoloration. Add the skins to the rice.

Core the apples and stand them in a deep casserole dish. Fill the centres with the black-currant jelly.

Whisking the rice and milk briskly, add the lemon juice slowly — the whisking will break any curds that form. Add the quartered Chinese dates and the lemon rind. Remove the apple skins and taste the mixture. Depending on the sweetness of your tooth, add sugar (Chinese dates are very sweet).

The rice should be quite creamy so, before all the milk has been absorbed, pour it around the apples. The rice should come about half way up the apples.

Put the lid on the casserole and bake the pudding in a moderate oven until the apples are tender, but not soggy.

APPLE SPONGE

6 large apples, preferably slightly green
1 tablespoon sugar — for apples
4 cloves (or 1 teaspoon cinnamon)
3 tablespoons butter
3 tablespoons sugar — for sponge
4 eggs
1 cup plain flour
2 teaspoons baking powder

Peel and cut the apples in halves, core them and slice them into thin crescents. Place the apples in a frying-pan, or shallow large-bottomed saucepan, sprinkle them with sugar, add the cloves (or cinnamon), and sprinkle them with a tiny amount of water. Put a tight lid on the pan, and cook the apple slices very slowly for 10 minutes, until they are soft and the sugar has dissolved. Try to time the cooking of the apple to dovetail with the making of the sponge, so you can put the sponge on top of very hot apple.

Cream the butter and sugar, and add the eggs, which have been beaten well separately. Beat this well again.

Sift the flour and baking powder, and add them to the creamed mixture slowly, stirring gently.

Put the hot apple mixture in the bottom of a hot large pie dish or casserole about 20cm (8in) square, and deep-sided. This is not a recipe suitable for the conventional, fairly shallow, round pie tin.

While the apple is still hot, tip the sponge mixture in on top of it, spread it around to cover the apple and be fairly even on top, then place it in an oven already well up to heat.

Bake at 210°C (400°F) for 20 to 25 minutes, until the sponge has risen and browned well.

Serve with hot custard sauce, or cream.

APPLE CHARLOTTE

6 large apples, preferably sweet-eaters
10 slices of white bread, well buttered on one side
2 cups cake crumbs
2 tablespoons caster sugar (or superfine)
1 teaspoon cinnamon
1 teaspoon allspice
125g (¼lb) butter, cut into thin slices

Peel the apples, core them, and slice them thinly. Put them in a saucepan and sprinkle lightly with a very little water. Put a tight lid on the saucepan and cook the apple very gently until you can purée it with a spoon; it isn't necessary to put apple in a blender.

In a fairly deep pie dish (2.5cm or 10in in diameter), or a 20cm (8in) square one, lay the slices of bread with their buttered sides against the dish, all over the bottom and sides, to form a shell.

Fill the shell with puréed apple, then sprinkle the cake crumbs deeply over the top.

Mix the sugar with the spices, and sprinkle this over the cake crumbs.

Lay the slices of butter all over the top.

Bake in a 175°C (350°F) oven for 40 minutes, or until the top is looking crunchy.

Serve the pudding with hot custard sauce or pouring cream.

BAKED CUSTARD FOR ONE

1 egg
few drops vanilla essence
2 teaspoons sugar
¾ cup milk

Beat the egg with 2—3 drops of vanilla.

Add the sugar and milk and continue stirring until the sugar is dissolved.

Pour into a buttered ramekin or a large cup that will withstand oven temperatures.

Stand the ramekin in a small container with hot water in the container reaching about half way up the ramekin. Cover the container with its own lid.

Cook for about 20 minutes with low heat, either in the oven, or on top of the stove until the custard sets.

Serve either hot or cold.

If you like nutmeg or cinnamon, this may be sprinkled on top of the custard before cooking.

CARAMEL CUSTARD (CRÈME CARAMEL)

If you have been dying to make caramel custard properly and have failed miserably because your toffee was no good, or your custard didn't cust the way a baked custard should, don't despair! We guarantee that if you read and absorb what we say here, you will have no trouble with toffee or custard.

1. The toffee
The chief complaints cooks have to make about their toffee are that it becomes crystalline, or it burns, or it never gets to the right colour and crackability.

What you have to understand first is that in making toffee you are attempting to put more sugar into a liquid than it can naturally accommodate. You are making, in effect, what chemists call a supersaturated solution. Then, having dissolved the sugar completely, you are attempting to change its structure from crystal to non-crystal — from glassy little grains to darkly transparent, solid rock. Of all cooking tasks, toffee-making is probably the closest to a true chemical experiment, and requires the same kind of care.

When Col was at her posh girls' school in Sydney around the late 1940s and early 1950s, the greatest treat the girls knew was 'toffees.' Fetes, holiday, any sort of festivity was an excuse to make and sell toffees. Price, one penny per toffee. All the girls made better toffee than most highly paid chefs; they regularly produced a glorious pale brown rock without the slightest tang of burn to it, and so hard it could only be broken by dashing it on the ground.

Perhaps because Col was as good a toffee-maker as the other girls, her crème caramel has always turned out superbly; in much-praised restaurants she habitually orders this dessert to see how the chef fares, and has discovered that with very few exceptions, even the highest-paid chefs either burn their toffee or else don't get to crackable temperature, and thus produce an anaemic sauce no darker than the custard it adorns. She then allows herself a quiet little smirk, and feels there is *one* haute cuisine feat she does better.

First, the equipment:

*1 medium-sized saucepan with a very heavy bottom and
    smooth sides — teflon or ironstone is ideal*
*1 asbestos mat if you haven't a heavy enough saucepan, or you
    can't get your stove heat right down*
1 jug of iced water
1 jug of hot water with a pastry brush in it
white sugar
water
450g (1 lb) white sugar
1 cup water

Put the sugar and water in the heavy smooth-sided saucepan and place it on the stove-top on low—medium heat. You must get all the sugar completely dissolved *before* the solution begins to boil, or the liquid will crystallise out, and keep on crystallising out. For this reason, we have stipulated more water than most recipes call for.

When the water is hot but not boiling, take the pan off the heat and stir until all the sugar is completely dissolved. There should not be one single tiny grain of sugar left!

Only when you have an absolutely clear liquid in the pan do you permit it to boil. Place the pan back on the heat, kept at low—medium until boiling begins, then reduced to as low as possible. There must be absolutely no foreign bodies in the liquid, so guard again minute flying insects! If you are a laboratory worker and you are making a supersaturated solution of salts, you soon learn to have the inside of your flask speckless and spotless. A mote of dust will suddenly turn into a forest of crystals. So work clean in a very smooth-bottomed and smooth-sided pan, have all the sugar dissolved before you bring the liquid to a boil and you will have no trouble with toffee.

Once the liquid does come to the boil, just let it boil. *Never stir it!* With this larger amount of water than usual, it will take anything up to an hour for the toffee to attain the right temperature. Water boils at 100°C (212°F), but sugar boils at about 190°C (315°F). So before your solution can turn into toffee, you have to boil off all the water. By the time you have toffee, there is practically no water left at all.

Every so often brush down the sides of the pan with a damp pastry brush, especially in the early stages while there is still a lot of water in the sugar and it is spitting quite viciously up the sides of the pan. As the amount of water is reduced by boiling off, the bubbles become much closer together and more sluggish in bursting, so they don't spit so far afield. Don't brush the pan sides with a very sloppy-wet brush, or water will trickle into the toffee and it will take longer to boil. Use the brush damp. The reason for brushing down the sides of the pan is simple — it prevents the drops from crystallising.

When boiling starts, the liquid is water-clear. So long as a fair amount of water remains, it stays water-clear. But as the water content becomes lower and lower, and the temperature of the solution creeps above the boiling point of water, the liquid begins slowly to darken. At this stage you have to watch for the slightest trace of burning, so if you have trouble regulating the low heat on your stove, slip an asbestos mat under the pan and turn up the heat slightly. It is very hard to burn anything through asbestos. (Incidentally, we know that asbestos is harmful to the lungs, but the few times in cooking when an asbestos mat is called for won't harm the cook at all.)

Don't bother with a sugar thermometer. It's a waste of money, and may form a focus for crystallisation. Until fairly recently people made toffee beautifully without one, and this old-fashioned way is still the best in our opinion. Indeed, after making toffee two or three times, you won't need to test for crackability at all. The right colour for perfect toffee is a deep amber in the pan, not brown and not yellow.

The crackability test is simple to do, and can be repeated as many times as necessary. Dip a clean dry spoon into the liquid, and drip the spoonful of liquid slowly into a jug of iced water. At first, while the solution is still pale, it will dribble off the spoon and disappear before it reaches the bottom of the jug. As the colour of the solution darkens, the toffee dribbled into the iced water will become harder and harder. At dark yellow, it forms a long hard thread in the water as it trickles off the spoon. At a good dark amber colour, it cracks very audibly as it hits the water.

The moment you hear it crack, take the pan off the heat and use it for whatever you want: coating a dish for crème caramel, all over the top of choux pastry puffs for Saint Honore cake, into paper patty-cake containers for school toffees.

2. Caramel custard (crème caramel)
toffee
6 eggs
3 tablespoons caster sugar (or superfine)
1 cup milk
1 cup cream
1 teaspoon vanilla essence
1 square Pyrex casserole, about 20 cm (8 in) on each side, and 5 cm (2 in) deep

When the toffee is to the cracking stage, a good dark amber in colour, take it off the heat and pour it into the casserole (no need to grease the casserole, just have it very clean and dust-free). When you have a thick pool of toffee on the bottom of the dish, pick up the dish and turn it in your hands, letting the toffee run as far up the sides as you can. Pour more toffee into the dish, and use it all up, every last bit; though this is a lot of toffee, it makes a deliciously ample amount of sauce, especially if you thickly coat the sides of the dish as well as the bottom.

Once you've used up all the toffee, put the casserole to one side to cool completely. It will take a long time to cool, as the toffee is so hot and the coating so thick, but *never* attempt to accelerate the cooling process by sitting the dish in cool or cold water, as it will, be it Pyrex or the best ovenware, crack into smithereens.

When the toffee is quite cold, break the eggs into the large bowl of an electric mixer (custard is so easy to make on an electric mixer, but you can use a French whisk or rotary egg beater), and beat them, adding the sugar a little at a time. Continue to beat until the eggs are a pale straw colour, and all the sugar is completely dissolved.

Heat the milk and cream combined, adding the vanilla essence at the beginning of heating. When the liquid just starts to simmer, turn the heat off and let it cool just a little. Then pour it into a heat-resistant jug, to make the next step easier to do.

Still beating the eggs, add the hot milk-cream in a very thin trickling stream as continuously as you can until it is all in.

Pour the custard into the toffee-coated casserole, and set the casserole in a roasting pan.

Put the roasting pan as far on to the oven shelf as it needs to be not to fall off, and fill the roasting pan with very hot water from a kettle or jug until the water level is half way up the sides of the casserole.

Push the pan all the way into the oven, and bake the mixture at 160°C (325°F) for 60 to 70 minutes. This temperature should ensure that the water in the roasting pan never boils, but open the door every 10 minutes or so to check, and if you do see the water in the pan bubbling vigorously, reduce the oven heat.

The custard is cooked when a knife thrust into its centre comes out clean, with no particles of custard adhering to it. The top should be slightly brown. Using a thick casserole dish means a longer cooking time than that usually given in such recipes, so be prepared for it to take at least the full hour, if not longer.

If you don't like bubbles on top of your custard, strain it through a fine sieve as you pour it into the casserole before baking. We rather like the bubbles so we leave them and the top becomes browner.

Once you can make toffee with confidence, this is such an effortless pudding to make (provided you have an electric mixer!) that you will be surprised into making it often. And, if you feel the toffee is too much trouble, the recipe made without the toffee coating inside the casserole becomes a plain but excellent baked custard.

CHARLOTTE RUSSE

2 cups made-up raspberry or strawberry jelly (Jell-o)
10 sponge fingers
1 teaspoon unflavoured gelatine
½ cup milk
1 cup cream
1 teaspoon vanilla essence
1 tablespoon caster sugar (or superfine)

For this you need a 4—5 cup jelly mould or basin, preferably one with fairly straight sides but a fancy bottom.

Have the jelly just cooled but not set.

Pour about 2.5 cm (1 in) of the red jelly into the mould, and chill it until set.

Arrange the sponge fingers around the sides of the bowl, so that they are standing up like the palings of a fence. Pour a little red jelly over them so they are fairly well stuck together, and chill again.

Dissolve the gelatine in the milk over heat, stirring so the milk doesn't boil. Allow to cool.

Beat the cream together with the vanilla essence and sugar until it is thick, then add the milk plus gelatine, and ½ cup of the red jelly.

Pour the mixture into the centre of the mould, and chill it until firmly set before turning it out.

PAVLOVA

This is a truly Australian—New Zealand dessert; as far as we know, it isn't made anywhere else save by homesick antipodeans. Unfortunately, most Australian and New Zealand restaurants seem to make a sort of ersatz Pavlova, consisting of soft meringue with a thin cream topping, sliced like a pie. Genuine Pavlova is made of crisp meringue, hard all the way through, and it is formed like a deep-cavitied shell which is piled high with whipped cream and fruit. Traditionally, the fruit is the passionfruit, its pulp of bright yellow dotted with glossy black seeds being strewn all over the top of the cream. The result is very pretty — and very tasty.

6 egg whites
2 cups caster sugar (or superfine)
1 cup cream

1 cup fresh or tinned passionfruit
white vegetable shortening

Very carefully separate the whites from the yolks of the eggs so that no yolk adulterates the white.

Without an electric mixer, it isn't easy to make a successful meringue, so we will describe this recipe as for an electric mixer. Place the egg whites in a large bowl, and put them on the mixer at medium speed. Beat until they are becoming stiff, then begin to add the sugar, a little at a time, beating continuously. Continue to beat after all the sugar is added, until the whites are so stiff they stand up in peaks; if necessary, increase the mixer's speed to maximum.

Put the mixture into a large pastry bag if you have one; about 4 to 6 tablespoons of mixture at a time will half-fill the bag and pipe easily. Don't over-fill your bag, or the mixture will ooze out of the top of the bag and on to your hands.

Spread a piece of aluminium foil over a baking tray, and tuck it well under the tray all around so that it doesn't slip. Using a cake-baking tin as a template, trace a circle on the foil with the wrong end of a pencil or something equally blunt so that you don't tear the foil. Grease the foil very well with white vegetable shortening.

If you are piping, use a very large rosette nozzle, and outline the circle with mixture. Then fill in the circle concentrically with the mixture, making sure that each circle of mixture is in good contact with the one on its outside. When you get to the middle, pipe a large rosette upright so it stands well up above the floor of meringue. Then pipe another circle on top of the outermost one, like a fence. On top of this, pipe a series of rosettes all around, so you end up with a fancy fence high around the edge of the meringue shell. If you have any mixture over, spoon it into high shapes somewhere on the foil away from the main shell.

Now hear this. Meringue isn't baked, it is just dried out in an extremely slow oven, below the boiling point of water. Never let the oven become hotter than 90°C (200°F)! Dry out the meringue at 90°C (200°F) for about 12 hours — yes 12 hours. Depending on how well your particular oven holds or loses heat (the very low temperature emphasises this), it may take even longer than 12 hours to dry out the shell completely. It is done when it sounds hollow when rapped gently with your knuckle, and keeps hard and unsticky upon cooling. If it gets sticky as it cools, put it back in the oven.

At this very low temperature the meringue will not brown. It may go a pale beige, or it may stay quite white, depending upon exactly how hot the oven is.

Store the meringue in a tighly lidded container until you want to use it.

Beat the cup of cream with 1 tablespoon of granulated sugar (powdered sugar ruins the creamy taste) until it is stiff, and pile it into the meringue shell. You can use a rosette nozzled pastry bag if you want a very posh-looking Pavlova. Then spoon passionfruit pulp over the top of the cream.

For those who are unable to get passionfruit either fresh or canned, any sort of fruit may be substituted: sliced strawberries, raspberries, sliced bananas, sliced peaches, etc.

This Pavlova will serve eight people comfortably.

TRIFLE

24 sponge fingers spread with a thin layer of raspberry jam (or
  2 large Swiss jam rolls cut into slices, or 1 large sponge
  sandwich joined together with jam, and sliced)
2 cups cream sherry (or sweet sherry)
3 packets raspberry jelly crystals (Jell-o)
3 cups boiling water
1 cup fruit juice
6 cups sliced or chopped fresh fruit, drained of juice
6 cups thick custard (either proprietary or see recipe in this
  chapter)
3 cups cream

For this party recipe, you will need a round clear plastic or glass dish, 25 cm (10 in) in diameter, with straight sides, such as a cake container or soufflé dish; however, the sides must be at least 13 cm (5 in) high. Many people use a small punchbowl, but we feel the sloping sides of this make it hard to ensure that everyone gets a fair share of the trifle's deeper layers, as the cake tends to get packed only in the middle of the bowl. We like to use a plastic cake-storing container. If you use a dish which isn't transparent, you lose the visual appeal of a trifle, but of course from the point of view of preparation, an opaque dish works just as well.

Pack the bottom of the dish densely with sponge fingers (or slices of Swiss roll or slices of sponge); the raspberry jam definitely adds to the flavour of the cake, so don't leave it out.

Pour the sherry over the cakes, until they are brown and swampy; unlike the Duchess of Duke Street, we think a trifle is not a trifle unless it is *loaded* with sherry. However, if you are part of a strictly teetotal family, sprinkle the cake with rum or brandy essence, then pour a cup of dark grape juice over it.

For a trifle, a more concentrated jelly than usual is needed because it has to set the entire fruit/cake layers, already wet from sherry and extra juice. Three packets of jelly should be made up with 6 cups of water, but for this recipe we want a harder jelly than that so it is made up with only 4 cups of fluid, 3 of which are water and 1 of fruit juice from the fruit used. Don't use more fruit juice than 1 cup, even if you have it; enzymes in the fruit juice tend to stop the jelly from setting if they are too concentrated. Gelatine, which is a jelly's setting ingredient, is a protein and is susceptible to acid sugar solutions like fruit juice.

Put the jelly crystals in a bowl, pour on the 3 cups of boiling water, and stir until the crystals have fully dissolved. Then add the cup of fruit juice, stir again, and let the jelly cool to lukewarm.

Spoon the sliced or chopped fruit over the sherry-soaked cake layer. We suggest you use whatever fresh fruits are in season, omitting apple (too hard) and banana (too soft), and limiting citruses such as orange and grapefruit to a very small proportion of the whole. Peaches, berries of all kinds, plums (peeled and stoned), nectarines, pineapple, mango, pawpaw (papaya), and melons of all kinds are suitable fruits. Our favourite combination is raspberry and peach, nothing else: we use fresh when we can, otherwise frozen but never canned. This trifle was made in Sydney during February, the best summer month for fruit, so we had nectarine, pawpaw, passionfruit, peach and strawberry.

When the jelly is lukewarm only, pour it on to the fruit and cake, which should be just covered and no more. Wait a little while after you have done this, because the jelly may soak down as the minutes pass, and need topping again. Put the dish in the refrigerator for about 1 hour to chill and set firmly.

The custard should be made and permitted to grow quite cold; it should be thick enough that it becomes quivery but not leathery upon chilling. Commercial powders (but only the better ones) do this upon 3 level tablespoons of custard powder to every 2 cups of milk. For your own homemade custard, you will need 4 eggs to 2 cups of milk, or 3 eggs to 1 cup of milk plus 1 cup of cream. Pour the cold custard over the chilled and set jelly layer, and return the dish to the refrigerator until you are going to serve the trifle.

Before you serve it, beat the 3 cups of cream with 1 tablespoon of granulated sugar until the cream is quite stiff. Never use icing (confectioner's) sugar to sweeten cream because it destroys the essential cream flavour.

If it is an occasion you are trying hard to make memorable, put the cream in a pastry bag with a large rosette pipe attached, and pipe the cream all over the top of the trifle in rosettes and shells. Otherwise, spread it around; it tastes just as good.

This quantity of trifle will serve fifteen to twenty people, unless they go mad about it, in which case it will only feed about ten!

We have given you a party-sized recipe because our feeling is that trifle is the kind of pudding people reserve for special occasions. If we are wrong, and you want to make a small dish for your family, use 12 sponge fingers, 1 cup of sherry, 2 cups of fruit, 1 packet of jelly crystals made up with 1½ cups water/juice, 2 cups of custard, and 1 cup of cream.

BLANCMANGE

Why has this ancient pudding been delegated to invalid cooking? It is easy to make, is very nutritious, lends itself to many variations, and above all it tastes good. Originally, it was made with flavoured milk thickened using isinglass. Isinglass is a very pure form of gelatine made from the air-bladders of freshwater fish, but modern commercial gelatine is an excellent substitute, and certainly cheaper. Cornflour (cornstarch) is also used in place of the gelatine. The recipe we give is for ginger blancmange, but experiment with other flavours such as coffee, vanilla, various fruit essences. The egg gives the blancmange a lighter texture, but it is not an essential addition. In fact, when you want a pudding and you have run out of eggs, blancmange will serve you well.

1 egg
1 cup milk
2 tablespoons caster sugar (or superfine)
1 envelope gelatine, unflavoured
1 cup less 1 tablespoon boiling water
1 teaspoon ginger essence

Beat the egg, put it with the milk and sugar in the top of a double boiler and stir until thickened.

Dissolve the gelatine in the water and make sure it is cold before proceeding.

Cool the custard to room temperature also.

When both custard and water-gelatine are cold, stir the two together, adding the ginger essence.

Pour into a fancy jelly mould and serve chilled.

Variations   In place of the cup of water, use a cup of strong black coffee, or drinking chocolate. Cornflour (cornstarch) gives the blancmange a different texture, and for the above quantities you will need 3 tablespoons.

ICECREAM

1 cup cream
2 cups milk
4 tablespoons instant full-cream dried milk
2 tablespoons caster sugar
3 eggs
¼ teaspoon vanilla essence
1 envelope unflavoured gelatine (½ tablespoon)

Using your electric mixer, combine the first six ingredients, i.e., everything except the gelatine. Beat them well until light and frothy.

While the mixture is beating, dissolve the gelatine in 1 tablespoon of hot water, and then add it slowly to the mixture.

Pour the creamy mixture into a freezing tray — the above quantities will half-fill two trays. Do not have the tray too full. Put into the freezing compartment of your refrigerator, having first turned the temperature to its lowest point.

Depending on the efficiency of your freezer chamber, in about half an hour the mixture will be mushy but not yet frozen. Remove from the freezer and beat well with a whisk. If you use your electric mixer, use the slowest speed.

Return to the freezer to complete the freezing.

Don't forget to re-adjust the thermostat after the icecream has frozen.

People do complain that homemade icecream does not have the smooth texture of the bought article, and this is often true. However, if you use a small amount of gelatine in your basic mixture and beat it at least once during the freezing process, you will have smooth, creamy icecream that is better than any bought variety and what is more you know it is made with cream, real cream. The secret of the old icecream churn was the churning all the time the mixture was being frozen, causing air to be incorporated and any crystals broken up. If you make a lot of icecream and have access to lots of cream, it may be worthwhile investing in an electric icecream maker — a neat little gadget that keeps the mixture churning while it is being frozen.

If you do not care for raw eggs in icecream, make a custard with the eggs, sugar and milk. Allow it to cool and then combine with the other ingredients in your mixer.

If you have no cream, susbstitute an equal quantity of unsweetened condensed milk.

You can vary the proportions of cream to other ingredients, but always remember that icecream should be a rich mixture, and because it is a frozen mixture it must be well flavoured and well sweetened. What tastes good at room temperature will have little flavour when frozen. However, do not go to the other extreme and add too much sugar because this will stop the mixture freezing properly. Likewise, if you use liqueurs for flavouring, too much alcohol will stop the freezing.

To add variety to your homemade icecreams, try some of the following.

Fruits At the time of the second beating of the icecream, add 2 or 3 tablespoons of fruit purée — apricot, persimmon, any berry fruit (having strained out the seeds), mango, mashed banana, etc.

Dried fruits and nuts Combined, these really do improve icecream. We always sauté the nuts in a spoonful of sunflower seed oil and drain them on kitchen paper. Pine nuts and almonds are our favourites, but pecans are also good. Add the dried fruits and the nuts during the second beating; but remember that because they are heavy they will sink to the bottom of the freezer tray, so when serving be sure everyone gets some from the bottom of the tray as well as the top.

A few notes on other frozen puddings:

Water ices These are made on a base of sugar and water syrup and flavoured with fruit juices, wine or liqueur.

Sherbets Make a water ice and then add whipped white of eggs. This gives them their fluffy texture.

Sorbets These are water ices that have been only half frozen; they are usually flavoured with liqueur. Serve them in tall glasses.

CUSTARD SAUCE

2 cups milk
1 tablespoon sugar
1 teaspoon vanilla essence
2 whole eggs
2 egg yolks

Bring the milk to the boil, add the sugar and vanilla essence and stir until the sugar dissolves. Leave to cool just a little.

Beat the eggs and egg yolks together until they are light in colour and foamy.

Transfer the milk to a jug to make the next step easier, and trickle the milk slowly into the eggs, beating continuously.

Transfer the mixture to the top of a double boiler, and stir until it goes thick and creamy.

Serve hot as a sauce over steamed or baked puddings, or serve cold with bananas cut up into it, or as part of a trifle, or with passionfruit stirred through it.

HOMEMADE CUSTARD POWDER

900g (2 lb) rice flour
450g (1 lb) arrowroot
⅛ teaspoon imitation saffron powder
2 drops oil of bitter almond
1 drop oil of neroli (or 5 drops oil of nutmeg)

Sift together twice the rice flour, arrowroot and powdered saffron.

Put about 1 cup of the mixture in a bowl, and drop in the oils. Pound with a pestle or some heavy-ended object. Add more flour, mix thoroughly, then add all the flour.

Sift again, and store in an airtight jar to prevent the powder losing its aroma.

HOT CUSTARD (WITH HOMEMADE POWDER)

2 level tablespoons powder
2 cups milk
2 tablespoons sugar

Put the custard powder in a small bowl, and add about 3 tablespoons of the milk to it, then stir well. The powder will stick to the bottom, but will come away easily, and dissolve rapidly.

Put the rest of the milk, nearly 2 cups, in a saucepan with the sugar, and bring it to the boil.

Take the saucepan off the heat, give the custard powder a final stir to get it all off the bottom (it has a tendency to sink down when it isn't stirred), and tip the dissolved custard powder into the very hot milk, stirring continuously.

Put the saucepan back on the heat and let it boil gently for about a minute, stirring all the time.

Turn into a bowl or jug to cool, or if needed as a hot sauce, pour it over the pudding before it grows too cool.

The custard will form a skin as it cools; most people don't like it, so skim it or lift it off before serving.

Note Commercial custard powders are made of very much the same sort of ingredients, and behave in the same way when mixed with milk to make a sauce. Some powders are better than others; in Australia we have found Uncle Toby's to be excellent, and in England we like Bird's (Bird's is available in the United States, marketed as Bird's Dessert Powder).

CHOCOLATE RUM SAUCE

225g (8oz) dark chocolate
2 tablespoons butter
3 tablespoons rum (or 1 teaspoon rum essence)

Melt the chocolate and butter together in the top of a double boiler, stir well, and add the rum, stirring again.

Pour over the top of plain steamed pudding, or use to top any pudding you think will go well with it.

BRANDY BUTTER

225g (½lb) unsalted butter
1 tablespoon caster sugar (or superfine)
1 teaspoon lemon juice, well strained
6 tablespoons brandy

Pound or mash the butter until it is very soft; under no circumstances must you melt the butter.

Add the sugar, and beat until there are no grains left in the mixture.

Add the lemon juice one drop at a time, beating; then add the brandy only a very few drops at a time continuing to beat all the while.

Pile into a dish and chill.

Serve with the Christmas pudding.

9. CAKES

We have noticed that homemaking of cakes is slowly coming back, either because shopmade cakes are now mostly made in huge factories instead of in small cake-shop kitchens, or because there are so many packaged cake mixes available, and cooks are discovering that it is much cheaper to make the cakes at home even when they use package mixes.

Making your cakes from scratch is even cheaper than using packaged mixes and the result tastes better than the mixes ever could. We feel that many cooks are frightened of making cakes from scratch, possibly because if they ever did, they had failures galore. But there's no need to have failures, especially now that inferior baking powders are practically non-existent.

There is a rhythm to cake-making, and a standard proportion of ingredients which renders failure much less likely if you understand what it is all about. You should be able to look at a recipe and tell whether it will work or not by the amounts of ingredients (butter or other shortening, sugar, eggs, flour plus baking powder), and what we hope to do in this chapter is to give you all the information you need to make that kind of judgement. This will be a long introduction, but bear with us if you can, because everything we write about has an important role to play in the production of excellent cakes.

Most cakes consist of shortening, sugar, eggs and plain flour plus baking powder. There are certain recipes which don't require eggs, others which don't require shortening, but all cakes require sweetening, usually with sugar, and all cakes require flour plus baking powder except those depending upon stiffly beaten eggs for leavening power; where flour isn't used in a cake, breadcrumbs are usually substituted, for a cake must have some sort of starchy body to it.

Usually, cakes are divided into three groups: plain or ordinary, sponge, and rich or complicated. Plain cake isn't necessarily plain, it can have raisins or nuts added to it, for example, but the balance of ingredients determines what group a particular cake falls into.

Plain cake Contains shortening and sugar which never weigh more combined than the flour does alone. Half a cup (115g) of sugar plus 115g (4oz) of butter may appear in a plain cake combined with 2 cups (225g) of flour, but the moment you put more shortening and sugar by weight in a cake than you do flour, you have ceased to make a plain cake.

Some authorities say that plain cakes should always have the shortening rubbed into the flour rather than creamed together with the sugar, but Col's grandmother and Jean's mother both preferred to cream shortening and sugar, no matter what sort of cake they were making. By creaming, the mixture is smoother, more homogenous, and more conducive to rising.

Sponge cake   Contains no shortening. It is very light and fluffy, and depends for its richness upon a larger number of eggs than is usually called for.

Rich cake   Contains a weight of sugar and shortening combined that exceeds the weight of the flour. Pound cake is a rich cake, not a plain cake, even though it is plain in the meaning that it has no frills added. The old recipe is a simple one: 1lb of butter, 2lb of sugar, 1lb of flour, and 1lb of eggs (anywhere from six to ten depending on the size of the eggs). To the flour was added 4 heaped teaspoons of baking powder. Chocolate cake made of melted chocolate is a rich cake, whereas chocolate cake made of powdered cocoa or drinking chocolate is a plain cake. Fruit cake is rich cake.

In our selection of recipes, you will see a fourth kind of cake that recipe books don't discuss, but which was extremely popular in the Australian bush. Probably its popularity was due to the fact that it was hard to keep butter cool, and also because this technique is easy, quick, and its results thoroughly reliable. We are talking about the boiled cake, where all the soft or liquid ingredients except the eggs were put in a saucepan together, and boiled for a few minutes. They were then cooled, the eggs were beaten in, and finally the dry ingredients, sifted together, were added. Such cakes require a fairly long and slow cooking time, but they are really delicious, and keep well.

If you eat it every day, cake is no good for you: unless you are working very hard physically and so burn it out of your body. We think of cake as a special-occasion or once-a-week treat, and if it is regarded as such, it is neither very harmful nor very fattening. Instead of buying hideous supermarket cakes stuffed full of chemical additives to keep them fresh long after any self-respecting cake would be healthily stale, produce a proper homemade cake once a week, and limit cake-consumption to that amount. While you are making your own cakes from scratch, you can control the quality of your ingredients.

SHORTENING

A few words about the various ingredients. Only one of the four basic ingredients of a cake possesses no ability to aid in rising — sugar.

Shortening is a loose term which covers all the fats and oils used in cooking. Oils are fats which are liquid at room temperature. Per gram, all these substances contain twice the calorie content of carbohydrates or proteins, that is, they can yield twice the amount of fuel energy. Of the shortenings, butter, margarine, white vegetable shortening, dripping and lard are used in cake-making. Which kind of shortening you use is purely a matter of personal choice and taste; we have used butter in testing our recipes, but all of the different shortenings listed above have much the same ability to assist the rising of a cake, so the substitution of margarine or dripping for butter will not ruin a recipe. Where they differ is in taste and texture, and butter is almost unanimously held to be superior for both. Cake made with butter is smooth, rich, tasty and well held together. Cake made with margarine is not as rich, nor as smooth, but holds together very well, and provided eggs are used there is little difference in taste. Cake made with white vegetable shortening tends to be dry and crumbly.

Cake made with any of the animal fats (beef dripping, lamb dripping or lard) has a taste we find unappetising, and quickly becomes stale.

All shortenings help to activate flour, and aid the gluten in flour to form a framework within the cake. As the shortening melts during the cooking process, it is absorbed by starch globules, which swell and burst, and contribute to the cake's rising.

SUGAR

Sugar is incorporated to give the cake sweetness; if it is not used, a substitute must be found, but non-granulated sugar substitutes are less successful in cakes. Honey, golden syrup, corn syrup, etc., are all liquid, viscous and a more complex mixture of sugars than the one we call sugar. Their heaviness and cohesiveness makes them unsuitable for cake-making except as an ancillary agent to impart some special flavour. Sugar is crystalline, and easily dispersed through the rest of the ingredients. If you do substitute one of the liquid sugars for granulated sugar, remember to reduce the amount.

There are various kinds of sugar, each of which is suitable for a particular kind of cake. Most recipes call for ordinary white granulated sugar, which is the most highly refined form of commercially produced sucrose (whether from cane or beet makes no difference); white sugar is bleached, deodorised, and water-free. There is a finer crystalline form of white sugar used for sweetening cold drinks and other tasks requiring rapid dissolving; it is called caster (sometimes spelt castor) sugar in British countries, and superfine sugar in the U.S.A. Brown sugar may be of several different kinds; generally speaking, the darker and wetter it is, the closer it is to the liquid form of sugar which come from treatment of sugar-producing plants by boiling under pressure. Crystalline sugars are spun out of the syrups by a kind of centrifugation, and the lighter in colour they are, the less water and harmless impurities they contain.

EGGS

Eggs are incorporated into cakes to help them rise, set the matrix of the cake's structure, and impart a special and rich flavour. The more eggs in a cake, the less baking powder the flour needs to contain, for the addition of an egg will significantly contribute to rising. When beaten, eggs can be broken up into millions of tiny air bubbles, and the protein/fat composition of the egg enables it to hang on to its air bubbles much longer than, say, a beaten solution of soap and water can. During cooking, as the mixture of wet and dry ingredients in a cake are altered by heat, and 'freeze' into their final structure, the bubbles of air contained in the egg swell (hot air occupies a bigger space than the same amount of cold air), and remain fixed in the cake by the setting of the cake's constituents around them.

The above accounts for every cookbook's constant exhortations to beat the eggs well into the mixture, or beat the eggs well separately before adding them to the mixture. The more an egg is beaten, the more air bubbles it contains, and the smaller these air bubbles are. When the air bubbles are extremely small, they are stronger-walled and take a lot of bursting. If by some chance disaster occurs and all the air bubbles do burst, your wonderful egg-built edifice will sag, flop and flatten. This is what you see the first few times you try a souffle, which depends for its rising entirely upon air bubbles in the eggs. Heavy substance like syrups, sauces, and melted chocolate put a strain upon beaten egg that isn't imparted by flour, granulated sugar or well-creamed shortening. Even when you break an egg straight into a mixture, you give it air bubbles.

FLOUR

Flour is a fascinating substance. By flour we almost always mean milled (ground) grains of wheat, other flours made from grinding other grains are usually qualified in some way: as cornflour, rice flour, rye flour, etc. Wheat flour is both fibrous and starchy (starch is a more complex form of carbohydrate than sugar), rich in vitamins, bulk, and nourishment. The more refined the flour is, the less fibre it contains, and usually the fewer vitamins, though the energy constituent, starch, is unimpaired. Flour contains starch globules and gluten, this last being the proteinaceous component, fibrin. It is fibrin which gives flour it tensile strength, and the human body bulk during digestion. Unfortunately it isn't as toothsomely good to taste as the starchy part, and some of it must be removed from all flours, even those called whole wheat. However, the gluten also contains the vitamin fraction of flour, and all of its nitrogen. Gluten received its name because of its form when removed from the flour by continuous washing in water; it is then very thick and sticky, *glutinous*, from the Latin word for glue. Home-baked white breads, for instance, have plenty of gluten, therefore fibre, in them; it is the highly processed commercially produced white breads which lack fibre so markedly.

So-called cake flour is a very low-gluten, high-starch flour sometimes recommended for cake-baking; we cannot see any advantage great enough to counteract the diminution in fibre content. Its chief advantages are its lightness and receptivity to rising; high fibre content diminishes rising. If you do use this kind of flour for your cakes, don't try to make bread with it, or any mix that calls for yeast as the leavening agent. In these latter, the gluten mesh is essential to trap the bubbles of gas evolved by the growing yeast.

Nowadays ordinary white flours are carefully balanced by millers to have as close to ideal a proportion of starch versus gluten as possible - - hence the term, all-purpose flour. This is good flour, and you can bake a cake with it as easily as you can bake bread. It has a good gluten content, yet has sufficient starch to satisfy most cake-bakers.

RISING INGREDIENTS

No matter what kind of flour you use, unless you spend a large extra slice of time attending to the eggs, you must help your cake to rise, and the best way to do that is to add a rising ingredient to the flour. Why add it to the flour and not the sugar, if the two substances, rising ingredient and carrier, are quite distinct and unrelated? The rising ingredient is added to flour because flour stays quite dry even when the atmosphere around it is very damp; sugar absorbs moisture from the atmosphere, so does salt. It is absolutely essential to keep the rising ingredient bone dry until it is activated by the water in whatever liquid ingredients the cake mixture calls for. None of the elements of the rising ingredient are in the slightest bit interested in flour, so the rising ingredient stays quiet and inert within the flour until such time as you, the cook, choose to cause rising to happen.

What is the rising ingredient? Why does it make a cake or a pudding or a pancake or a scone expand to almost double its size during cooking? In the bread section we have discussed yeast as a rising ingredient, and in pastry we have shown you the expansion of chilled air when heated as a rising ingredient. In sponge-making and soufflé-making you will see how effective stiffly beaten egg can be as a rising ingredient. But all those are rather specialised ways to make a substance rise and expand; by far the commonest way is to add baking powder.

In cooking, to make a substance rise and swell and increase in size, we do things with gases. We heat a gas, cold air, which is already present in pastry, and in so doing we cause it to expand, swelling the pastry and creating tiny pockets of space within it. We take a small item such as the contents of an egg, we beat it, and we persuade it to absorb air within itself in the form of bubbles, so that what started out as about a tablespoon of white and yolk can end up as half a basinful of froth. If we are careful, and we don't break too many of the bubbles in the froth when we fold it into a mixture, we can increase the size of the mixture enormously in exactly the same way as we do pastry-air; heat it, and cause the air to expand.

Baking powder produces a gas. The gas is carbon dioxide, the same one we produce as a by-product of our oxygen metabolism. In large quantitites, and especially if breathed, it is highly poisonous. But in small quantities, and when eaten rather than breathed, it is harmless.

There are two opposing constituents in baking powder.

Unless triggered, the two substances coexist peacefully; but add water and heat to them, and they begin to react. They attack each other, use each other up, and end as two or three different things. One of these end-products is the gas carbon dioxide. The space they occupied when they were not reacting is much smaller than the amount of carbon dioxide they produce, so that when they are trapped inside a network of flour, fat and protein and sugar, the gas they evolve puffs itself into bubbles, and the whole mass expands, rises, grows bigger. Despite its new size, it is much lighter and more porous than it was before cooking, like a fine sponge full of tiny holes.

The baking powder you buy, or the baking powder which is included in self-raising flour, is a beautifully balanced combination of acid, alkali and what is called a filler or carrier substance. Modern baking powder is somewhat different in composition from the baking powders of other ages, because it has been improved enormously, and standardised.

Sodium bicarbonate is a substance which is present naturally within our bodies, and it has remained the alkali of choice in baking powders. Other carbonates have been used from time to time, but when they react with the acid component they produce unsavoury and sometimes harmful end-products, so that their use has been abandoned commercially.

A word of warning: if you are not using a commercial baking powder, but instead are using some old and cherished recipe of grandma's which you make up yourself, make sure it contains sodium bicarbonate. If it contains some other carbonate, throw it away and never use it again.

The acidic component of the older commercial baking powders is either cream of tarter or tartaric acid. Tartaric acid is stronger than cream of tartar, and less predictable. It is more easily triggered off into reacting with the bicarbonate, and its use has gradually given way to the potassium salt called cream of tartar. (Real name, potassium tartrate.) Cream of tartar is slower to react, and more easily controlled.

However, most of the commerical baking powders of today don't contain a tartrate acid; they contain a phosphoric acid derivative, usually mono-calcium phosphate, $CaH_4P_2O_8$ which is more commonly called acid calcium phosphate. In the United States baking powders must by law detail all their ingredients, but in Australia this is not law, and our tin of baking powder has 'phosphate aerators' on its side, with no reference to what sort (we presume acid calcium phosphate), and no reference to the sodium bicarbonate, or the amount of filler, or the nature of the filler.

According to Dr J.M.Hammill, the ideal baking powder is one which remains stable (that is, fully active) after the tin is opened, produces a maximum of carbon dioxide gas *only upon heating*, and leaves no nasty taste or undesirable change in the texture or colour of the item being raised.

In order to keep the acid and alkaline components peaceful in the tin, even after it has been opened, a neutral filler-substance is always added. This can be rice flour or cornflour (cornstarch), but rice flour is generally held to be the better of the two; cornflour when present at the reaction of bicarbonate and acid salt to produce carbon dioxide gas can give the item being raised an unappetising taste.

The best commerical baking powders are usually marketed in small tins, for they contain only the minimum amount of filler-substance necessary, and this filler is rice flour; products which come in a big tin are often inferior in quality, and contain much higher percentages of filler.

Some baking powders contain too much sodium bicarbonate, on the theory that the more bicarbonate there is, the more carbon dioxide gas will be evolved during cooking. Whereas only as much sodium bicarbonate as there is acid substance to react with it is useful; extra bicarbonate just sits there and gets incorporated into the human body, which doesn't need it and may find it harmful. Too much sodium bicarbonate in a baking powder makes the item being baked have a yellow, mottled appearance, and a soapy taste. Soap is a fatty alkali, so if you put too much sodium bicarbonate into a cake containing butter or other shortening, of course you will get some soap in it. (A cake of soap, ha ha.)

Acid substances other than tartrates and phosphates have been used in baking powders; alum, which is a double sulphate of aluminum and potassium was once extremely popular. However, research has proven that the breakdown products of alum during baking are harmful to health. So if your private grandma-recipe for making your own baking powder contains alum, throw it out.

No matter what its composition, any baking powder must be stored with a tight-fitting lid; whether you make it yourself or buy it from the supermarket, don't leave the lid off. Don't dip a damp or wet spoon in it, either.

Baking powders vary in how much you must use to how

much flour; ours stipulated 1 teaspoon to 1 cup of flour, or 4 teaspoons to 1 lb of flour. But yours may be different, so look at the label of the tin to check it before you use it.

If you would like to make your own baking powder, we suggest you don't bother. Just keep a packet of sodium bicarbonate and cream of tartar (preferably in bottles or jars with tight-fitting lids) in your kitchen, and use 2 teaspoons of cream of tartar to 1 teaspoon of sodium bicarbonate and mix it just before using.

SELF-RAISING FLOUR

Now to discuss self-raising flour. Most Australian women prefer to use SR flour, as they call it, than to add baking powder to plain flour. Most of the recipes in our book are not cooked with self-raising flour, but in most cases it can be substituted. The sorts of things which shouldn't be made with SR flour are biscuits (which require about one-fourth the amount of baking powder normally used for cakes), pastry (only one-eighth of a teaspoon of baking powder), sponges (egg leavening), rich heavy cakes (requiring more rising ingredient than usual). You will be able to tell where SR flour can be substituted by looking at the amount of baking powder we have stipulated and comparing it to the amount of flour. SR flour substitution can occur where the baking powder is 1 teaspoon per cup of flour, this being what our particular brand of baking powder recommended on its label. More or less baking powder means you ought to use plain flour plus baking powder.

When you think about it, using plain flour plus baking powder isn't difficult. It also serves one other useful purpose; it ensures that you sift the flour. If the baking powder is already in the flour, we know many cooks who peek into the packet, think it's beautifully sifted already, and don't sift at all. That isn't good. No matter how well sifted the flour is when it leaves the miller, it has been sitting compressed in a packet for who knows how long, and if added unsifted to a mixture, it will be lumpy.

Most self-raising flours are made of flour containing less gluten than plain flour does, so it is a soft, very white flour of lowish fibre-content. It contains rising ingredients which are usually acid calcium phosphate or sodium pyrophosphate, and sodium bicarbonate. Its release of carbon dioxide remains at between 12 per cent and 13 per cent gas by weight of baking powder.

There has been a lot of interest lately in the fibre-content of flour, and this is directly related to the amount of gluten (protein) in the flour. One British authority says that it contains something which enables the body to metabolise its fats more efficiently, with less danger of producing high blood cholesterols and fatty deposits along artery walls. He calls it fibre, and deplores the modern tendency, especially among commercial manufacturers, to bleed wheat flours of their gluten content.

Packaged cake-mixes contain even softer flours than self-raising flour, so if you use them, you must remember that you are not contributing much fibre to your diet.

MAKING AND BAKING A CAKE

Most cakes can be made, partially at least, on an electric mixer. Unless we are folding flour into a sponge, or raisins into pound cake, or something similar, we use our big electric mixer-on-a-stand: we put the bowl under the beaters, add our ingredients as they are called for and at the time they are called for, and mostly walk away from that part of the kitchen until we are going to do something else to the cake.

In the early stages, like creaming butter and sugar, or beating eggs, you can't possibly harm a cake by using the electric mixer. Great debates occur as to whether flour should be added to any cake mixture on an electric beater; a lot of people insist flour must be added by hand, and the mixture stirred gently by hand. Provided you aren't relying heavily upon lots of air bubbles in beaten eggs for your cake's main rising power, there is no reason why you can't put the flour in using your electric mixer at its slowest speed.

We decided that if cakes made from scratch were going to compete with packaged mixes, they would have to be made like a packaged mix, entirely on an electric mixer. So, barring sponges and the last stages of cakes having nuts or raisins and so on in them, we made all our cakes entirely on an electric mixer, and they were fine. The one thing you have to remember is to alter the speed at which you beat; very fast for eggs and egg whites, medium for creaming butter and sugar, and the slowest speed for adding flour. However, be warned: the electric mixer will not work for adding the flour to a sponge!

There are several things you ought to know about actually baking the cake. First, the kind of container you bake it in.

Heavy, rich mixtures like the chocolate cake receipes we give are best baked in a ring mould or Bundt mould (a Bundt mould is made of heavier material than an ordinary ring mould, and is generally contoured into pretty shapes, though it is still basically a ring mould), because if they are cooked for a long time, as fruit cakes are, they become too dry. Since the middle of a cake bakes slowest, eliminate the middle of a heavy and rich cake by baking it as a ring.

Generally, the cake batter should be just thick enough that it can't be poured out in a stream, but has to be helped along by being pushed out of the mixing bowl, and as it is pushed, it plops and slops irregularly into the cake tin. The cake tin you plan to bake it in should be about half-full of cake batter; don't fill the tin too much beyond the half-way point, or you will have cake all over the bottom of the oven.

Our recipes were designed to fill a large ring mould if to be baked in a ring, or a fairly deep-sided 10 cm (4 in) tin, 20 cm (8 in) in diameter, or a square deep-sided 10 cm (4 in) tin, 20 cm (8 in) by 20 cm (8 in). Sponge mixtures are baked in tins having much shallower sides, and our sponge mixture has been designed to half fill two tins 10 cm (8 in) diameter, with sides about 4 cm (1½ in) high. Our Lamington mixture has been designed to fill a rectangular tin 20 cm (8 in) by 30 cm (12 in), its sides being shallow like a sponge tin, about 4 cm (1½ in) deep.

Use good quality cake tins for baking, not thin old tins that cause the cake's sides and bottom to burn long before the middle can be cooked.

A cake tin must be well prepared if the cake isn't going to stick to its sides and bottom during baking. We keep a block of white vegetable shortening just for this kind of job and, using a piece of kitchen paper, adequately smear the inside of the cake tin with this (it is cheap, it has no salt, and it seems to work best), taking care that corners get a little bit more shortening, and that the paper we are using hasn't missed the junction between sides and bottom. Then we put about a tablespoon of plain flour into the tin, and shake it around until every bit of the shortening has flour stuck to it; then we rap the tin smartly to collect all the unused flour in one spot, turn the tin upsidedown over a piece of paper, or the sink, or a container, and shake all the surplus flour out, rapping the tin's bottom smartly to make sure there is no flour only partially sticking to the shortening. If there are any spots where the flour is not sticking, we know we have missed that spot with the shortening and this is remedied.

Cakes done like this will not stick, unless they are left in the tin too long during cooling. There is a happy medium; you should remove a cake from the oven and leave it for about 5 to 10 minutes in its tin, this depending upon the thickness of the cake; the thicker, the closer to 10 rather than 5 minutes. Then carefully turn the tin upside-down over a wire rack, or place the wire rack over the top of the tin, and carefully turn the whole thing upsidedown.

Don't use butter or margarine to grease a cake tin — white vegetable shortening works much better.

Large fruit cakes are cooked slightly differently. Here, the object of the exercise is to stop the cake's outsides burning during the enormously long and slow baking process. Take a large sheet of strong thick brown paper and a pair of scissors. Fold the brown paper double. Trace the outline of the cake tin's bottom on the paper, and cut out two thicknesses of paper in the shape of the tin's bottom. Measure the sides of the tin, then cut out a long double-thick strip of paper three times as deep as the sides of the tin.

Put the shapes of paper down on a space where getting a bit of grease around doesn't matter, and smear both thicknesses of brown paper very well with white vegetable shortening. Then put the two shapes meant for the bottom, both greased, into the tin; they should fit snugly.

Take the long piece of double thickness paper you have cut three times as high as the sides of the tin, and put it inside the tin to line the sides. Since it is so much taller, it will protrude high above the top of the tin's sides. Make sure the strip is long enough to meet, and have a few centimetres (or an inch or two) of overlap.

After you have put the mixture in the tin, take the scissors and cut the protruding high sides of brown paper into ribbons about 2½cm (1in) wide (a bit like a child's paper party hat). Then crease the ribbons just above the tin's top and fold them inward towards the centre of the cake, but don't let any of the ribbons actually touch the cake surface and stick to it. The object of these ribbons bending inwards over the cake's top is rather like opening an umbrella in bright sunlight — for shade from the heat. Unless you protect the top of the cake as well as its sides and bottoms, it too will burn, and these brown paper ribbons bent inward do a good job.

The temperature at which a cake cooks depends upon its type. Sponges cook hottest and shortest, because they are the thinnest and lightest of cakes; fruit cakes for weddings and Christmas cook slowest and longest, because they are the biggest and heaviest of cakes. A good cake recipe indicates the temperature at which the cake should cook, but sometimes, if you are working from an old book especially, there is no indication as to what sort of oven is necessary, or how long baking should continue. Sponges are usually baked at 210°C (400°F), plain cakes and heavy cakes at 175°C (350°F), and fruit cakes at 150°C (300°F), or even lower, if the fruit cake is a massive bottom tier of a wedding cake.

Swiss roll cakes (and other sorts of cake you want to do things with immediately after they come out of the oven) must be baked on brown paper, because you can't leave them to cool in their tins for that little time necessary to turn a cake out of its tin without sticking.

To make a Swiss roll, you bake the cake in a rectangular tin about 20cm (8in), by 30cm (12in), well lined with a single thickness of brown paper greased with vegetable shortening. Immediately it is cooked, it is turned out on to a piece of aluminium foil sprinkled with caster sugar (superfine granulated) its edges are trimmed away, it is spread with jam or butter cream, and then rolled up. If butter cream is used, you must wait for the cake to cool a little, and it will then be more difficult to roll up, but if you have used a mixture rich in eggs, it will still roll when cool without cracking. Wrap it in foil so it can't unroll, until it is quite cold and set into its shape.

Don't line cake tins with aluminium foil. Use only heavy brown paper or unwaxed kitchen paper. Aluminium foil is a heat insulator, and will not permit the cake to bake at the true oven temperature.

How can you tell when a cake is properly cooked, even in its middle? Our mothers always had a straw broom handy, and if you ever look at a straw broom, it has wee bits of straw poking out of it, well above the dirty level. Mother would pluck such a straw out, and thrust it into the middle of the cake; if it came out clean, the cake was cooked. Nowadays, cooks mostly use a thin steel skewer, and thrust it into the cake in the same way. When it comes out, you mustn't merely look at it; run your fingers down it, too. Cakes which are properly cooked often shrink away from the sides of the tin; they may also crack and fissure on their tops, though this usually means too much baking powder was added.

Little cakes bake in a 210°C (400°F) oven for about 15 to 20 minutes; any of the recipes given in this chapter can be made into little cakes if you would prefer, though some sorts of mixtures aren't suitable, and we advise you to choose carefully. We have given only two recipes for little cakes, Lamingtons and fairy cakes, which are two traditional Australian versions. But if you like little cakes better than big ones, go right ahead and choose another of our recipes.

POUND CAKE

225g (8oz) butter
1 cup sugar
6 large eggs
2 cups plain flour
2 heaped teaspoons baking powder

If you have one, you can use an electric mixer for the whole of this recipe, but remember to drop the speed to the lowest setting when you begin to add flour.

Cream together the butter and sugar.

Beat the eggs separately, then add them to the creamed butter and sugar, and beat well again.

Sift together the flour and baking powder, then add it gradually to the mixture, stirring or mixing gently.

Turn the mixture into a deep-sided round or square 20cm (8in) tin, which has been well greased and floured.

Bake in a 180°C (350°F) oven for 45 to 50 minutes, or until a skewer thrust deeply into the middle of the case comes out without mixture adhering to it.

Turn the cake on to a wire rack to cool. Traditionally, pound cake is not iced or otherwise decorated; when served it can be buttered and 'jammed' as if it were bread.

Pound cake gets its name from the amount of ingredients used — 1 lb butter, 1 lb of sugar, 1 lb of flour, 1 lb of eggs — but most recipes, as this one does, cut that mixture in half, so perhaps it ought to be called half-pound cake.

SEED CAKE

250g (8oz) butter
1 cup sugar
6 large eggs

3 tablespoons caraway seeds
2 cups plain flour
2 heaped teaspoons baking powder

This is another recipe which can be made entirely in an electric mixer. Remember to use the lowest speed setting when you begin to add the flour.

Beat together the butter and sugar until they are creamed and pale in colour.

In a separate bowl, beat the eggs well, then add them to the creamed butter and sugar, again beating well.

Add the caraway seeds.

Sift the flour together with the baking powder, then add them gradually to the mixture, mixing gently on the lowest speed if you are using an electric beater, otherwise stirring gently with a large wooden or Melamine spoon.

Turn the batter into a well greased and floured deep-sided round cake tin with 20cm (8in) diameter.

Bake in a 180°C (350°F) oven for 45 to 50 minutes, or until a clean dry skewer thrust deeply into the middle of the cake comes out smooth and not sticky.

Turn on to a wire rack to cool. This cake is never iced or filled with cream but served quite plain.

AN ALL-PURPOSE CAKE MIXTURE

225g (½lb) butter
1½ cups sugar
4 eggs
1 cup milk
3 cups plain flour
3 teaspoons baking powder

Cream the butter and sugar, then add the eggs one at a time, beating each well in before adding another, and beating the last one well before adding the milk, which should be trickled in while you beat.

Sift together the flour and baking powder, then carefully and gradually stir it into the mixture.

This mixture can be used for almost anything; patty cakes, slab cakes, as a basis for fancy mixtures, for Lamingtons, or whatever you like.

If you want to flavour it, add 1 teaspoon of essence to the milk before beating the milk into the mixture.

If you want to colour it, add the colouring a couple of drops at a time to the batter before adding the flour.

You can add 1 cup of desiccated coconut, and it turns into coconut cake.

One cup of raisins turns it into Australian brownie.

Baked in a big shallow rectangular tin, it can be used as the basis for a Swiss roll.

Add 1 tablespoon golden syrup (or honey), plus 2 teaspoons ground ginger, and you have a ginger cake.

Divide it in three, add red colouring to one-third to turn it pink, plus a little strawberry essence; put a tablespoon of drinking chocolate in another third, and leave the last third plain. You then have the basis for rainbow cake or marble cake.

For rainbow cake, bake each third separately in a small rectangular tin, then sandwich together the three layers with mock cream or butter cream, and a thin layer of jam.

For marble cake, colour and flavour the three parts separately, then tip them all back into the same bowl, and very gently stir them into big swirls, only once or twice, twisting the spoon in your hand as you stir. In this way, the three colours will be swirled all through the cake without being very mixed together.

For patty cakes, or a thin large-area cake like Swiss roll or rainbow cake, bake in a 210°C (400°F) oven from 15 minutes (patty cakes) to 25 minutes for the bigger, thicker layer squares.

If you put the cake mixture fairly thickly in a tall-sided tin, bake it at 175°C (350°F) for about 35 to 40 minutes.

LAMINGTONS

1. The cake
¾ cup sugar
180g (6oz) butter (or margarine)
4 eggs
3 cups plain flour
3 teaspoons baking powder
1 cup lukewarm water

Cream together the butter and sugar (in a mixer if you have one).

In another bowl, beat the eggs until foamy and light, then add them to the butter and sugar, and beat again.

Tip the cup of barely warm water into the bowl, and beat again until it is well mixed.

Sift together the flour and baking powder, then add it to the mixture a small amount at a time, stirring gently or using the electric mixer on its slowest speed.

Pour the batter into a well greased and floured rectangular tin, 20 cm (8 in) by 30 cm (12 in), and bake at 175°C (350°F) for 30 to 35 minutes, until a skewer thrust deeply into the middle comes out clean and dry.

Turn the cake on to a wire rack to cool, let it get thoroughly cold, then slice it with a very sharp knife into blocks about 5 cm by 7½ cm (2 by 3 in).

2. The covering icing
2 cups sifted icing sugar (confectioner's)
3 tablespoons powdered drinking chocolate (or cocoa)
1 cup runny chocolate syrup, such as icecream topping
½ cup very hot water

Sift together the icing sugar and then the powdered drinking chocolate in a bowl, then add the chocolate syrup and stir until there are no lumps. Tip in the hot water, beating as you do so, and continue to beat until the mixture is smooth and very runny.

3. The putting-together
blocks of cake
runny chocolate icing
2 cups desiccated coconut

Pour the chocolate icing mixture into a small tray with low sides.

Put the desiccated coconut into another tray.

Take a block of cake, and sit it in the runny chocolate icing for about a minute, then turn it over, let it sit a minute, and keep turning it until all its sides have been soaked in the icing; the icing should actually soak into the cake, rather than coat it.

Take the cake out of the icing, and very thoroughly, but gently, roll it in the coconut.

Put each block on a wire rack to dry, about 1 hour, then store in a tightly lidded tin.

This recipe makes about fifteen blocks.

STRAWBERRY LAMINGTONS

This is the same recipe, except that instead of using chocolate in the icing, use strawberry icecream topping syrup, and omit the chocolate powder from the icing sugar.

MADEIRA CAKE

225g (½lb) butter
1 cup caster sugar
4 eggs
2 cups plain flour
½ teaspoon baking powder — optional
lemon essence
candied orange (or citron peel)

Madeira cake is often erroneously called a plain cake because its flavouring is only lemon essence and it contains no fruit. It is really a rich cake, as you can see from the quantities of eggs and butter to flour. Do not be confused by the optional baking powder — if you beat your eggs thoroughly you will not need baking powder; however, if you are in a hurry, it is wise to add that half teaspoon of baking powder.

Prepare an oblong loaf tin, 20cm by 10cm (7 by 3½in).
Cream the butter and sugar.

Add the eggs, one at a time, beating continually until the mixture is uniform and stiff.

Fold in the flour (sifted with the baking powder, if you are using it). The mixture should be soft so that it will drop easily from the mixing spoon. If you have added too much flour, 1 teaspoon or 2 of milk will not spoil the end result, but be careful not to make the mix too thin.

Add the lemon essence, the quantity depending on your own preference for strong lemon flavour or gentle lemon flavour.

Transfer the mixture to the prepared loaf tin and bake at 175°C (350°F) for 1½ to 1¾ hours, or until the testing skewer comes out clean.

The traditional decoration for a Madeira cake consists of candied orange or citron peel on the top. However, wait until the cake is partly cooked, i.e., the mixture has set, before adding the peel, otherwise it will sink into the cake.

Turn on to a wire rack to cool.

We have given the basic Madeira cake recipe, but you can experiment with different flavouring essences or even with liqueurs.

JEWISH CAKE

4 tablespoons butter
8 tablespoons sugar
3 eggs
2 tablespoons milk
1 cup plain flour
1 heaped teaspoon baking powder
2 heaped teaspoons cinnamon

Cream the butter and sugar thoroughly, then add the eggs one at a time, beating each well into the mixture.

Add the milk and beat again.

Sift together the dry ingredients, then gradually and gently stir them into the mixture.

Grease and flour a rectangular 20cm by 30cm (8 by 12in) tin, and pour the batter into it.

Bake at 210°C (400°F) for about 20 minutes.

Turn the cake on to a wire rack and cool, then split the cake in half with a very sharp knife, and spread it with raspberry jam before sandwiching the halves together again. Dust the top of the cake with icing sugar.

RICH CHOCOLATE CAKE

225g (8oz) dark chocolate
4 eggs
¾ cup sugar
115g (4oz) butter
2 cups plain flour
2 heaped teaspoons baking powder

If you have one, you may use an electric mixer for the entire cake-making.

Break the eggs into a bowl large enough to accommodate, eventually, the whole of the cake mixture. Beat the eggs until light and frothy, then start gradually adding the sugar, and continuing to beat. We beat together our eggs and sugar for 30 minutes on the electric mixer.

Melt together the chocolate and the butter over hot water

in the double boiler, or if you don't possess one, put the chocolate and butter in a small saucepan, and sit it in a larger saucepan half-filled with boiling water. As the butter and chocolate melt, you will see small bits of white fat in the butter, but as you keep stirring they diappear. If you clarify the butter first, you won't see this, but we preferred not to clarify the butter, since this is a cake mixture, and butter for incorporation in cakes is not clarified.

Let the chocolate and butter mixed together cool to room temperature; if you do this melting process at the same time as you start to beat your eggs, just keep beating eggs and sugar until the chocolate is cool again.

Slowly trickle the chocolate when cool into the egg and sugar mixture, and continue to beat until it is all well mixed.

Gradually add the flour, folding it rather than stirring.

Turn the batter into a ring mould or Bundt pan, well greased and floured, and bake in a 175°C (350°F) oven for about 40 minutes, or until a skewer thrust deeply into the cake comes out clean and dry.

Turn the cake on to a wire rack to cool, and when cold ice with real chocolate icing.

REAL CHOCOLATE ICING

225g (8oz) dark chocolate
2 tablespoons clarified butter (or ordinary butter)

In the top of a double boiler, or in a small pan sitting in a larger one half full of boiling water, put the chocolate and the butter, and let them melt thoroughly.

Stir them until they are properly blended, then trickle the liquid over the cake, and when set, trickle another layer over the top of the first. You can build up layers of chocolate until you've used up all your mixture. The cake will keep fresher if you manage to coat every bit of it with the chocolate, thus sealing it from the air.

Chocolate made with butter is glossy. There is no reason why you can't substitute white vegetable shortening for the butter, but it tends to make the chocolate taste less appetising, and will be dull in finish. Hot water or hot milk added to the chocolate will also thin it, but when it sets again it will be leathery, and again it will be dull in finish. However, if you wish to use a substitute for butter, to every 225g (8oz) of dark chocolate, add 2 tablespoons of white vegetable shortening, or 2 tablespoons of hot water, or 2 tablespoons of hot milk.

Note   Chocolate will dissolve in water provided that the chocolate is melted first and the water is very hot when added. Never use more than 3 tablespoons of water to 225g (8oz) of chocolate if you want it to set again. We prefer butter or white vegetable shortening to water or milk.

ACCIDENTAL CHOCOLATE CAKE

This is what we made out of the chocolate cream which turned to butter when we were making the Saint Honore cake, rather than waste 2 cups of cream just because it went to butter. This 'accidental cake' will rank among the best chocolate cakes you have ever encountered. It can be made entirely with an electric mixer, except for its covering coat of chocolate.

2 cups cream
2 tablespoons powdered drinking chocolate
1 tablespoon sugar
4 eggs
3 cups plain flour
3 heaped teaspoons baking powder
1 cup chocolate syrup (as used for icecream topping)

Beat the cream with the powdered drinking chocolate and the sugar until it gets very stiff, and then begins to curdle; it is now at the first stage of butter, but do not take it any further or it will begin to separate and ooze watery fluid.

Break the eggs into the mixture all at once, and beat until the eggs have been well assimilated by the near-butter. Add the cup of chocolate syrup and beat the mixture again. The mixture, which will have looked smooth after the eggs were beaten in, will now begin to look a little curdled again.

Turn the mixer speed to its lowest setting, and slowly add the flour and baking powder, which have been sifted together. Do not add too much flour at once, and make sure that what you do add is well mixed before adding more.

Turn the mixture, which should be a smooth thick batter needing a helping hand to move into its tins, into two shallow-sided 20cm (8in) cake tins, well greased and floured. Bake at 180°C (350°F) for 35 to 40 minutes, or until a clean dry skewer thrust into the middle of the cake comes out without mixture adhering to it.

Ice with real chocolate icing (page 243).

SPONGE CAKE

6 eggs
¾ cup sugar
1½ cups plain flour
⅛ teaspoon baking powder

Put the eggs and sugar together in a bowl, preferably one attached to an electric mixer, and beat them for 40 minutes (Col's grandma used to beat her eggs and sugar together for a whole hour without stopping — by hand!)

At the finish of beating, the mixture should be more than twice its original volume, pale straw in colour, and so light it is difficult to see bubbles in it because they are individually so tiny.

Sift together the flour and tiny bit of baking powder, and add it to the beaten eggs and sugar very, very slowly and carefully; use the biggest spoon you have, and turn the mixture over rather than stir it — the less you disturb the bubbles in the egg, the better the cake will rise, and the lighter it will be.

Turn the mixture into two 20cm (8in) shallow-sided tins which have been well greased and floured, and bake in a 210°C (400°F) oven for about 20 minutes, or until the tops are lightly browned, and the cakes have shrunk slightly away from the sides of their tins. *Don't open the oven door during the first 15 minutes of cooking.*

Turn the cakes on to a wire rack to cool. If you have really succeeded, they will be so light you will have trouble getting them out of their tins.

When the cakes are thoroughly cold, sandwich them together with jam and cream, or whatever filling you fancy. You can ice the top if you wish, but a true sponge is not iced, it is just dusted with icing (confectioner's) sugar and served as soon as possible after baking. You can make the sugar-dusting into patterns by placing one of those paper mats, embossed and cut to look crochet work, on top of the cake before you dust; when you remove the mat you will have the pattern in sugar-dusting on the cake.

FAIRY CAKES

These are miniature sponge cakes, and are made as a sponge cake is. They don't rise very much during cooking, but have a delightfully even-topped appearance which is easy to ice. Unlike a large sponge, they must be iced — half of them with pale pink icing, half with white.

4 eggs
½ cup white sugar
1 cup plain flour
⅛ teaspoon baking powder
icing sugar and a little water for frosting afterwards

Combine the eggs and sugar, and beat them together for 30 minutes (using an electric mixer if you have one), until the mixture is pale straw in colour, and stiff, with very tiny air bubbles.

Sift together, the flour and smidgin of baking powder, then add this very carefully and gradually to the mixture, using the biggest spoon you have, and turning the mixture over rather than stirring it. You must try not to break up the bubbles in the egg. Don't use the electric mixer!

Turn the batter a spoonful at a time into two trays of patty tins, making sure you have greased and floured the tins first. Fill each tin just to the top with batter.

Bake in a 210°C (400°F) oven for 10 to 15 minutes, until the little cakes are a light golden brown. Don't open the oven door during the first 10 minutes!

Turn the little cakes on to a wire rack to cool, and when they are quite cold, ice them with a fairly runny mixture of the icing (confectioner's) sugar and water, but don't forget to divide it in half and ice half the cakes with pale pink, and half with white.

Store tightly lidded; this recipe makes about twenty-four fairy cakes.

BOILED FRUIT CAKE

5 tablespoons butter
1 cup water
3 cups sultanas (raisins)
½ cup chopped peel (citron)
1 cup dark brown sugar

¼ *teaspoon nutmeg*
¼ *teaspoon cinnamon*
¼ *teaspoon salt*
1 *teaspoon cocoa powder (or powdered drinking chocolate)*

Put all these ingredients into a large saucepan and bring them to the boil, then boil them gently for 3 minutes, stirring occasionally.

Let the mixture cool off.

1 *tablespoon coffee essence (or instant coffee powder)*
2 *eggs, well beaten*
2¼ *cups plain flour*
1 *teaspoon baking powder*
1 *teaspoon bicarbonate of soda*
2 *tablespoons sherry (or brandy or rum)*

Sift together the dry ingredients.

Stir the eggs and liquor into the cooled boiled mixture, then add the sifted dry ingredients. Mix well.

Line a 20cm (8in) tall-sided tin with one layer of greased brown paper, bottom and sides, and make sure you have enough paper higher than the top of the tin to cut into ribbons.

Put the mixture in the tin, fold the ribboned top of the paper inwards over the centre of the cake, and bake in a 175°C (350°F) oven for about 90 minutes.

The cake is cooked when it is firm and springy to pressure of the fingers, or when a skewer comes out without any mixture on it — the skewer will be sticky, because of the fruit in the cake.

Cool the cake in its tin. When it is quite cold, you can add ½ cup of brandy (or rum) to the cake by piercing it gently in a few places with a skewer, then trickling the liquor over the cake's top.

If you prefer your cake without added liquor, after it is cold and has been turned out of its tin, and the paper peeled away, ice it thinly with a mixture of icing (confectioner's) sugar mixed with orange or lemon juice instead of water.

We are indebted to Mrs Joyce Byfield of Merriwa, N.S.W., for this recipe.

PINEAPPLE FRUIT CAKE

1 cup sugar
1 can (450g) pineapple, crushed
3 cups sultanas (raisins)
1 teaspoon bicarbonate of soda
1 teaspoon mixed spice (or spices of choice)
115g (4oz) butter

Boil together all these ingredients for 3 minutes in a saucepan.
    Let the mixture get quite cold.

2 eggs, well beaten
2 cups plain flour
1 teaspoon baking powder

Stir the eggs into the cooled mixture, then sift together the
dry ingredients and add them gradually, mixing well.
    Line a 20cm (8in) high-sided round pan with brown paper
that has been well greased; make sure the paper is much higher
than the sides of the tin.
    Pour the batter into the tin, then cut the paper top into
ribbons and bend them inwards over the top of the cake,
making sure none of them actually fall into the mixture.
    Bake for 2 hours at 160°C (325°F), then let the cake grow
cold in its tin before turning it out and peeling the brown
paper away.
    Ice with a mixture of icing (confectioner's) sugar and pine-
apple juice.

DATE AND NUT SQUARES

2 eggs
½ cup sugar
½ teaspoon vanilla essence
¾ cup plain flour
¾ teaspoon baking powder
½ teaspoon cinnamon
1 cup walnuts, chopped
2 cups dates, finely chopped

Beat the eggs until foamy, then beat in the sugar and the
vanilla essence.
    Sift the flour, baking powder and cinnamon together, then
add it slowly and gradually to the cake mixture.
    Finally add the walnuts and the dates, and mix well.
    Spread in a rectangular tin, 20 by 30cm (8 by 12in), which

has been well greased and floured first, and bake at 160°C (325°F) for about 25 to 35 minutes, until the top has a dull crust.

Turn out the cake on to a wire rack, and when it is cold, cut it into squares.

CLAUDIE'S CHEESE CAKE

1. The cracker crust
8 wholemeal biscuits (grahams)
3 tablespoons sugar
6 tablespoons soft butter
1 teaspoon cinnamon

Crush the wholemeal biscuits to fine crumbs — they will make about 1⅓ cups of crumbs. Mix together the butter, sugar and cinnamon until they are well blended.

Stir the crumbs into the mixture, and tamp it into a doughy mass.

Press the mixture all over the bottom and sides of a 20 cm (8 in) spring-pan with fairly high sides, so that it is about 6 mm (¼ in) thick.

Chill it in the refrigerator for 30 minutes.

Then bake the crust at 160°C (325°F) for 10 to 15 minutes, until lightly browned.

Cool it in the pan.

2. The cheese filling
750 g (1½ lb) Philadelphia cream cheese
1½ teaspoons vanilla essence
1 cup sugar
5 egg yolks
5 egg whites

Let the cream cheese stand at room temperature for about 6 hours, or until it is very soft.

When it is very soft, cream it with the cup of sugar, then one by one add the egg yolks, beating continuously and thoroughly between each one. At the end of the egg yolks, add the vanilla and beat again.

In a separate bowl, beat the egg whites until they are stiff enough to stand up in peaks.

Gently and carefully fold the egg whites into the main mixture.

Pour the filling into the pan containing the baked crust, and bake in a 190°C (375°F) oven for 30 minutes. Carefully remove it from the oven and let it stand in the mould for 10 minutes.

Increase the oven temperature to 240°C (450°F).

3. The topping

1 cup sour cream
1 teaspoon vanilla
2 tablespoons caster (or superfine) sugar

Mix the sour cream, vanilla and sugar together, then slowly and carefully spread it on top of the cheese cake, evening it out.

Make sure the oven heat is well up to 240°C (450°F) and bake again for 5 minutes to set the topping.

Remove the cake from the oven and cool it thoroughly in the mould. Let the cake stand in the refrigerator for 12 hours before turning it out of its mould and serving it.

AUSTRALIAN BROWNIE

This is one of the shearer's cook specialties, and was a great favourite with all Australians during colonial days. It is not like American brownie, because it contains no chocolate.

2 cups sugar
2 cups sultanas (raisins)
1 cup water
225g (½lb) butter
¼ teaspoon salt

Put the ingredients into a saucepan, bring them to the boil, and boil gently for 3 minutes, stirring. Let the mixture get quite cool.

4 cups plain flour
1 teaspoon bicarbonate of soda
2 teaspoons baking powder
1 teaspoon allspice
1 teaspoon nutmeg
1 teaspoon cinnamon
1 teaspoon ginger

Sift all these ingredients together, gradually stir them into the cooled mixture, and mix well.

Take the dish you use to roast a leg of lamb or a piece of beef in, and line it with two layers of greased brown paper. Pour the batter in and even it out.

Bake it at 170°C (350°F) for 60 minutes, then turn it on to a wire rack and cool, leaving the paper around it until it is cool before peeling away the paper.

Serve it sliced and buttered.

If you prefer, you can turn the mixture into papered loaf tins instead of the roasting pan, and bake at the same temperature for about 55 minutes, or until a skewer comes out clean. However, the shearer's cook never carried such things as cake or loaf tins, and did all his baking in the same dish, no matter whether it was a roast of meat, brownie or scones!

We are grateful to Mrs J.M.Hodgson of Eulabar, Merriwa, N.S.W., for this recipe.

10. BISCUITS (COOKIES)

Home-made buscuits (cookies) have fallen sadly out of fashion since young girls no longer undergo an apprenticeship in mother's kitchen, and since manufactured biscuits have become available in such variety. Biscuits used to be a child's first step on the road to good kitchencraft, for they're very easy to make, and the taste is ample reward for the labour involved. Biscuits also teach the learner-cook a lot about ovens, textures of finished products, the difference between crispness and softness, what dough is, how to roll things out without sticking, and how to organise space and time.

The most wonderful thing about biscuits is that they rarely fail to live up to their recipe-book promise; there's no falling-in-the-middle syndrome, and about the worst fate that can befall them is over-cooking. However, since it doesn't matter how often the oven door is opened while they bake, nor how soon after they're put in, even this risk of burning is minimal. We think the best burners of biscuits are not the beginner cooks, but the old hands at it, who aren't tempted to peek and who go off to do something else without remembering that biscuits only take ten minutes.

When Col was a little girl, living in the super-tropical horrors of North Queensland, her mother devised a new biscuit recipe, and tried it out on her own offspring as well as a number of other children. The biscuits were a dismal failure, but all the kids adored them; they were rock-hard, and you might have thought quite indigestible. But all the kids christened them 'dog biscuits', and used to beg for more, much to Mother McCullough's chagrin. On the other hand, when she made meltingly light and eminently edible biscuits, no one showed much interest or enthusiam. The moral of this story is that children love very hard and crunchy things — maybe it's teething!

So when it came to biscuits, we thought the best course of action was to give you a basic recipe, and follow that up with some of the variations on this basic theme; only after that have we branched out into a few specialised recipes for the biscuit classics of our youths.

We have used butter, but you can substitute margarine or even soft white vegetable shortening, and still produce proper home-made tasting biscuits.

We haven't used self-raising flour, for on the whole biscuits require less leavening than cakes or scones, and therefore the amount of rising ingredient in self-raising flour is too much. For routine biscuits, about one-fourth the quantity of baking powder needed for cakes is used. Biscuits don't (and shouldn't) rise very much, for if they do, they lose their essentially biscuity crunch. They are one of the few kinds of food meant to be crisp all the way through. Unless you're making kisses or melting moments or shortbread, this is a pretty hard and fast rule.

There are very few ways in which you can go wrong. Perhaps the commonest way is to make the dough too wet, and then you'll be struggling with sticky glop. However, the basic recipe we have given (and most of the specialised ones also) contains only one source of moisture, a large egg, and it shouldn't be necessary to add any further liquid. When you've got all the flour (sifted together with its baking powder) in, the mixture will look too dry, and you may be tempted to add a little milk before beginning to knead. Don't. Before you resort to that, knead your crumbly dough, and you'll see it begins to form nicely, and that your hands aren't terribly sticky as a result of kneading. If you still think it's too dry, pick the wad of dough up in your hands and press it around between your palms a few times. This melts the butter or other shortening a bit, which will enable you to get every loose crumb into the main ball. If it cracks on the sides during rolling out, don't worry; it blends back together again easily, and you can avoid the cracked edges when cutting your biscuits out. When you've cut the first lot of biscuits, you'll find your dough compresses and fuses back together just as easily in preparation for a second rolling-out and the cutting of more biscuits; it will do so a third time, and at no stage should you need to add further moisture, in spite of the extra flour incorporated by rolling.

If you have a pastry-sheet, use it for rolling out, just as you would for pastry. And if you have a cold-water rolling pin use it too, only you needn't fill it. Biscuit dough contains nothing to resist the weight of a feather-light pin.

Use an egg flipper-overer (we would love to know if there is a proper name for an egg flipper-overer, but no one seems to know of one, so we oscillate between calling it an egg flipper, an egg turner, and usually add overer onto the end) to slip under your cut-out shapes on the pastry sheet, and slide them onto the baking tray in the same movement.

Grease the tray with a little white vegetable shortening on a piece of kitchen paper; it is not necessary to flour the tray as well.

The baking temperature for most biscuits is fairly high, around 210°C (400°F) for flat thin biscuits, and 185°C (375°F) for the thicker biscuits made from balls of dough and pressed a little in the middle.

Biscuits can be wonderfully 'tarted up' with thin icing drizzled over them in various colours, hundreds-and-thousands (nonpariels) sprinkled into the still-damp icing, coloured sugars sprinkled onto an egg glaze; they can have nuts or cherries pressed into their tops; they can be sandwiched together with icing or jam, or both; they can be coated all over with chocolate; they can be cut into marvellous shapes and made with icing and piping to look like anything from Christmastime Santas to spaceships to gingerbread men. At children's parties, they very often turn out to be the most popular food item on the loaded table, especially if you're gifted at decorating.

BASIC BISCUIT MIXTURE

8 tablespoons (115g, 4ozs) white sugar
115g (4ozs) butter, margarine or other shortening
1 large egg
2 cups (225g, 8ozs) plain flour
1 heaped teaspoon baking powder

Cream the butter and sugar together, then add the egg to them and mix well.

Sift the flour and baking powder together, and add them to the mixture a little at a time, again mixing well.

By the end of the stipulated quantity of flour, the dough should be just right for rolling out, and it should not be necessary to add further moisture. However, if you find it too stiff and crumbly to work, add a teaspoon of milk, knead again, and see what it's like before adding another teaspoon of milk.

You can now proceed in one of three ways:

1. Flat Biscuits
Roll the dough out as thinly as you can (3mm or ⅛ in) should not be beyond the capability of the dough), and cut out the biscuits with a glass tumbler or special cutters.

Bake on a greased tray in a 210°C (400°F) oven for about

ten minutes, or until the brown of the undersides starts to creep up over the edges onto the tops — they always brown first underneath, so if you let them get very brown on top, they'll be burned underneath.

Turn them out onto a wire rack to cool, and store them in a tightly lidded container so they don't lose their crispness. They can be decorated or sandwiched together as you wish.

This recipe makes about 40 biscuits.

2. Balled Biscuits

Shape the dough into a lump, and pinch bits off it with your fingers. Each bit is to be rolled into a ball about 25mm (1in) in diameter, or, if you're not the mathematical type, into a ball about halfway in size between a marble and a ping-pong ball. You could perhaps use a melon-baller; this would give a ball about the right size, but you'd have to roll it between your palms a bit more, to push the particles in it more firmly together.

Place each ball on a greased baking sheet with plenty of space around it, and gently press your thumb into the centre-top of the ball, squashing it outwards and flattening it a little.

Alternatively, you can roll each bit into a ball, and use an egg flipper or a spatula to squash the balls into fairly flat rounds, but you mustn't squash them so much their edges crumble; biscuit dough tends to crumble at the edges when too much pressure is applied.

Bake at 185°C (375°F) for about fifteen minutes, or until the outsides are beginning to brown; watch the lowest parts of the sides, as these brown faster than the top.

Turn them onto a wire rack to cool, and store in a tightly-lidded container.

This recipe makes about 30 biscuits.

3. Cylinder-rolled and cut biscuits

Roll the dough into a long, fat cylinder shape, and using the sharpest knife you possess, slice coins about 3mm (⅛ in) thick off it. If you can manage to make your slices this thin, you can proceed as if they were flat biscuits as to baking temperature and time; the thicker your coin slices are, the closer the oven temperature should be to 185°C (375°F), and the longer they will take to cook.

Using this same method, you can roll your dough out fairly thinly, then sprinkle it with chopped nuts, chopped raisins or sultanas, chopped cherries, etc, before rolling it up into a cylinder. If you have stuffed the roll in this way, cut the coins thicker, about 6mm (¼in), and bake at 185°C (375°F).

VARIATIONS ON THE BASIC THEME

Custard Biscuits
Add 2 tablespoons of custard powder to the flour and baking powder before sifting (so you can sift them all together) and proceed as for flat biscuits.

Chocolate Biscuits
Before sifting, add 2 tablespoons of powdered drinking chocolate to the flour and baking powder, sift together, and proceed as for flat biscuits.

Orange or Lemon Biscuits
Add 1 teaspoon of dried powdered orange or lemon peel to the flour and baking powder before sifting, sift them all together, and proceed as for flat biscuits.

Plain Ginger Biscuits
Before sifting, add 1 tablespoon of gound ginger to the flour and baking powder, sift them all together, and proceed as for flat biscuits.

Spiced Biscuits
Add to the flour and baking powder before sifting 1 teaspoon of cinnamon and 1 teaspoon of allspice, sift them all together, and proceed as for flat biscuits.

Malt Biscuits
Before sifting, add 2 tablespoons malted milk powder (such as Horlicks) to the flour and baking powder, sift them all together, and proceed as for flat biscuits.

Coffee Biscuits
Add 1 tablespoon powdered instant coffee to the flour and baking powder before sifting, sift together, then proceed as for flat biscuits.

Coconut Biscuits
Add 1 cup of desiccated coconut to the dough, work it in thoroughly, roll out and cut as for flat biscuits.

Peanut Biscuits
Before adding the sifted flour and baking powder, put 2 tablespoons of peanut butter in the bowl with the sugar, butter and

egg mixture, and beat it through well. Then proceed to make a lump of dough, and either make a cylinder out of it, or pinch bits off and make them into balls.

Fruity Biscuits
Add 1 cup of currants or sultanas to the dough when it is finished, and knead it well. Then proceed as with balled biscuits. You can also proceed as for cylinder, rolling the dough out, sprinkling it with the currants or sultanas, then rolling it up and cutting slices off.

Tollhouse Cookies
To the chocolate biscuit variation (2 tablespoons of drinking chocolate sifted in with the flour and baking powder), add 1 cup of dark chocolate buds to the finished dough, knead the buds well through it, and proceed as for balled biscuits. If you prefer the chocolate buds through a plain mixture, just add them straight into the basic recipe.

Nutty Biscuits
To the finished dough add 1 cup of finely chopped nuts (it doesn't matter what sort — anything from almonds to macadamias to walnuts, or mix a few varieties together), work them well through by kneading, and proceed as for balled biscuits. You can also use the cylinder attack, rolling the dough out fairly thinly, sprinkling it with the nuts, then rolling it up and slicing it into coins.

Jam Drops
Make the plain basic recipe, and roll it up into balls on a greased tray, leaving plenty of space between each one. Press a much deeper yet not so spreading dent in the top of each one, put a little red jam (raspberry or strawberry) into it, then pinch the edges over it so the jam doesn't burn during baking. Bake as for balled biscuits.

Essences can change the flavour of the basic dough, without your needing to add so much you destroy the firm texture of the dough. At most, you will need ¼ teaspoon of any essence (the colours, if you wish to colour your dough, should be added only a drop at a time, and will not need more than 3 to 6 drops) to give the dough a subtle hint of whatever it is. There are many, many essences.

Almond	Coconut	Vanilla
Coffee	Ginger	Ratafia
Aniseed	Orange	Rosewater
Lemon	Lime	Rum

These are just a few of the more popular ones, and they are all highly concentrated, designed to be added in such a small amount that they change neither colour nor consistency.

You may be able to think of other things you would like to do to this basic recipe, and we say — go right ahead! It will be very difficult to spoil your attempts, provided you remember the principles of what tastes good with what.

CHOCOLATE BISCUITS

40 round biscuits made from the basic recipe, or the basic recipe plus 2 tablespoons drinking chocolate, or the basic recipe plus
¼ to ½ teaspoon rum essence
225 to 335g (8 to 12ozs) sweet dark chocolate
2 tablespoons white vegetable shortening
some seedless red jam, raspberry or strawberry, which has been dried out a little in a low oven to thicken it.

Join the biscuits together with a little jam, and press them together gently (don't press too hard and break them) to make sure there isn't jam oozing out of their edges. Leave them to settle for a while.

Melt the chocolate and the shortening together in the top of a double-boiler, or in a small saucepan resting in a larger one half-full of boiling water. Stir the two together well to mix, and leave over the hot water.

Drop each biscuit into the pan of liquid chocolate and turn it over to coat it well on all sides, lift it out and leave it to set on a greased sheet of foil.

Note 1:   You can coat single un-jammed biscuits in the chocolate just as well as jammed ones, and thus produce good plain chocolate biscuits.

Note 2:   You can sandwich two biscuits together with a little icing or butter-cream, and then coat them with the chocolate.

MONTE CARLOS

115g (4oz) butter, margarine or other shortening
8 tablespoons (115g, 4ozs) white sugar
1 large egg
½ cup desiccated coconut
2 tablespoons golden syrup or honey
2 cups plain flour
1 teaspoon baking powder
a little seedless red jam which has been thickened in a low oven
a little white icing, fairly stiff in consistency

Cream the butter and sugar together, then break in the egg and beat well.

Add the golden syrup or honey and the coconut, and mix well again.

Finally add the flour and baking powder sifted together, knead it into a smooth dough and then form the dough into a lump.

Break pieces off and roll them into balls about 25mm (1in) in diameter, about the size of melon balls, and place the balls on a greased tray with plenty of room between them.

Press the back of a large eating fork into the top of each ball to flatten it out somewhat, and leave ridges in the dough. The shape, because the fork is longer than it is wide, will be more oval than round.

Bake each tray of biscuits at 185°C (375°F) for about 15 minutes, or until they are browning on top.

Turn them onto a wire rack to cool, and when cold turn them all so that their flat sides are facing up. Spread half of them with jam, and half with icing, then sandwich a jam one and an icing one together.

This recipe makes about 20 biscuits.

HARD DOERS (ALSO CALLED REAL OLD TIMERS)

1 cup and a bit of sugar
1 cup beef or lamb dripping (you can substitute lard)
3 eggs
3 cups plain flour
2 teaspoons baking powder
pinch of salt
1 cup sultanas (raisins)
1 tablespoon golden syrup or honey

Sift the flour, salt, and baking powder together, and then rub the dripping into it (or cut it in with a pastry-blender) until the dripping is lying all through the flour in crumbs. Add the sugar, and mix well with your hands.

Break in the eggs one by one, and mix each one well in before adding another.

Add the golden syrup or honey and mix again, then add the sultanas.

Divide the mixture into two halves, and roll the first half out as thinly as you can. Cut the biscuits out with a tumbler.

Place the rounds on a greased tray and bake at 185°C (375°F) until golden-brown.

Repeat with the second half of dough, and then use up all the scraps.

Turn onto a wire rack to cool, and store in air-tight tins. This makes about 60 biscuits.

We are indebted to Mrs Russell Collins of Merriwa, N.S.W. for this recipe, which is a real old bush favourite. It was high on the request menu of every shearer's cook and riverboat cook in the Outback. You can substitute butter or margarine for the dripping Mrs Collins stipulates; we tested it with dripping and again with butter, and confess that we do prefer the butter ones, but found the dripping ones amazingly good in taste, though inclined to stale quicker.

RATAFIA ESSENCE

This is the last modern remnant of what once constituted a great part of Georgian cooking; it began to fall out of favour during the Victorian era, and survived at this time only as a mild flavouring ingredient for biscuits and cakes. During the Georgian era, however, it was among other things drunk by ladies as an alcohol substitute (ladies did not imbibe of spiritous or fermented potations in those days), and appeared as a much-liked constituent of punches, puddings, cakes and candies.

For your amusement, we include a recipe for making ratafia which dates from the reign of George III.

'Take of nutmegs, eight ounces; bitter almonds, ten pounds; Lisbon (castor or superfine) sugar, eight pounds; ambergris, ten grains; infuse these ingredients for three days in ten gallons of clean proof spirit (70% alcohol, 30% water) and filter through a flannel bag for use. The nutmegs and bitter almonds

must be bruised, and the ambergris rubbed with the Lisbon sugar in a marble mortar before they are infused in the spirit.'

The bracketed bits are ours; we would conclude from the preparation that the prim-and-proper ladies of Georgian England, America and Australia were probably doing better from the booze point of view, even when the ratafia was diluted with water, than their wine-imbibing masters or their gin-drinking servants!

RATAFIA BISCUITS

3 tablespoons (85g, 3 ozs) butter
5 tablespoons (140g, 5 ozs) sugar
1 large egg
1 teaspoon ratafia essence
2 cups plain flour
2 teaspoons baking powder

Beat the butter and sugar to a cream, then break in the egg and add the ratafia essence. Beat well together.

Add the flour and baking powder sifted together, and work the mixture into a dough.

Break small pieces off, roll them into balls, place the balls on a greased tray with plenty of room between, press their middle-tops into a dent to spread them a bit, and bake at 185°C (375°F) for about 15 minutes, or until the biscuits begin to turn brown from their bottoms up.

Turn onto a wire rack and cool.

This makes about 30 biscuits.

Ratafia is ancient stuff, and hard to come by these days. Once a year it would pay you to visit a speciality store catering for essences and colourings and cake decorations, and stock up on the items you think you'd like to have in a cupboard, just to break the monotony of everyday recipes. Ratafia is a rather pungent, overwhelmingly almond-smelling and almond-tasting essence which flavours cakes and biscuits requiring almond flavouring better than the labelled essence of almond does.

ALMOND MACAROONS

6 egg whites
2 cups caster sugar
2 cups almond meal

1 teaspoon ratafia or almond essence
1 cup plain flour
1 teaspoon baking powder

Beat the egg whites until stiff. Add the sugar fairly gradually, then the almond meal, and the essence.

Mix thoroughly but lightly, then add the flour sifted together with the baking powder.

Put in a pastry bag and force through a large plain nozzle onto a greased tray. The mounds of mixture should be at least 7.5 cm (3 in) apart to allow for spreading. Put a blanched almond in the centre of each one.

Bake in a 160°C (325°F) oven for 30 minutes, until browned and risen.

Turn onto a wire rack to cool, and store tightly lidded.

GARIBALDIS

2 tablespoons butter
3 tablespoons sugar
a little milk
2 cups plain flour
2 teaspoons baking powder
1 cup very finely chopped raisins

Rub the butter into the flour, or cut it in with a pastry-blender, until the butter lies all through the flour in small beads or crumbs. Add the sugar, and rub it or cut it through the mixture. Make sure you've sifted the flour and baking powder together before beginning!

Make this dry mixture into a stiff dough by adding a little milk, about 1 tablespoon to begin with — if that isn't enough, add more milk in teaspoons only. Work the dough with your hands to soften the butter, and then knead the dough until it's nicely smooth and free from stickiness.

Roll the dough out very thinly, and sprinkle half of it with the chopped raisins. Lift the other half and place it on top of the raisined half, then apply your rolling pin and fuse the two layers together, without pushing the raisins all the way through the dough, though the raisins will show a bit here and there. Roll it out until the dough is almost as thin as it was in the beginning, and then cut it into triangles or rectangles.

Place on a greased tray and bake at 210°C (400°F) for about 15 minutes, or until the biscuits are browning.

Turn onto a wire rack to cool, and store in a tightly lidded container so the biscuits don't become soft.

This makes about 20 to 25 biscuits.

OATMEAL BISCUITS

8 level tablespoons flour
8 level tablespoons fine oats
4 tablespoons butter
¼ teaspoon salt
2 tablespoons sugar
1 egg
1 teaspoon baking powder

Sift the baking powder and the flour together in a large bowl, then add the oats and mix thoroughly. Rub the butter into the dry ingredients with your palms, or cut it in with a pastry-blender; it must be very well distributed and finely crumbed.

Add the sugar to this and mix well, then break the egg in and work the mixture to a firm dough.

Roll out thinly, and cut with a tumbler into rounds or ovals.

Place on a greased sheet, and bake in a 210°C (400°F) oven for about 10 minutes, or until they begin to brown.

Turn onto a wire rack to cool, and store tightly lidded.

This recipe makes about 30 biscuits.

KISSES

1 cup sugar
115g (4ozs) butter
1 large egg
½ cup (125 ml, 4 fl ozs) fresh milk
about 3 cups plain flour
½ teaspoon bicarbonate of soda
1 teaspoon cream of tartar

Cream the butter and sugar, break in the egg and beat well. Add the milk, and beat to a smooth consistency.

Sift 2 of the cups of flour with all of the cream of tartar and bicarbonate of soda, and reserve the other cup of flour for use if needed; this is a recipe where the amount of flour has to be adjusted to the stipulated amounts of fluid, instead of the other way around.

Enough flour must be used to make a stiff, light dough,

about the consistency to drop off the end of a teaspoon with a bit of a push behind to encourage it.

Drop teaspoons of the mixture onto a greased sheet, and bake in a 210°C (400°F) oven for about 10 to 15 minutes, until the little cakes turn light golden-brown.

Turn onto a wire rack to cool, and when cold sandwich two together with raspberry jam.

This makes about 15 to 20 kisses.

MELTING MOMENTS

450g (1lb) butter
5 tablespoons icing (confectioner's) sugar
4 tablespoons cornflour (cornstarch)
200g (7ozs, 14 level tablespoons) plain flour
1 teaspoon baking powder

Beat the butter until it is white and very creamy (an electric beater is a great help), then add the icing sugar and beat well.

Add the cornflour, beat again, and lastly add the plain flour sifted together with the baking powder. You should have a very stiff, plastic dough; work it with your hands to melt the butter a little, and make the dough less stiff, more easily worked.

If you have a biscuit forcing syringe and fancy nozzle, force rosettes of the dough out onto a greased sheet. If you have a pastry bag and a rosette nozzle, use this to force the dough into rosettes. If you possess neither, then roll the dough into balls, put them well apart on the tray, and press them down with the back of an eating fork.

Bake at 175°C (350°F) for about 20 to 25 minutes, or until the biscuits are beginning to brown lightly.

Turn onto a wire rack to cool, and when quite cold, sandwich two together with a little stiff white icing.

This recipe makes about 20 biscuits.

SCOTTISH SHORTBREAD

225g (8ozs) butter (no substitutes for shortbread!)
1 cup (225g, 8ozs) sugar
2 cups plain flour
2 tablespoons arrowroot
2 teaspoons baking powder
a little milk if necessary

Soften the butter without melting it, and cut it into the sugar with a pastry-cutter, or rub it in between your hands. Get it well distributed, not clumped.

Sift the flour, arrowroot and baking powder together, then add them slowly to the butter and sugar, mixing with your hands and working it all into a very stiff dough. The proportion of butter is so high compared to the other ingredients that you shouldn't find the dough very crumbly, even when all the flour is in.

Only if you can't get a nice plastic ball of dough should you add a little milk to it, but it is preferable to work the mixture between your palms to melt the butter a bit and then add extra liquid, if necessary.

Shape it into a ball, then roll or press it out into a rough round about 12 to 18mm (½ to ¾in) thick. Take a cake tin or something similar with a sharp edge a bit smaller than the round you have of dough, and press it down on the dough to cut out a perfect circle.

Press your thumb all around the edge to crimp it, then trace grooves in the top like the spokes of a wheel (use a blunt knife rather than a sharp one), making the grooves deep enough to aid in breaking the shortbread into wedge-shaped slices after it is cooked. Prick the surface of each wedge with a fork, in a pattern if you like.

Place on a greased tray and bake at 165°C (325°F), which is a fairly low oven, for about 1 hour to 90 minutes, or until the slab is beginning to brown.

When it has been cooled on a wire rack, tie a piece of tartan ribbon into a bow, and fix it at the centre of the cake. If you have a sprig of purple or white heather, or a Scots thistle in flower, tie the bow round it before fixing it to the cake.

Shortbread is traditionally served absolutely plain; no jam, no icing of any kind, so if you like to ice yours, or decorate it in some other way than we have described make sure there's no MacPherson or Gordon or Grant or MacLeod among your eaters!

If you prefer small biscuits to the single round cake, roll the dough out about 6mm (¼in) thick, and cut it into rectangles about 10cm (4in) long and 5cm (2in) wide; if you have a toothed cutter, trim the ends into teeth but not the long sides, and then draw two deep grooves lengthwise down the middles, so you've divided each biscuit into three finger-sized slices, but haven't actually cut them.

Bake at 175°C (350°F) for about 30 minutes, or until the biscuits begin to brown slightly underneath; they should never be very brown.

Turn onto a wire rack to cool, and store tightly lidded.

ANZAC BISCUITS

1 cup (225g, 8ozs) sugar
1 cup desiccated coconut
1 cup flaked fine oats
¾ cup (85g, 3ozs) plain flour
2 teaspoons golden syrup or honey
½ cup (115g, 4ozs) butter, margarine or other shortening
2 tablespoons boiling water
1 level teaspoon bicarbonate of soda

Mix the sugar, coconut, oatmeal and plain flour together in a bowl.

In a saucepan melt the butter or other shortening, add to it the golden syrup or honey, the boiling water and the bicarbonate of soda. Stir over low heat until all the butter is melted and the liquid is well mixed.

Wait until the hot liquid cools to almost room temperature, then pour it into the dry ingredients, and knead well. The dough should be firm and stiff. If it isn't, add a bit more flour to it and knead well again.

Roll the dough into a cylinder and cut coins off it with a very sharp knife, about 6 mm (¼ in) thick, or less if you can.

Place the rounds on a greased tray and bake at 210°C (400°F) for 10 to 20 minutes, depending upon the thickness of your rounds. Watch them carefully and remove them from the oven when they are beginning to brown.

Turn onto a wire rack to cool, and store airtight.

This makes about 35 biscuits.

DIGESTIVE BISCUITS

3 tablespoons butter, margarine or other shortening
3 tablespoons sugar
1 egg
1 cup plain flour
1 cup wheatmeal
1 heaped teaspoon baking powder

Rub the butter through the sugar, or cut it into the sugar with a pastry-blender, then break in the egg and beat well.

Sift the two flours together with the baking powder, and add gradually to the mixture, finishing with a firm dough you can roll out fairly thinly.

Cut with an oval cutter if you have one, otherwise use a tumbler or something similar.

Place on a greased sheet and bake in a 210°C (400°F) oven for about 10 minutes, until they begin to brown.

Turn onto a wire rack to cool, and store airtight.

This makes about 40 biscuits.

ARROWROOT BISCUITS

3 tablespoons butter, margarine or other shortening
⅔ cup (170g, 6 ozs) sugar
1 egg
a little milk if necessary
1 cup flour
1 cup arrowroot
1 teaspoon baking powder

Cut the butter into the sugar with a pastry-blender, or rub it through with your hands, until it is well broken up into crumbs.

Break the egg in, and beat the mixture well.

Sift the flour, arrowroot and baking powder together, and add gradually to the mixture, beating with a spoon until it becomes too stiff, and you have to use your hands. This quantity of dry ingredient shouldn't need extra fluid to make it into a firm, workable dough, but if you wish, add milk a teaspoon only at a time until you're happy.

Roll the dough out very thinly, to 3mm (⅛ in), and cut it with an oval cutter if you have one, otherwise use something round.

Bake in a 210°C (400°F) oven for about 10 minutes, until they are beginning to brown.

Turn onto a wire rack to cool. These are delicious eaten with a bit of butter spread on them.

The recipe makes about 40 biscuits.

When we were babies, these biscuits made babies' pap. Mother broke a few arrowroot biscuits into a bowl, and added suffi-cient hot water to mash them into pap, which was ruthlessly spooned into our mouths. Oddly enough, we both love arrow-root biscuits to this very day!

BRANDY SNAPS

Many cooks baulk at the thought of making brandy snaps, but if you organise yourself well, and don't try to do anything else while you're making them, you won't have any trouble. By using three or four baking sheets at a time, you can set up a process line.

2 tablespoons butter
½ cup (55g, 2ozs) plain flour
⅓ cup (85g, 3ozs) brown sugar
⅓ cup golden syrup or honey
1 level teaspoon ground ginger
1 tablespoon finely grated rind of lemon, no white in it
½ teaspoon brandy essence, otherwise rum essence

In a small saucepan put the butter, sugar, golden syrup or honey, lemon rind and ginger and brandy essence. Stir over very low heat, or swill the saucepan round gently, until the butter melts.

Remove from the heat and beat well with a wooden spoon, or use an electric mixer.

Add the sifted flour gradually, blending it through until the mixture is smooth and free from lumps. *Make sure the liquid mixture is well cooled before you begin to add the flour, or you'll cook the flour prematurely and your biscuits won't spread during baking!*

Grease three or four baking sheets with a little white vegetable shortening smeared on a wad of kitchen paper, and have them ready and waiting.

If you're likely to be interrupted, stop the process at this point and refrigerate your mixture until you can carry on in peace and quiet; it doesn't matter if this doesn't occur until the following day.

Drop a teaspoonful of the mixture onto a greased baking tray, and then one more teaspoonful on the same tray, well away from the first. Both should have room to spread. Content yourself with just two on this first trayload, because what happens the moment the tray comes out of the oven can be most exasperating if you've too many to cope with, and three can be too many on your first try.

Bake in a 210°C (400°F) oven for about 5 minutes, until they are set. The snaps should look very thin and a deep golden-brown in colour on their bottoms.

Take the tray out of the oven, and lift the two snaps off the tray onto a wire rack with a spatula, or egg flipper.

Allow a few moments for setting, then wrap one around the greased handle of a melamine or wooden spoon, tamping its edges together, and holding it there for a few seconds to keep the shape. Then slide off the spoon handle.

This is where the production line comes in. If you have several greased sheets ready and waiting, you can move the numbers along faster; don't cook too many at the same time, or they'll set faster than you can mould them round your spoon handle. Should they set too quickly to mould, a few seconds back in the oven will soften them up again.

Leave them to grow cold on a wire rack, then pack them in an airtight container with foil or waxed paper between the layers in case they get a little sticky.

Before use, fill a pastry bag with whipped slightly sweetened cream (or butter cream), attach a rosette nozzle to it, and pipe each snap full of cream.

This recipe makes about 20 snaps.

OLD-FASHIONED GINGER NUTS

4 tablespoons butter or margarine
5 tablespoons soft dark brown sugar
1 large egg yolk
¼ cup (2 generous tablespoons) treacle or molasses
2 heaped cups of plain flour
1 tablespoon ground ginger
½ teaspoon salt

If the sugar has lumps, force it through a strainer by pushing and stirring it with a spoon — discard only the very few congealed solids which won't go through on pushing, and replace these discarded bits only if they amount in total to more than one teaspoon. Ours didn't, they amounted to about ¼ teaspoon at most.

Cream the butter and sugar together until you have a soft, smooth paste (dark brown sugar is a joy to cream with butter, it melts and blends beautifully). Add the egg yolk and mix it in thoroughly, then add the treacle or molasses and do the same.

Sift the flour, ginger and salt together, then add it gradually to the mixture, stirring it in; this is a rather sticky-looking and acting mixture, and can be difficult to stir though you can use your hands if you find it easier.

When all the flour is in, you will have a dough which seems awfully sticky, and yet when you pick it up in your hands it doesn't really stick to your skin at all. It isn't a stiff dough that you can roll in a big lump, it's loose and pliable.

Pluck bits off the mixture as it sits in the bowl, and roll them between your hands to form a sort of a ball; you won't be able to form perfectly shaped balls, so be content with something less than perfection, it doesn't matter with this recipe at all.

Put the balls on a well greased baking tray, with plenty of space between. Then put the palm of your hand flat on top of each one, and squash it down to a rather thin, flat coin. You'll find this very easy to do, and the mixture doesn't crack at its edges.

Cook in a 210°C (400°F) oven for approximately 10 minutes; it is difficult to tell when they are ready to come out, for they're brown to begin with. They should *look* cooked, which isn't much help to you, is it? However, they'll smell cooked, and they will have risen slightly in their middles, and if you look closely at their edges you'll see them well browned. Don't leave them in until their tops darken much, or their bottoms will be burned.

Turn onto a wire rack to cool, and store in a tightly lidded tin.

This recipe makes about 40 biscuits.

Thank you, Mrs Joyce Byfield, of Merriwa, N.S.W.! We have tried many recipes looking for a really good ginger nut, and this one wins our award for best ever. We could tell how good they were long before we could taste them; of all the smells that ever emanated from a kitchen, this one must rank right up there with the best. Gorgeous! The taste lived up to the smell, and they turned out to be as hard and gingery as a ginger nut ought to be.

WATER BISCUITS

1 tablespoon butter or margarine
4 tablespoons water

pinch of salt
2 cups plain flour
2 teaspoons baking powder

Sift the flour, baking powder and salt together into a large bowl.

Put the water and butter into a small saucepan, and heat it very gently until the butter has entirely melted, rolling and swilling the contents around to hasten the melting process and prevent the mixture getting too hot.

Wait until the mixture is quite cool, then pour it into the flour and knead until it turns into a smooth, plastic dough.

Turn it onto a floured sheet and roll it out very, very thinly, less than 3mm (⅛ in) if you can. Cut it into small rounds with a tumbler.

Transfer the rounds to a greased baking tray and bake in a 210°C (400°F) oven for about 15 minutes, until the biscuits are beginning to go dark brown at their edges — water biscuits should be cooked until they just escape burning, so you have to be very vigilant.

Cool on a wire rack, and store in a tightly lidded tin so the biscuits retain their crispness; if they should accidently soften, pop them in the oven for a minute to crisp up before serving.

This recipe makes about 50 biscuits, depending on the thinness of the dough.

CHEESE BISCUITS

2 tablespoons butter
½ cup iced water
2 cups plain flour
2 teaspoons baking powder
4 tablespoons grated mild cheddar or other hard cheese
    (e.g. Gouda)
½ teaspoon salt
¼ teaspoon coarsely ground black pepper

Sift the flour with the baking powder, salt and pepper, then rub in the butter, or cut it in with a pastry-blender, until it lies all through the flour in small beads.

Add just enough water to work the mixture into a stiff but pliable dough; don't put all the water in at once, add about half of it and then add the rest a teaspoon at a time. Knead the dough well; it doesn't matter if you handle it, which is where it differs from pastry.

If you don't know how to make puff pastry, look it up before you begin the next step, for you're going to put the grated cheese into the dough much as you would butter into puff pastry.

Roll the dough out very thinly into an oblong shape, and mentally roughly divide it into three sections.

Sprinkle grated cheese thinly over the middle third of the oblong and the third farthest away from you, then fold the unsprinkled, clean third closest to you over the middle third. Then fold the third farthest away (press its cheese into it gently to prevent it falling off as you lift) over the top of the other two. Lift the small packet of dough up, turn it sideways, press its edges together with the rolling pin, and roll it out into the same sized oblong as before.

Repeat the cheese sprinkling, folding and rolling out until all the cheese has been used up, then roll the slab of dough out very thinly, and cut it into small squares, triangles and rectangles.

Bake the biscuits on a greased tray at 210°C (400°F) for about 10 minutes, until the crackers turn brown on their under-sides, and are beginning to brown on top.

This recipe makes about 20 to 30 biscuits.

INDEX